T0354354

REVELATION

GOD'S FINAL PROPHECY SUMMARIZED

DR. MICHAEL W. COTIE

Author Credits: Pastor, thD

Scripture taken from the King James Version of the Bible.

WestBow Press books may be ordered through booksellers or by contacting:

WestBow Press
A Division of Thomas Nelson & Zondervan
1663 Liberty Drive
Bloomington, IN 47403
www.westbowpress.com
1 (866) 928-1240

ISBN: 978-1-5127-8115-1 (sc)
ISBN: 978-1-5127-8116-8 (hc)
ISBN: 978-1-5127-8114-4 (e)

Library of Congress Control Number: 2017904691

Print information available on the last page.

WestBow Press rev. date: 3/27/2017

DEDICATION

To my wife Debra, without whose encouragement the series of books on Revelation would not have been accomplished. The book dedicated to her for her encouragement of me to write these and her support and dedication to the time and resources for this series to be written.

As I was teaching through Revelation, she commented on how this was the most in-depth study of Revelation she had been through, and that it would be great in book form, thus the series was born.

To her for having been by my side for forty one years of marriage. For the Love and support as the helpmate God intended her to be for me, I give her my undying love and deep appreciation for the inspiration to write.

CONTENTS

INTRODUCTION

Many people have read the book of Revelation and feel totally mystified. Dr. Michael W. Cotie in *Revelation: God's Final Prophecy Simplified* provides a simplified insight into scripture while providing an in-depth view of Christ messages to the churches.

The prophetic message The Lord Jesus gave the church in these messages to the churches is revealed in this insightful book. Each church represents a phase the true church was to go through as the Bride of Christ. One day soon as seen in the section *THE SNATCHING AWAY OF THE BRIDE* author Dr. Michael W. Cotie reveals how Christ will return in a moment in the twinkling of an eye when the trumpet sounds and the Bride is called home.

The other Sections show God's plan as seen for mankind through as the events of God's Judgment unfold. The prophetic message of Jesus to the churches guides the believer through exactly how the events of God's plan will work for believers of today and those of future periods of time. Come follow the plan of God and see how it was given not to scare but to motivate believers to serve God to the fullest and to be the Witness God has made them to be.

REFERENCES

1. William Newell
2. Matthew Henry
3. John Gill
4. John Darby
5. H. A. Ironside
6. M. R. DeHaan
7. J. Vernon McGee

SECTION 1

The Snatching Away of the Bride

CONTENTS

INTRODUCTION

John was in the isle called Patmos, exiled there by the Roman emperor. Of course, the Lord had sent him there for a purpose, which is revealed in the vision and the revelation of Jesus coming to him. The Lord came to him and instructed him to write. We now see the "things after these." The scene in chapter 3 is the progression of the church into apostasy. This is seen in the time of the church age and shows how the church progressed into the apostate church of today. A remnant is holding fast the truth. The progression of the apostasy was over an almost-two thousand-year period it is the apostasy which currently exists in the church.

In verse 1 of Revelation 4, we are told John heard a voice as if a trumpet. The voice John heard after the sound of a trumpet makes a clear and concise command for us because it is saying, "Come up hither." John looked and saw a door open, coinciding with the voice as if a trumpet. "After this I looked, and, behold, a door was opened in heaven: and the first voice which I heard was as it were of a trumpet, talking with me; which said, Come up hither, and I will shew thee things which must be hereafter" (Rev. 4:1). A clear and concise call, but whom or what is called up hither? Is it John or is it typifying the call for the snatching away of the church?

I like to use the term "Rapture of the church," but there are folks who want to say the word *rapture* isn't in the Bible, which is true; but the term "snatching away" is, and that is what the Rapture, termed by many biblical scholars, means. Let's cover a few things that must happen before you can receive the message, which is the Holy Spirit's purpose for you reading this book. Before you can receive the message and serve God as He commands, before you can walk for Him, you must have a personal, intimate relationship with Him. Romans 10:13states, "Whosoever shall call upon the name of the Lord shall be saved." Acts 16:31 says, "And they said, 'Believe on the Lord Jesus Christ, and thou shalt be saved, and thy house.'" Of course, John 3:16 is known by almost everyone, but verses 17 and 18 state, "For God sent not his Son into the world to condemn the world; but that the world through him might be saved. He that believeth on him is not condemned: but he that believeth not is condemned already, because he hath not believed in the name of the only begotten Son of God."

You must admit you are a condemned sinner because of not having believed. You also must believe and then call upon Christ for salvation. Next, if you are a believer, you must practice 1 John 1:9: "If we confess our sins, he is faithful and just to forgive us our sins, and to cleanse us from all unrighteousness." Before you can receive God's message, you need to confess all known sin, and God will forgive that sin and all the things that you don't realize are sins or, as I like to say, unknown sins.

1

The Church of the Rights of the People

The first thing we need to understand here is the message to the last church, which is seen in Revelation 3:14–22, the church in Laodicea. Jesus's message is clear to them, for He says, "I know thy works, and they are neither hot nor cold." We have in many churches today people who call themselves Christians, but they preach a watered down message. That watered-down message is one that is lukewarm. Many, not all, are lukewarm, just as the church in Laodicea.

We have in the final message to the churches in chapters 2 and 3 the end of the time of the church, the church that exists at the time Christ will return for His bride; the last and worst church of all the churches. Christ is the Great Amen we see in Revelation 3, and as such, He is the foundation of that church Paul told us in 1 Corinthians 3:11. He is the unchanging God of the universe, the head of the church. We see through Scripture He never changes in His purpose or in His promise. The message to the church in Laodicea concludes the messages to the churches. It brings an end to the time of the church on the earth. The name Laodicea means "the rights of the people."

That sounds like the church we have today. That sounds like our society today. Today it seems the church is all about the rights of the people to do as they please; the time of the rights of the people to worship as they feel right about instead of worshipping as God has commanded.

We see this in our world today; the authority of God and His word are being denied. God has been removed from school textbooks. God's word, the Bible, is being removed from public view in public buildings. People are fighting to get prayer removed totally from schools and even in public. That is the Laodicea period of the church age.

Many prominent pastors in our time are turning from biblical truth, preaching and teaching a lukewarm gospel. One that says "faith in Jesus" is not necessarily the only means of salvation.

You see, that goes against what the Bible tells us. As seen earlier in the introduction, I placed this set of scriptures which apply at this point: Romans 10:13 and Acts 16:31.

Look at it. Do you see any other gospel taught? Any other gospel apart from faith in Christ is a lie, an attempt by Satan to keep people from accepting Christ as their savior. God will ensure that the ones who preach it are disciplined. Galatians 1:8–9 applies to these men and, now we must say, women.

Do you see what Paul said? Those who are preaching anything other than salvation by grace through faith are to be accursed. A person who has truly accepted Christ as their personal savior by grace through faith brings salvation, as we see in Ephesians 2:8–9. Paul made it extremely clear here in this passage, you cannot work your way to heaven. See here what Scripture tells us. Look at what is being preached today.

Do you see the doctrine of the Laodicean church? We are in the final days before the church will be snatched away. Christ said in Revelation 3:15 that He knows their works just as He knew the works of the other churches, the phases of the church age, and the apostasy that would progress in the church. The Laodicean church was neither hot nor cold, it was lukewarm. Christ wishes they were cold or hot, but the church in the final period will be indifferent. How many churches today are just that indifferent! They are neutral and tolerant churches; a church for all even if they don't turn from their sin. This is a sad picture for the church at the end of the age, and it is a sad picture in our world today, but these types of churches exist today. We see in Revelation 3:16 just how bad this church has become. Many churches of today are lukewarm, have no power, and have become the worst of all sicknesses. Christ reproves their lukewarmness. He reproves their indifference. They are not hot, that is, not on fire for Him like the Philadelphian church was. No burning zeal like the Philadelphian church. Their zeal and fervor are for organization; the organization of their religion is what is most important. They are not cold, and they are indifferent to the Gospel of Christ.

This is the church God will reject. He'll spew it out of His mouth while the church in Philadelphia had the promise that they will be snatched away before the hour of tribulation. Revelation 3:10.

Now let me interject here; many who don't believe in the Rapture of the church will say that this verse only applies to the church in Philadelphia. Christ's promise goes further. He will keep them from the hour of temptation. Here is the first definite promise that the church will escape the Great Tribulation. How can this be stated dogmatically, some might ask. From the church in Thyatira to the church in Laodicea, the church would continue in the world simultaneously until the coming of the Lord.

Only the church in Philadelphia is, as it says, to be kept from the hour of temptation, snatched away; kept from the hour of temptation that is coming upon the world after the snatching away (i.e., the Rapture). Those who keep the word of Christ's patience will be kept from the hour of temptation. If we limit this to just the church in Philadelphia, then we must limit that church to the only one that has kept the word of Christ's patience. The study light interlinear translation states it like this:

"Seeing that you keep saying of the endurance of me I also you shall be keeping out of the hour of the trial of the being about to be coming on the inhabited earth whole to try the ones dwelling on the earth." This sounds like we will be kept from the Tribulation.

Let's see if I can make it better grammatically: "See that you keep on talking of the endurance of Christ, I also shall keep you out of the hour of trial that is about to come on the whole inhabited earth to try the ones dwelling on the earth." Notice we are to continue to talk about enduring in the faith and truth about Christ in order to be kept from the time of trial. That time of trial is coming not upon the church in Philadelphia but upon the whole inhabited earth, not just the region around the Philadelphian church. The time of Jacob's trouble seen in Jeremiah 30:7, the great time of

Tribulation, which is coming upon the whole inhabited world. It is coming upon all those dwelling on the earth at that time.

Daniel 9:27 Daniel saw seventy weeks of seven years each; the Tribulation we see in Revelation the last seven years, the final week of Daniel's seventy weeks. The tribulation is not seen in chapters 1–3 but in chapters 6–19. We see according to Daniel 9:24–26, seventy weeks were determined for Israel to complete before the Messiah would come and reign in His kingdom. The Messiah would come when seven plus three score and three weeks had occurred after the decree to rebuild Jerusalem. That would be sixty nine weeks or 483 years. Then from that, we are told the Messiah would be cut off (killed) after sixty-two weeks, so seven weeks forty-nine years, the city would be rebuilt and complete, then following 434 years after the completion was the Messiah cut off.

It happened just as Daniel's prophecy said it would. Christ came and ministered for three and a half years, and then He was cut off, crucified. Do you see that the time of temptation or trial is the tribulation, and *all* those who keep the word of Christ's patience, "keep on talking of the endurance of Christ," will be kept from the hour of temptation? Those who place their faith and trust in Christ in the church age will be kept from the Tribulation.

Peter gives us a little hint of all this too. Second Peter 3:8 virtually God has given mankind seven thousand years of time, divided up into one week, the first thousand was the Sunday of that week; it began with Adam being placed in the garden. The final week is when Christ's thousand year reign begins and ends as it is. Completed, this would be the Saturday of that seven-thousand-year week, the day of rest, with the Lord ruling the earth. Now let's pick back up on the churches' apostasy. The church in Thyatira would be thrust into tribulation, and the church in Laodicea will be rejected by Christ. Cast off as worthless to Him, the general body is judged by the world. Christ disowns and rejects this church, which is lukewarm.

The church in Laodicea receives a severe punishment. As lukewarm water turns the stomach, so this church turns Christ's stomach. Understand the word *spew* here in the Greek means "to vomit." One of the meanings of *vomit* in *Webster's* is "to eject violently."

Christ is sick of the Laodicean church. He can bear them no longer; they shall be rejected. How much are we seeing the church being disrespected by people? Almost all in the rights of the people, church will not be snatched away in the Rapture because they have denied the Gospel of Christ! Even their spiritual leaders will not avoid the time of trial.

Revelation 3:17 shows us their major problem. What do you see here? "Thou sayest," that is, they talk about themselves; they are proud, and even, as it appears, they are arrogant. They look at what they have and see riches. They saw themselves well furnished, in goods, and believe that is God blessing them. They had worldly riches this was true and they were thinking that they have need of nothing from God. They were the self-satisfied church. What do we see of many megachurches today—feel good, self-satisfying churches? Many are proud and self-righteous; they have no idea how God sees them. The rights of the people must be followed while the rights of Christ are trampled on or not thought of; that is, they have stopped "talking of the endurance of Christ."

Just look at all the vacant seats in many churches today, especially on Sunday nights and midweek services. How many churches have stopped having a service during the week and/or a Sunday night? People don't have time for those services anymore. They are too busy with other things, things of the world.

Many carry on a religious program without the Holy Spirit leading them. As the Laodicean church had shut out Christ, so too have many churches today. Christ describes here just how He sees this church: "Knowest not that thou art wretched, and miserable, and poor, and blind, and naked" (Rev. 3:17b). They were a wretched church, but they never saw themselves this way. Their state called for pity and compassion from others; they were proud of themselves and felt they needed no one's pity. They never realized that riches for the body will not enrich the soul. They were in a miserable state and never knew it. They were poor and blind. They had no justification, no righteousness in their account, because they denied the faith in Christ. They were blind spiritually, in a state of spiritual death.

In 1 Corinthians 2:14, Christ describes to them their condition, but they didn't see it. They seem to be natural men, unsaved and blind; not just blind but naked. They had no spiritual clothing. If they were saved, then they had suffered operational death, no production in time. James 2:26, Revelation 3:18 also tells us Christ's great council to them to buy gold tried in fire. True riches come from God and Christ's deity, seen in the gold, which represents those riches. This is saying you need salvation. This shows they were not in a state of operational death but were not even saved. They must buy this gold tried by Him, by His efficacious work on the cross.

Christ knows them; He knows their works. They cannot buy it with worldly riches nor with works of righteousness that they had done (Titus 3:5). They needed to part with something in order to buy this gold. They needed to part with sin and self-sufficiency. They needed to come to Christ with a sense of poverty and emptiness that they may gain gold tried by Christ's death on the cross. They were naked, uncovered, with no house, no place of safety, and no peace. They were without God and needed raiment; not just any raiment but white raiment, as Christ said to the church in Sardis, "Those who overcome shall have white raiment." They must put off filthy rags, as Isaiah states that "man's righteousness is." This is seen in Isaiah 64:6.

Put off the righteousness of man, a righteousness that they thought they could gain by works. Remember Titus 3:5. Righteousness comes by grace through faith, putting off the old man and his deeds and receiving the new man through faith in Christ Jesus the Lord. They were blind and needed eye salve; put off their own reason and wisdom, which came because of being a natural man who cannot receive the things of the Spirit of God, as seen in 1 Corinthians 2:14. The eye salve of faith in Christ would open their eyes to spiritual truth. They can only see spiritual things when they become spiritually alive in Christ. For the believer in temporal or operational death, sight comes through confession of sin. This seems to say that almost all the people in that church were not saved, just as many pastors today aren't saved, yet they are in the pulpit, preaching every Sunday. Other folks are in church, teaching Sunday school, and aren't saved, but they have the answers.

Revelation 3:19–20 tells us Christ rebukes those He loves. If you haven't been rebuked or haven't been chastened by Christ, you need to check up on your salvation and make sure it is by grace through faith. Christ rebuked them out of love just as He does for all who have truly received Him as their savior. Christ loved their souls—hated their sins but loved their souls. They needed only to comply with His rebuke and chastening; to turn from their spiritual blindness and nakedness to see the salvation gift Christ has for them. Christ is knocking at the door for them. Christ continues to deal with them in grace. Those who were saved and in operational death, they must repent and come to Him, and He will sup with them. Anyone who hasn't trusted Him can come to Him and sup with Him.

But there is no wholesale revival in this church of the rights of the people. No major turning or returning to Christ; it is near death, except for a small remnant. The masses have rejected Christ. Look at our world today—prayer removed from schools, God's word removed from court houses, Nativity scenes challenged when placed on public-owned property. Christians who speak against sin are labeled a bigot. Soon some may even be charged under hate crime legislation. The age is closing with the rejection of Christ and sound doctrine. Christ finds a door closed against Him in the heart of the sinner, but when He finds that heart shut, He continues to knock.

Paul's teaching to Timothy in 2 Timothy 4:3 is seen here in the Laodicean church. That time has come! How many are flocking to churches where they don't have the truth and they don't endure sound doctrine? Do you see the Laodicean church here in this verse? Many Baptist churches aren't holding to sound doctrine anymore. Thank God, the folks at the church I pastor want to hear sound doctrine, and those reading this book are hopefully seeking the guidance of the Holy Spirit to find the truth. Christ knocks in vain to so many. Matthew 22:14 says,

"For *many are called*, but few are chosen" (emphasis mine). All have the opportunity to be saved, but many reject and aren't chosen because of that rejection of Christ, and many are seen here in the Laodicean church.

Revelation 3:21–22 tells us those who hold fast to sound doctrine will overcome. The overcomer will be granted to sit with Christ in His throne. Just as Christ overcame death and the cross and now sits on His Father's throne, we too who overcome in these last days will sit with Christ on His throne; seated with Him when He judges the whole world at the great white throne. They will sit down and rest from their labor in the truth. So it is important to listen to what the Spirit says to the churches, very important to let the Spirit show us the truth of Scripture.

We see the church of the last days I believe we are in those last days. Notice Christ didn't give them any type of commendation, only condemnation to this church! If they failed to heed His advice, failed to turn to Him, judgment was coming. Christ is knocking on the heart of believers to return to the truth, return to sound doctrine. We need to hear what the Spirit says to the churches, and the Bible is what the Spirit says to the churches, just as much as chapters 2 and 3 of Revelation are to be heeded. We need to hear and heed what the word of God says. The Holy Spirit inspired it and had it written for our understanding. The church in Laodicea was the church of the rights of the people, the church that would not be brought great revival. In this church we see how the Gospel is rejected, how the Lord and His truth were shut out with a closed door. It is occurring just as it was predicted by Christ with the church in Laodicea and the church today in the last times.

2

The Church from Pentecost to the Sixth Century AD

John was in the isle called Patmos. The Lord came to Him and instructed him to write. We now see the messages to the seven churches in Asia Minor. The messages are from the Lord Jesus Christ Himself. They both condemn and praise the churches of that early time at the close of the first century AD. In verse 1 we see the church in Ephesus. Paul had written to them years earlier, and we have the Epistle to the Ephesians showing Paul's instruction to them; now we see Jesus's message to them in Revelation 2:1. The message is to the messenger of the church in Ephesus.

There is a change seen here from chapter 1 to chapter 2, changing from that which you have seen to the things that are. The order of things in the Bible is important. The messages to the churches are prophetic and revelatory. They represent the progression of the church in this age. Ephesus represented the church of the first century. Smyrna represented the persecuted church of the second and third centuries. Pergamos represented the church from AD 312 to AD 500. Thyatira represents the church of the Dark Ages to the sixteenth century. Sardis is the church of the Renaissance and the Reformation. Philadelphia is the church of the revival starting in the nineteenth century.

Laodicea, as we saw in chapter 1, is end-time church of apostasy. Ephesus, the first church mentioned, is the church Paul had started in the book of Acts, the church the Epistle of Ephesians was written to. Ephesus is the church Timothy had been left at to install bishops and deacons, and the first church in the progression of the church of this age. We see Revelation 2:2 describing the apostolic church. Remember, its name means "desired one"! The zeal of the first love was in it. It was the church that loved and sought after the truth of God's word, the one who sought out false teachers and found them to be liars. Thus, Christ was commending them for this. This was the desired place of the church.

Remember Paul's command to Timothy 1 Timothy 1:3: "As I besought thee to abide still at Ephesus, when I went into Macedonia, that thou mightest charge some that they teach no other doctrine." Christ says He knows their works and labor. Christ knows our work and labor. He knows our vision and desires. He knows all about us, whether we are true or whether we lie. They had patience in waiting on God and ensured that no false teachers could seduce them. Timothy accomplished his mission with them. They were able because of the strong teachings of Timothy and John to root out those who were false teachers.

The early church was walking in separation from the world. The word for *church* in Greek is *ecclesia*. It means "called-out ones." The church in Ephesus was doing just as God's ideal church is to do, separate from worldly influence. Today we see the church where discipline has nearly come to an end. They were loyal to the truth. Look at churches today; many teach a contrary doctrine, or one that makes people feel good when they attend, creating large numbers.

The church in Ephesus unmasked these types of pastors who called themselves apostles. They showed their evil teaching, which exposed them for the liars they were. Revelation 2:3 tells us they had borne; they were suffering for the sake of truth, patiently enduring the suffering for the Lord's sake. They had not given up the ship, hadn't lost their vision; they had kept on keeping on for the sake of Christ. They continued in labor, not fainting from it. They didn't give up. What a desirable church they were. Christ saw the good, complemented them on the good, but we now get to Revelation 2:4 where Jesus had something against them.

They had left their first love. They had lost their zeal. Their desire was declining; they had lost their warmth. We see the early decline of the church even in Ephesus. Their hearts drifting from Christ, that decline has continued. We see it today. We see it in the churches where people choose to leave sound teaching and go to that which makes them feel good.

Today we need to heed Revelation 2:5 where Christ advised them "Remember your first love. See how you have fallen away from it. See where you stand on spiritual things. Think back to when you were first saved. Repent, turn back to your zeal, and get back on fire for Christ." I remember the joy I felt the day I was saved. I wanted to shout it out to the world. If you have left that first love, be grieved that you left that first Love. "Examine yourself," He tells them. "Do the works you once did. Be renewed in heart, in soul, and in strength."

The church theme for 2014 of the church I pastor had this verse on it—"Mount up on wings of eagles and be renewed"—as Isaiah 40:31 states. Pray as Psalm 51:10 tells us. Christ warns there are consequences for being non-repentant. Christ says He will come quickly. Remember how John saw him as judge. If the people and churches don't repent, He will come in judgment. He will remove their light, their witness, and possibly even their church from them.

In Revelation 2:6, Christ again commends them. Although they left their first love, they hated the deeds of the Nicolaitans. The Nicolaitans were a sect who called themselves Christians, yet they held hateful doctrines. They were guilty of hateful deeds, were hateful to Christ and hateful to all true Christians. They placed stumbling blocks in the way of the truth. Eating meat that had been offered to idols and participating in orgies—these were among their deeds. The point, we are to hate the sin not the sinner. Notice He said that the church hated the deeds of the Nicolaitans, not the Nicolaitans themselves. Revelation 2:7 tells us to hear what the Holy Spirit says to the churches.

What does He say? Repent of those things that pull you away from your first love. Turn back to your zeal, get on fire for God! Ensure we are on fire and wanting God to bless us. Be a witness and invite unbelievers to receive Christ and come to church. Invite those who are away from God; be ready for God to work. What was said to the church in Ephesus applies to churches today. If we fail to repent, judgment will come. If we fail to heed the Spirit, we won't accomplish Christ's mission for us. The Christian life is warfare against sin. We all are tempted; we give in to temptation many times.

We can apply what 1 John 1:9 said: confess our sins, and God forgives and cleanses. We need to never yield to our enemies, never compromise the truth of God's word, and never let the Doctrine of the false teachers affect our lives. Revelation 2:7b says, "To him that *overcometh* will I give to eat of the tree of life." We overcome the world when we receive Christ. We gain rewards for faithful service.

We gain spiritual knowledge when we continue to resist temptation. We grow as we study God's word and when we heed what the Spirit said to the churches. So we see the early church in the church in Ephesus. They had lost their zeal, their fire, for doing God's will; for listening, learning, and applying God's word. The Bible is what the Spirit says to the churches as much as chapters 2 and 3 of Revelation. We need to hear and heed what the word of God says, for the Holy Spirit inspired it and had it written for our understanding. The church in Ephesus was the desired church in its beginning but in the end had lost its zeal and fire for service. Smyrna represented the persecuted church of the second and third centuries. Jesus introduces Himself here as the first and the last, then He carries it further; He was dead but is now alive. That is why we are to place our faith in the truth of the Gospel.

We see a church of suffering, the persecuted church, which went until about AD 312. Tens of thousands of Christians were put to death for their faith and their testimony; yet despite the bloodshed, they remained faithful. Notice Jesus gave her no condemnation. This period of the church found the believers faithful even to death. They were to have a short period of tribulation. Understand this is not the Tribulation that follows in Revelation 6 to 19. It is a short period of extreme persecution the church would endure and be found faithful.

In 1 Peter 1:6, do you see Peter said the suffering was for a little season? He is referring to our suffering as believers, not the Tribulation; that is also what we see here for the Smyrna church. This is the persecuted church, but there is reward for this church, first for enduring persecution and being faithful to the end. The reward would be the crown of life. We see this also in James 1:12 and Hebrews 12:2 and 3.

When we endure trials and temptations, we receive this crown. Then

Jesus concludes with the promise of not suffering the second death. The second death can only be suffered by those who are not saved. The second death is eternal separation from God. These believers in Smyrna, as all believers, will not suffer the second death because they have received Christ as their Lord and Savior by grace through faith.

We now see the third message to the third church in Asia. The messages are from the Lord. They both condemn and praise the churches. In verse 12 we see the church in Pergamos. In verses 12–17 we find Jesus's message. In Revelation 2:12, Jesus introduces himself to the church in Pergamos as the one who has the sharp sword with two edges. He comes with judgment. He comes with the Word. We saw Smyrna representing the persecuted church, and then we see from history that Constantine the Great came to power as Roman emperor from ad 306 to 337.

The persecuted church lasted until about ad 312. Tens of thousands of Christians were put to death for their faith and their testimony, yet they remained faithful. In AD 312, Constantine the Great, Emperor of Rome, was carrying on his conquest of the world. He was suffering serious losses until one day he announced he had seen in the sky a giant cross; over it were these words: "In this sign thou shalt conquer." This pagan emperor took this to mean that if he embraced the cross, he would be victorious. So in what probably was an act of desperation, he professed to have become a Christian. He decreed that the religion of the Roman Empire must henceforth be Christianity.

After his victory, he made the religion of Christianity the state religion. He compelled all his armies to be baptized, thus beginning a new era of church history, which, by many historians, is considered a great blessing, but in reality it became the greatest curse that could have ever occurred.

The church became the dependent of the state. The Roman Empire became a father to the church and supported it financially. Church and state became one. Soon the emperor became the head of the church. The church, now in a state of marriage to the Roman government, began to dictate not only the power of religion but also the powers of the government. Almost everyone accepted Christianity. Many were paid in gold coins to be baptized. How many actually embraced Christ, we don't know; possibly very, very few. From this date, we can track the decline of the spiritual power of the church.

Pergamos is the third church; in its name we have two meanings: marriage and elevation. In AD 312, we see the church joining the state in a marriage type of agreement. AD 312 to approximately AD 500 represents the time in which the church was elevated to a place of power.

The church was virtually married to the world. It was a time when the church and state were united under Constantine and his successors.

The Lord comes to Pergamos to judge by His word. The two-edged sword seen as the word He speaks judged men. It judges now and in the last days. Here we see the church delighting in this union. The churches rise in the power of the clergy. They became as dictators over the members. The history of this period is a gloomy one spiritually. Revelation 2:13 tells us Christ knew the works of Pergamos. He knew where they were dwelling. They were even seated on Satan's throne.

What was Satan's throne? The people of Smyrna would say it was the Roman emperor's throne. The church was filled with men of corrupt minds. Look at Revelation 2:14. They see how God deals with the believer. Christ had a few things against this church. The doctrine of Balaam was being taught as well as the doctrine of the Nicolaitans. False teaching was now in the church.

The doctrine of Balaam is seen in Numbers 24:1–9. Balaam taught Balak in Numbers 24 to cast a stumbling block before the sons of Israel. He did this by leading them to make unholy alliances with the Midianite women, thus the unholy alliance of church and state seen here. As you just read in Numbers 24:1–9, the doctrine of Balaam was a doctrine of tolerance.

Sound familiar? Balaam encouraged Israel to blend in with the Gentile world, just as the church in Pergamos was doing, just as the church did in ad 312, thus causing the loss of a separated position. We are told to be holy (i.e., separate). We are to be in the world but not of the world.

The church in Pergamos as well as the church from AD 312 to AD 500 had married the world. They held fast to Christ's name. He says that, "Thou hast not denied my faith." False doctrine, false teaching, had crept in, but they had some who didn't deny their Christian faith. Satan, with the persecution, had sought to destroy the church by destroying the believers. Now he changes his tactics; he attempts to destroy their testimony by using external worldly factors and introducing false doctrine from within the church. It is far more dangerous for the church to be supported by the world than for the world to be openly against it.

Remember the doctrine of the Nicolaitans (Rev. 2:15)? They were a sect who called themselves Christians, yet they held hateful doctrines, were guilty of hateful deeds, were hateful to Christ and hateful to all true Christians. They placed stumbling blocks in the way of the truth, the doctrine of Balaam. Eating meat that had been offered to idols and participating in orgies were among their deeds.

The point is we are to hate the sin, not the sinner. The Greek word *Nicolaitans* actually means "rulers over the people." That is what the church became when Constantine united church and state. The church in Pergamos had been greatly deceived with these false teachings. When the persecution ended for the church, the world began to look upon them with satisfaction and came to them with open arms and a smiling face instead of a sword and a frown.

Understand when the church was persecuted, she flourished, but when the union took place with the world, decline set in. With the teaching of Nicolaitans, the church suffered greatly. We still see the church suffering from this even today. This brought about a period where the clergy was accepted as being of divine origin; therefore they must be knelt down too. This made the clergy dictators, in many cases, as well as the false idea that all witnessing and all evangelistic efforts are to be accomplished by the clergy when just the opposite is true. The pastor is on equal ground with the members. All should be involved with witnessing and evangelism.

The answer for the Pergamos church—repent (Rev.2:16–17). Change your doctrine, change your ways. Repentance is the duty of every believer as well as every unbeliever. Repentance, for the believer, restores fellowship, for the unbeliever, repentance brings salvation. If there is no repentance, Christ would judge the church. He will come against them with a sword in His mouth. Remember, He told them He was the one with the sword with two edges. The word of God is a sword; it is an offensive as well as a defensive weapon. For this church, it would be in the hand of God, able to slay both sin and sinners. It is a sharp sword. No heart is too hard; it is able to cut it. It can divide asunder between the soul and the spirit, between the soul and those sinful habits. God can cut the false out of the church and leave the truth, or He can destroy all who will not seek after the truth.

It is a sword with two edges. It can cut out the infection in order that the church will be healed. There is no escaping this sword.

In verse 17, again we are told to hear what the Spirit says unto the churches. When repentance occurs, great favor belongs to the repentant soul. "To him that overcometh will I give to eat of the hidden manna, and will give him a white stone, and in the stone a new name written, which no man knoweth saving he that receiveth it" (Rev. 2:17, kjv). All are for those who repent and overcome. The hidden manna, the filling of the Spirit, comes to those who are saved. The indwelling of the Spirit is for the believers too. When we sin, we lose the filling, but confession of sin restores the filling or fellowship we have with God through the Holy Spirit.

The white stone and the new name written on it show that when we receive Christ, we are no longer guilty of sin and our sin debt. We are a new creature upon salvation. We have a new name in glory—we are the adopted children of God. We see the church from AD 312 to AD 500 in the church in Pergamos.

Notice Christ gave one condemnation to this church! He praised them for holding His name and faith in Him. He promised them a judgment if they didn't repent and fellowship with the Holy Spirit and freedom from the guilt of sin if they did. We need to be listening, learning, and applying God's word. We need to hear and heed what the word of God says, for the Holy Spirit inspired it and had it written for our understanding.

The church in Pergamos was the church that married the world and was exalted. In this church, we see how the church would marry the state and corruption would set in. False doctrines and teaching would be found in that church. It occurred just as it was predicted by Christ with the church in Pergamos and the church from AD 312 to 500.

3

The Church from the Sixth Century AD To the Reformation

In verse 18 of Revelation 2, we see the church in Thyatira. We see Jesus's message to them in verses 18–29. In Rev. 2:18, Jesus introduces himself to the church in Thyatira as the Son of God, making clear His deity; his eyes like a flame of fire showing His holiness, his feet like brass showing His righteousness—the Son of God with eyes like fire.

He is God as much as the Father, the eternal only begotten Son, who was equal to God in every way yet subordinate by becoming a man or the God-man and in coming to die on the cross for the salvation of mankind! We see His eyes like flame signifies piercing, penetrating, perfect knowledge; and His thorough insight into all people and all things. His feet like that of brass show that His providence is steady, pure, and holy. He judges with perfect wisdom. He acts in perfect strength and steadfastness. We saw the church through Pergamos last chapter, and the church in Pergamos represented the marriage and exaltation of the church.

We see in the name Thyatira a continual sacrifice. It can also mean an incense offering. This is the church in the Dark Ages from AD 500 to the Reformation. It represents the result of the union of the church as we saw with Sardis. In the seventh century AD, we see through historical documentation that the bishop of Rome was first regularly recognized as Christ's vicegerent and visible head of the church. This was, properly speaking, the beginning of the papacy. There was no Roman Catholic Church, in the full sense, until the pope was the acknowledged head of Christendom. It is important for Protestants to keep this in mind. You will often hear papists say, "You know, the first church was the Roman Catholic Church, and all the different branches of the Protestant church have simply broken off from Rome. There was no Protestant church until the days of Luther."

That is an absolute fraudulent claim. There was no such thing as the papacy until the seventh century of the Christian era. For six centuries before that, the church was becoming more and more corrupt and drifting farther away from the Word of God. Then in the seventh century, men professing themselves to be servants of God were ready to acknowledge the pope as head of all Christendom. The churches started by Paul and the other apostles and early Christians were the original churches.

Each ERA following the persecution saw more and more degeneration. I have been to several funerals in the Catholic Church; my dad's family was mostly Catholic. The pastor who my wife and I grew up with was saved out of the Catholic Church! Both my father and pastor said that the church was filled with rituals; they knew because they had been in them. The priest, in conducting Mass, claims to offer a continual sacrifice—the continual sacrifice for the sins of the living and the dead. Christ is the only sacrifice for our sins; thus, the continual sacrifice doctrine denies the finished work of Christ.

As we saw, Christ states in verse 18 that He is the Son of God. Christ is the propitiation for our sins and not for ours alone but the sins of the whole world. First John 2:2 tells us that. Romans 3:25 tells us that God set forth Christ to be a propitiation through faith in His blood, and we see that He also came to declare His righteousness for the remission of sins that are past through the forbearance of God.

In 1 John 4:10 we see: "Herein is love, not that we loved God, but that he loved us, and sent his Son to be the propitiation for our sins." Where in this does it say that men must make a continual sacrifice for sin? That is what is taught by the Catholic Church, and it was in Thyatira. Revelation 2:19 tells us the Lord now gives them a commendation. He knows their works just as He knows our works. He knows their charity or love. He knows their service, faith, patience, and He says their last works are more than their first works. He mentions this because they had a doctrine of works added to salvation. They had a religion of works, not grace. The Lord gave them credit for a great deal that is good.

From the seventh century and forward, there has been a great deal of good accomplished by the Catholic Church and the underground churches that continue to exist. Many Roman Catholic monks and nuns have been ready to lay down their lives for the needy and sick, some more than Baptists and Protestants. Centuries before Luther, every hospital in Western Europe was a Roman Catholic monastery or convent. The Lord does not forget all that. Where there is a little bit of faith, His love takes note of it all. Hearts that are even in the Catholic Church yet have faith in Christ are met with His grace for salvation and His love toward them.

The honorable character of the commendation Christ gives the church is seen here in verse 19. The ministry and the people receive great commendation from the Lord. He mentions their charity or Love their disposition of good to all men. Further, to the household of faith, He commends their love. He commends their service, their ministration, their officers in the church who labored in the Word and doctrine. He commends their faith, which was by grace, which brought on all the rest both charity and service. He commends their patience for those who showed charity to others, are diligent in their service to others, are most faithful.

Many were fruitful and growing wiser and better. Yet now in Revelation 2:20, we see His condemnation. They allowed the woman Jezebel to seduce the church. In the Old Testament, Jezebel was a wife of King Ahab. She persecuted the prophets of God and led the people to worship Baal. Her goal was to unite the religion of Israel with that of Phoenicia. Just as the Roman emperors mixed their pagan religion in with the church, the church became very accommodating in the fourth, fifth, and sixth centuries. They begin to compromise with heathen rites and rituals. It became so bad it was hard to tell Christian from pagan worship. These seducers had two things which brought agony to them: They made use of the name of God to oppose the truth of his doctrine and worship; this very much aggravated their sin.

They abused the patience of God to harden themselves in their wickedness. This was the church in Thyatira's great sin. She was accused of being like that woman Jezebel. Why was the church in Thyatira compared to Jezebel? It was because the church required her to seduce the people of the city. As a church, they had no civil power to banish or imprison her, but they had ministerial power to censure her, to excommunicate her; neglecting to use their power made them partners in her sin.

Revelation 2:21 tells us that Christ gave them time to repent, but they repented not. Repentance is necessary to prevent a sinner from destruction. Repentance requires time. When God gives time for repentance, He expects fruits for repentance. When the time for repentance is lost, the sinner perishes with a double destruction.

Revelation 2:22–23 tells us the seductress will be cast into a bed along with those who commit adultery with her. Spiritual adultery will be punished. The church in Thyatira was punished. She will suffer in the Great Tribulation. A key for us to understand here: those who are not of the faith but are following the seduction of salvation by works will go through the Great Tribulation. "I will kill her children, those who follow her, unless they repent." Her children will be killed. Unbelievers will die the second death, leaving no hope of a future life with Christ or the Father, no resurrection from the lake of fire, only shame and everlasting punishment.

In Revelation 2:24–25 we now see Christ's encouragement to those who remain faithful. The Lord promises blessing to the faithful. The false doctrines of those who aligned with Jezebel in Thyatira are called the depths of Satan. Satan's false doctrine always brings punishment, but not holding to those doctrines brings blessings. No new mystery would be given to the faithful. No new doctrinal truths would come. All had been written by the New Testament writers.

In verse 25 are the doctrinal truths you have to hold on to; hold fast to the truth of God's word. Don't give in to the deception of Jezebel; the delusions and devices that those who taught this offered. So tender is Christ's promise to his faithful ones here. Hold fast till Christ comes. This is the coming at the Rapture, the snatching away of the church, prior to the Tribulation. This is the first time we see Christ mention His return to these churches. Thyatira is the first that will continue even in her wicked state until the coming of the Lord. The wicked worshippers shall pass through the Tribulation, but the faithful ones have the promise that they shall rule and reign with Christ when He comes.

Revelation 2:26–27 contains the promise that those who overcome by faith, those who even after salvation keep on working for Christ to the end of the church period, will rule and reign with Christ during the kingdom. He will give power over the nations. Christ in His kingdom will rule with a rod of *iron*. He will break them! "And I will give him the morning star. He that hath an ear, let him hear what the Spirit saith unto the churches" (Rev. 2:28–29). He will give those who overcome the morning star.

The Gentile nations that ruled will be crushed. The heathen elements that infiltrated the church will be destroyed. The King, who shall reign in Mount Zion and in Jerusalem, will destroy all these. He, as the morning star, is given to the people of that time. We will shine along with Him as He reigns. Here we have the hope of Christ's return. Here we have the promise that we will rule and reign with Him. If we receive Christ by grace through faith, not of works, lest we can boast in our works, we will have Him with us. The bright and morning star will be reigning right here on earth, and we will be with Him in all His glory, in all His power. We see the church, from AD 500 into the Reformation, in the church in Thyatira. Notice Christ gave several commendations to this church! He praised them for holding the faith in Him. He promised them he would bring judgment if the seducers didn't repent. We need to be listening, learning, and applying God's word. The church in Thyatira was the church that mingled truth and falsehood while the world exalted her. In this church, we see how the church, having married the state, had corruption set in. False doctrines and teaching were found in that church. It occurred just as it was predicted by Christ with the church in Thyatira and the church from AD 500 to the Reformation.

4

The Church of the Reformation

We now see the fifth message to the fifth church in Asia. The messages are from the Lord. He both condemns and praises the church in Sardis. In verse 1 of chapter 3, we see the message beginning to the church in Sardis. Jesus's message to them: "I know thy works you have a name that thou livest and art dead" (Rev. 3:1). Jesus introduces himself to the church in Sardis as He that has the seven Spirits of God, and He has the seven stars. He has the Holy Spirit with all His various power, grace, and operation.

To every church and minister, there is a dispensation and measure of the Spirit given to them for edification. The measure given is a spiritual influence for the minister and the church. Faithfulness keeps the Spirit's power and influence at work in the church unless they forfeit it by mismanagement. They had an early return to biblical principles. The ministers are Christ's ministers, not the churches' ministers. Yet even in the Reformation period, this truth was not completely understood because of the fact that the ministers of Christ are subject to Christ without humans as intermediaries.

We saw Thyatira representing the union of church with the state. We saw in the name Thyatira a continual sacrifice, which can also mean incense offering, in the church in the Dark Ages from AD 500 forward.

Now we have Sardis, which means "remnant" or "that which remains" or "those who have escaped." We have prophetically seen the church of the Reformation. These churches escaped from Rome only to eventually fall into cold, lifeless formalism. The Renaissance begins with this church. *Renaissance* literally means "rebirth." Yet we see an indictment of this church here in the first verse, "thou livest" or "came alive," the revival and blessing of the Reformation days.

Historically, the state churches included the population of a given country who were supposed to be made members of the church and kingdom of Christ by infant baptism. These churches would therefore have people still dead in trespasses and sins. Baptism never saved anyone, and yet these churches practiced this. The churches would have people banded together, baptized, and called Christians, taking the sacrament of the Lord's Supper. They are zealous in Christianity yet void of a personal relationship with Christ and not having been saved. They do not have faith in Christ but rather believe baptism as an infant made them Christians rather than the new birth, which comes by grace through faith.

The Reformation began in the fourteenth century and continued into the sixteenth century in Europe. Many things brought about this reformation; the Holy Spirit, of course, was the driving force. Man's inventions set the stage for the Reformation. Certain discoveries fed it too: the discovery of America, the invention of the printing press. The Scripture now could be given to everyone in printed form. Until the invention of the printing press, the Scriptures were unknown to the common people. Each copy of Scripture, to this point, had to be transcribed by hand, thus limiting the number of Bibles available.

The printing press came to the forefront in the middle of the sixteenth century. John Gutenberg of Germany invented the printing press in about ad 1550. The first completed book, printed in Latin, is known as the Mazarin Bible, or the Bible of forty-two lines, because there were forty-two lines to a page. God gave man the ability to print His word. With this God-given, God sent, and God-timed invention of printing, a new study of the Bible began. Lost truths were rediscovered.

Unbiblical errors were exposed and so set the stage for the church in Sardis—the church of the Reformation. It swept Europe under the leadership of the following well-known men:

a. Luther,
b. Erasmus,
c. Zwingli,
d. LeFevre,
e. Calvin, and
f. others.

Luther's influence spread through Germany and Scandinavian countries. Calvin's influence was found in France, Switzerland, and the Dutch countries, and John Knox later in Scotland. Understand that the Reformation fell short of accomplishing all that it could have achieved. While it was a protest and reaction against the rigid ecclesiastical hierarchy of Thyratira, it went to another extreme, becoming free of restraints of absolute vicars and potentates of the church. It was split by the abuse of liberty and freedom and split into various sects and denominations.

Christ says of this confusion, "Thou hast a name that thou livest, and art dead." God's estimate of the church as a whole was they had a name and lived but were dead, but there is a remnant of true believers as with each church and era. The church in Sardis had a great reputation; it had a name, a very honorable name. It was a flourishing church. It had a name for a vital and lively region, for purity of doctrine, and for unity among them.

Everything appeared well outwardly, but it was not really what it appeared to be. They had a name to live, but they were dead. They had a form of godliness but no power from God. Second

Timothy 3:1–7, especially verse 5, centers on this. They had a name that upheld them, but not a principle of life. They appeared to have great lives, but their souls, service, and spirits were dead.

They needed a renewal of heart, soul, and strength. In Revelation 3:2, Christ's advice to the church in Sardis is to be on guard, ever watchful; to strengthen the things that remained. The reason they were dead is that they had lost their watchfulness. When we are off our watch, when we let our guard down, the things of sin creep in, and we lose ground in our advancement for the Lord. We must be watchful against sin, Satan, and his destructive forces (1 Peter 5:8).

Satan doesn't want to just devour believers but churches that teach and preach the truth. We need to renew our strength on those things that remained. We need to retain our integrity. We need to remember the truth we have been taught, the truth we have heard. We need to hold on to that truth.

The message of the Reformation churches tells us the great truths of God's word. We have a doctrinal statement for the church I pastor. I have a personal doctrinal statement of what I truly believe. These are the ones set in stone for us and for me. The Southern Baptist have their Baptist faith and message, and the New Hampshire Declaration of Faith. They hold these fast. We as believers are to hold the truths in our lives. We have men in churches and places of authority, even in the Baptist faith, who would destroy everything for which their denomination stands; Baptists who want to deny the inspiration of the Bible, Baptists who seek to destroy churches that won't align with the false teachings they bring.

God sometimes purges out those who won't follow the truth. He purges out the bad because the remnant seeks and holds the truth. What you have received and heard, hold it fast! Failure to do so will bring judgment (Rev. 3:3). Christ's judgment comes quickly; the churches of the Reformation learned the truth. The Bible being printed helped them to understand biblical truth and falsehood. The great truths were committed to the churches of the Reformation. They were called on to repent—repent of the slack way they treated God's truth, the truths received in past teaching.

Warning for not being watchful is given. Christ will come like a thief, and we won't know when He will come. We see this verse as compared to 1 Thessalonians 5:4. Paul said Christ would come and take the church home. We will meet Him in the air. The dead shall rise first. We who are alive and remain shall be changed and meet them in the air; that is the snatching away of the bride. Here Christ will come in judgment of the church and believer. He will come as a thief to strip them of their remaining enjoyments and mercy.

Hebrews 12:5, 7, and 11 tells us the Lord chastens us. "And ye have forgotten the exhortation which speaketh unto you as unto children, My son, despise not thou the *chastening* of the Lord, nor faint when thou art rebuked of him" (v. 5, emphasis mine). We don't know when, but we can know He will chasten. He will judge the churches that turn from the truth and have stopped preaching the truth.

In Revelation 3:4, Christ commends those who remain faithful; those who haven't defiled their garments, who haven't given in to false doctrine. His promise—"they shall be with me in white." They are part of the bride of Christ. They will have the white robes of justification, justified by grace through faith in the Lord Jesus Christ; white robes of adoption as the adopted children of Christ, white robes of comfort, white robes of honor and glory in eternity.

Revelation chapter 3 tells us they will walk in white, for they are worthy (v. 4). Those who overcome will be clothed in white raiment (v. 5). Let's look ahead in Revelation 4:4: "And round about the throne were four and twenty seats: and upon the seats I saw four and twenty elders sitting, clothed in *white* raiment; and they had on their heads crowns of gold" (emphasis mine).

Revelation 19:7–8 says, "Let us be glad and rejoice, and give honour to him: for the marriage of the Lamb is come, and his wife hath made herself ready. And to her was granted that she should be arrayed in fine linen, clean and white: for the fine linen is the righteousness of saints."

Revelation 19:14 says, "And the armies which were in heaven followed him upon white horses, clothed in fine linen, white and clean." So tender is Christ's promise to his faithful ones here. He will not blot their names out. The purity of grace shall be rewarded with the perfect purity of glory. God will not blot your name out of the book of life. True believers will never lose their salvation. Men may blot you out of church membership, but Christ will produce this book of life and confess the names of those written in it. Because they overcame by faith in Him, they overcame the world.

Revelation 3:6 tells us to hear what He is saying. Be faithful and gain reward. Be an overcomer by placing your faith in Christ, and all these things will be added unto you. So we see the church of the Reformation in the church in Sardis. Notice Christ gave several commendations to this church! He praised them for their faith in Him. He promised them that if they would be watchful, He would reward, but if they failed to watch, He would come in judgment.

We need to be listening, learning, and applying God's word. The church in Sardis was the church of the remnant, those who escaped. In this church, we see how the remnant was faithful and held the truth while others sought to be with the world. It occurred just as it was predicted by Christ with the church in Sardis and the church of the Reformation.

5

The Church from the Eighteenth Century Into the Twenty-First Century AD

We now see the sixth message to the sixth church in Asia. The Lord says nothing of the works of the church in Philadelphia. In Revelation 3:7–13, we see the church in Philadelphia. Jesus's message to them, "I know thy works," He set before them a door. In verses 7–13 we find Jesus's message.

In Revelation 3:7 Jesus introduces himself to the church in Philadelphia as He who is holy, He who is true, He who has the key of David. What he opens, no man can close; and what he closes, no man can open. His personal character is seen in the introduction. The church in Philadelphia is the church of brotherly love, for that is what *Philadelphia* means. The holy one is speaking to the loving church.

Christ's nature is holy; He cannot be anything but true to His word. He has the key of David that is to the kingdom age, even more as the one who has the key to government and authority in the churches. Christ opens doors, of that we can be thankful. He opens doors of opportunity for churches. We need to step through that door and utilize that opportunity. He opens a door of utterance to His ministers. He gives us the messages He has for the churches. He opens a door of entrance, which is to salvation and to fellowship for the believer. He opens the heart's door for those who need salvation. He opens a door of admission into the visible church that lays down the terms of communion or fellowship with Him. In the end, the church in Philadelphia would eventually fall into cold, lifeless formalism. Christ opens the door to the triumphant church according to His plan of salvation; He also shuts doors. If He wills it, He shuts the door of opportunity, so we need to be very careful to enter through the door of opportunity when it is open.

He opens the door of utterance; He leaves obstinate sinners shut up in the hardness of their heart. He shuts the door of fellowship to the unbeliever. We see the church in Philadelphia; this is the church of the eighteenth, nineteenth, the end of the twentieth century, and maybe it stretched to the twenty-first. With the God-given, God sent, and God timed invention of printing, a new study of the Bible began. God began to work afresh in a mighty power. There were marvelous awakenings all over Northern Europe and the British Isles it then swept into America itself. Spirit-filled servants of Christ went through these various countries as crusaders of the Lord, calling on sinners to repent.

We see Billy Graham as the best known to many of us. They called saints to awaken to their opportunities. God began to arouse many of His people to a deeper sense of value of His word in all sufficiency, in guidance for His people. For His name, thousands of people left all human organizations and began to meet, simply seeking to be guided by the Lord. Prior to the nineteenth century, the blessed hope of Christ's return, the premillennial return of the Lord, was seldom stressed. The truth was believed by many of God's faithful remnant. Seldom though was it preached or taught and was utterly unknown to the masses of church members.

Over two hundred years ago, the truth of the imminent return of Christ was revived. As a result, the true Christians were inspired and fired up with their responsibility. God raised up men full of power, zeal, and passion for souls to awaken the dead church in Sardis to its responsibility.

These men were

1. Whitefield,
2. Wesley,
3. Edwards,
4. Moody,

5. Darby,
6. Spurgeon, and
7. Henry.

As a result of these men, revivals swept the continent. They swept the world with great results from these revivals. During the twentieth century, surging and great missionary movements began. Powerful missionary societies were born. The protest to the deadness of the church in Sardis ignited missionary fire, and the following names broke out:

1. Livingston,
2. Taylor, and
3. Graham.

Many others bear testimony to the zeal and love of the revived church, which was what the church in Philadelphia represented.

Revelation 3:8 tells us that Christ again knew the works of this church in Philadelphia. He had set a door in front of this church; no man could shut it. The church in Philadelphia had little strength, yet they had kept the word of God and not denied Christ. Many of us who grew up in the twentieth century saw churches hold fast to the truth of salvation by grace through faith. There is one and only one true church. It is neither Protestant nor Catholic; it is neither Presbyterian nor Baptist. It consists of all those rich and poor, Jew and Gentile who have, by grace through faith in the Lord Jesus Christ's shed blood, become members of that one church, the church whose assembly is made up of the firstborn whose names are written in the Lamb's book of life.

Observe these important characteristics of the church in Philadelphia. His word was kept, his name confessed. The keeping of His word involves a great deal more than just believing the Bible or reading and studying it. It implies obedience to the revealed will of the Lord. It is a blessed thing to realize "All scripture is given by inspiration of God, and is profitable for doctrine, for reproof, for correction, for instruction in righteousness: that the man of God may be perfect thoroughly furnished unto all goods works" (2 Tim.3:16). How immense is the scope for faith to act upon.

When we teach and preach the truth, like the Philadelphian church, we can be sure Satan will attack. Some, even some Baptist groups, want to deny the inspiration of the Bible today in our time. Some, even many Baptists, want to destroy churches that won't align with the false teachings they bring. They are here in our world today. Christ set an open door and kept it open. Anyone who wanted to step through could and still can. Revelation 3:9 tells us Christ's great promise: He will make the enemies of His church subject to her; those enemies described to be of the synagogue of Satan, saying they were Jews, but they weren't. They lied. They were pretenders. Christ knows them; he knows their works. They profess Christ but are not truly His.

Christ will, in the end, convince them that they were wrong; that the church that kept Christ's name, the church that kept His word was the true church. They will admit their wrong, and Christ will show them that He loved the church that taught and preached the truth. The greatest honor and happiness a church can enjoy is in the unique love and favor of Christ. Christ can show this favor to His people in such a way that their enemies will see it. They'll be forced to acknowledge it. This, by the grace of God, will soften their hearts and make them eager to be admitted into communion with them.

In Revelation 3:10, Christ's promise goes further. He will keep them from the hour of temptation. Here is the first definite promise—that the true church will escape the Great Tribulation found in the book of Revelation. From the church in Thyatira to the church in Laodicea, the church would continue in the world simultaneously until the coming of the Lord.

As we saw in a previous chapter, only of the church in Philadelphia is it said that they will be taken out and kept from the hour of temptation. That is coming upon the world after the snatching away (i.e., the Rapture) of the bride. Those who keep the word of Christ's patience will be kept from the hour of temptation. The study light interlinear translation goes like this: "Seeing that you keep saying of the endurance of me I also you shall be keeping out of the hour of the trial of the being about to be coming on the inhabited earth whole to try the ones dwelling on the earth." This sounds very much like we will be kept from the Tribulation.

The time of Jacob's trouble can be seen in Jeremiah 30:7: "Alas! for that day is great, so that none is like it: it is even the time *of Jacob's trouble*, but he shall be saved out of it" (emphasis mine). This is the great time of

Tribulation, which is coming. To be sure, it is coming upon the whole world. It is coming upon all them dwelling on the earth at that time. Daniel 9:27 says, "And he shall confirm the covenant with many for one week: and in the midst of the week he shall cause the sacrifice and the oblation to cease, and for the overspreading of abominations he shall make it desolate, even until the consummation, and that determined shall be poured upon the desolate."

Daniel saw seventy weeks of seven years each; the Tribulation we see in Revelation will last seven years, the final week of Daniel's seventy weeks. Daniel 9:24–26 says, Seventy weeks are determined upon thy people and upon thy holy city, to finish the transgression, and to make an end of sins, and to make reconciliation for iniquity, and to bring in everlasting righteousness, and to seal up the vision and prophecy, and to anoint the most Holy. Know therefore and understand, that from the going forth of the commandment to restore and to build Jerusalem unto the Messiah the Prince shall be seven weeks, and threescore and two weeks: the street shall be built again, and the wall, even in troublous times. And after threescore and two weeks shall Messiah be cut off, but not for himself: and the people of the prince that shall come shall destroy the city and the sanctuary; and the end thereof shall be with a flood, and unto the end of the war desolations are determined.

Seventy weeks were determined for Israel to complete before the Messiah would come and reign in His kingdom. The Messiah would come when seven plus three score, or sixty weeks and two weeks, had occurred after the decree to rebuild Jerusalem. That would be sixty-nine weeks or 483 years. Then from that, we are told the Messiah would be cut off (killed) after sixty-two weeks, so seven weeks forty nine years the city would be rebuilt and completed, then following 434 years after the completion was the Messiah cut off. It happened just as Daniel's prophecy said it would.

Peter gives us a little hint of all this too: "But, beloved, be not ignorant of this one thing, that one day is with the Lord as a thousand years, and a thousand years as one day" (2 Pet. 3:8). Virtually God has given mankind seven thousand years of time, divided up into one week. The first thousand was the Sunday of that week; it began with Adam being placed in the garden. It ends when Christ's thousand-year reign is complete on the Saturday, the day of rest, with the

Lord ruling the earth.

It is promised He will come quickly (Rev. 3:11). Note here the Greek word for *quickly* means "speedily." He comes speedily; that is how He will come. The original reads, "Be perceiving I am coming swiftly be ye holding which you are having that no-one may be taking the Wreath of you." This is, of course, telling us to hold fast the truth of His return at the snatching away, i.e., the Rapture of the bride. Do not let a false teacher with a doctrine of Him already having come take your crown of righteousness away from you. You gain the crown of righteousness by looking forward to the return of Christ for His bride.

Luke 12:37–38 tells us, "Blessed are those who are watching for the Lord's return." Christ said that. It means we need to be faithful in watching for the snatching away of the church, the bride. In 2 Timothy 4:8, Paul said there is a crown of righteousness for all those who love His appearing. To gain the crown of righteousness, you must hold onto the truth of His return. If you follow after any other doctrine, the false teacher will take your crown; they will cause you to lose it.

Revelation 3:12–13 tells us that those who overcome will have stability in the heavenly temple. We shall no longer lose our fellowship but remain with God, worshipping Him. We will have an intimate family relationship with God. New Jerusalem will be our eternal home, so it is important to listen to what the Spirit says to the churches, very important to let the Spirit shows us the truth of Scripture.

We see the church of the eighteenth to twentieth century; maybe it can be stretched into the twenty-first century. Notice Christ didn't give any condemnation to this church! He praised them for their faith in Him. He promised them that if they would continue to hold onto the faith, they would not go through the time of temptation or trial that is coming upon the earth and upon all mankind. If they failed to watch, that is, keep on watching for Him, they would lose their crown, the crown of righteousness. That is, they would not gain it because they failed to earn it under the conditions laid down in Scripture. We need to be listening, learning, and applying God's word.

We need to hear and heed what the word of God says. The Holy Spirit inspired it and had it written for our understanding. The church in Philadelphia was the church of the brotherly love, the church that brought great revival. In this church, we see how the Gospel spread, how they held on to the patience of the Lord and His truth. It occurred just as it was predicted by Christ with the church in Philadelphia and the church of the eighteenth to twenty first centuries.

What now of the twenty-first century? We can still see a small remnant of those holding the truth, but it is nothing like it was in the eighteenth and nineteenth centuries. In fact, we saw at the end of the twentieth, starting in the mid-seventies, a decline in holding fast the truth, a decline in faithfulness to God. It has progressed to people being too busy in the twenty-first century to remain faithful to God, to church, and to accomplishing God's will.

Many people in their fifties and above have returned back to God, but what do we see? When a young person reaches their twenties, they seem to stray from God. Many return when they reach their forties, but they seem to be getting fewer and fewer.

We have now the Laodicean church, the church of the rights of the people. The verse that was shown in chapter 1, the verse in which Paul states to Timothy in 2 Timothy 4:3, is seen here in the church of the twenty-first century, the Laodicean church: "For the time will come when they will not endure sound doctrine; but after their own lusts shall they heap to themselves teachers, having *itching* ears" (emphasis mine). How many are flocking to churches where they don't have the truth and they don't endure sound doctrine?

Do you see the Laodicean church here in this verse? Even many Baptist and Bible churches aren't holding to sound doctrine anymore. Thank God, there is a remnant of believers who want to hear sound doctrine, and those reading this book are hopefully seeking the guidance of the Holy Spirit to find the truth. Christ knocks in vain to so many. Soon—yes, very soon—He will be coming for His bride to snatch her away and take her home to heaven. Then the hour of temptation will come to pass. The trumpet will sound, and the dead in Christ shall rise, and we who are alive and remain, that is, we who have been saved by grace through faith and are living, will be snatched away; the bride that is the true church going to be with her husband, Christ Jesus.

6
The Church the Bride Snatched Away

The scene now changes. There is now a voice like a trumpet. In Revelation 4:1, John hears a voice after the sound of a trumpet, saying, "Come up hither." He saw a door open and heard the voice as it were of a trumpet. We don't see the spewing out of the church in chapter 4. We do see, prior to the beginning of chapter 4, an openly apostate church; people wanting their rights no matter what the Bible commands. Sounds like today's church? We saw a lukewarm church.

Christ was ready to spew them out of His mouth, that is, vomit them out. The church of today is the apostate church, as seen with Laodicea, which is the church that will be in existence when Christ returns for His bride; the last and worst church of all. These conditions need not alarm us, nor should they confuse us, for the closing of the Laodicean church is assigned to us in these last days of the church period. It signals the opening of the door in heaven. Remember, the end of Revelation 3 showed a closed door that Christ was knocking on.

No need for alarm, chapter 4 shows an open door. The age of the church comes to an end here in chapter 4, which will occur after this present age, and this is set to begin as the church of the rights of the people comes upon us full force. Second Thessalonians 2 tells us to stand fast in this apostate time, which is upon us. We are to hold fast the truth of God's word. Now we see in chapter 4 the second vision John saw.

Verse 1 starts with "After this." After what one might ask? After the vision of Christ with the golden candlesticks and the messages and cycles of the church, after John had handwritten the messages to the churches, after he sent the messages to the several churches. That vision closed, John now sees the next vision. John says, "Behold, a door was opened in heaven." Whatever is transacted on earth, it is first designed and settled in heaven. John, a member of and representative of the true church, is called now to see the things that will happen after this age. He escorts us into the realm of these things to come.

Now the scenes of the world are gone for us; we now look into heaven. We have the third separation of the book with the things hereafter, the wonders we will see, both heavenly and earthly. The end of the church age and the history of the church on earth ended. From here on, we will not see the church mentioned as being on earth again until late in the book of Revelation. We see saints mentioned, but they are distinct from the church of the present age; the scene in heaven here in chapter 4. We will see a shift back to God working through Israel. We see Gentiles saved in the age, but there is no church, that is, no bride of Christ, on earth; no body of Christ; no bride of the Lamb any more on the earth unless Christ is on earth.

John states in Revelation 4:1, "And the first voice which I heard was as it were of a trumpet talking with me; which said, Come up hither, and I will shew thee things which must be hereafter." Let's look now at what the dispensationalist calls the Rapture (others say Rapture is not mentioned in Scripture, so "the snatching away," as the Greek calls it) in 1 Thessalonians 4:16–17: "For the Lord himself shall descend from heaven with a shout, with the voice of the archangel, and with the trump of God: and the dead in Christ shall rise first: Then we which are alive and remain shall be caught up together with them in the clouds, to meet the Lord in the air: and so shall we ever be with the Lord."

Notice the similarities in Revelation 4:1. John represents the church, which is called up. He hears a voice, and he described it as sounding like a trumpet. Paul in Thessalonians says a voice and the trump of God will be heard. John hears a voice as if a trumpet; that represents those who are alive and remain. First Corinthians 15:52 says, "In a moment, in the *twinkling of an eye*, at the last trump: for the trumpet shall sound, and the dead shall be raised incorruptible, and we shall be changed" (emphasis mine). John sees the open door in heaven in which the believer will then pass through. His attention is turned from earth to heaven. Yes, Jesus is coming again. Praise God!

Many scoff; some say He came in ad 70, many Christians have never heard this teaching, and many believe in His second coming, but not this coming for the church as His bride. Others place it in the middle of the Tribulation, mid-tribulationalist. Scripture states that He will return. In Acts 1:9–11, the disciples were told He shall come just as He left; that is the Second Coming. In John 14:1–3, Christ promised to return to take us to heaven; this is the snatching away (i.e., Rapture). He is right now preparing a place for us as part of the bride of Christ. We see many scoffers today or those who say He has returned, as prophesied in 2 Peter 3:4. We are told of this day, this day of apostasy, in these final days of the church.

However, His imminent return is sure. Just as it was in the days of Noah, Peter reminds us in 2 Peter 3:5–6: "For this they willingly are ignorant of, that by the word of God the heavens were of old, and the earth standing out of the water and in the water: Whereby the world that then was, being overflowed with water, perished." Christ Himself stated this of His return. Matthew 24:37 says, "But as the *days of Noah* were, so shall also the coming of the Son of man be" (emphasis mine). Then when all is complete, God will renovate the earth with fire; Peter tells us in 2 Peter 3:10.

The first promise of the Bible must be seen in spite of all the denials the Lord will return; first for His bride the church, then in judgment at the great white throne. The first promise in the Bible after man fell has to do with the first and second coming of Christ. Genesis 3:15 says, "And I will put enmity between thee and the woman, and between thy seed and her seed; it shall bruise thy head, and thou shalt bruise his heel." After pronouncing the curse upon Adam that he would work by the sweat of his brow and upon Eve for pain in childbirth, Jesus turned to the serpent and also gave a promise to Satan. God would send Adam and Eve a seed. That seed of woman was Jesus, who will crush Satan's head. Satan bruised Christ heel with the death on the cross, but when Christ returns, He will cast Satan into the lake of fire and crush his head. Here we see the first advent of Christ and Satan bruising the seed of woman's heel. We see His second coming to crush Satan's head. Half of this has already been fulfilled.

In Romans 16:20 we are told "God shall bruise Satan under your feet shortly." We see that Genesis 3:15 is more than the promise that a redeemer would come; it includes both Advents. The final will be the seed of woman in final triumph over Satan. We see that Scripture shows a return in the air, first for the bride, in that the things that shall be can began.

Revelation 4:2 Notice again the similarity of verse 2 with 1 Thessalonians 4:16–17, and 1 Corinthians 15:52. Then we will be with the Lord forever. What a great day that will be. As the song says, "There is coming a day when no heartache will come; no more sickness, no pain, no more crying over there. What a day that will be when my Jesus I shall see. What a day, glorious day, that will be."

John says he was changed. Look back at the 1 Corinthians 15:52 verse: we shall all be changed; we have a new body. "For this corruptible must put on *incorruption*, and this mortal must put on immortality" (1 Cor. 15:53, emphasis mine).We will be changed from our corruptible body, one that sees death, changed to a body that is incorruptible and immortal, that will never see death. Paul started in 1Corinthians 15:51 with these words: "Behold, I shew you a mystery; we shall not all sleep, but we shall all be changed." We won't all see death. Some believers will be alive when the Lord returns, but those who are alive and remain will be quickly changed. John was in the Spirit as He entered into heaven.

John's words being, "And behold, there was a throne *set* in heaven" (Rev. 4:2, emphasis mine). We see John doing just as he was commanded in Revelation 1:19. He has written, and we have seen him write as Christ commanded. He wrote what he had seen. He wrote the things that are now occurring in the church. He wrote the things that shall be, starting here in chapter 4. John was in the spirit, and now we see the throne in chapter 4 verse 2. It was a seat of honor, a seat of authority, a seat of judgment. Thus, we see 1 Corinthians 3:11–15: "For other foundation can no man lay than that is laid, which is Jesus Christ. Now if any man build upon this foundation gold, silver, precious stones, wood, hay, stubble; every man's work shall be made manifest: for the day shall declare it, because it shall be revealed by fire; and the fire shall try every man's work of what sort it is. If any man's work abides which he hath built thereupon, he shall receive a reward. If any man's work shall be burned, he shall suffer loss: but he, Himself shall be saved; yet so as by fire." We will face the bema seat of Christ.

Second Corinthians 5:10 says, "For we must all appear before the *judgment seat* of Christ; that every one may receive the things done in his body, according to that he hath done, whether it be good or bad" (emphasis mine). Thus, we are facing the throne of Christ, but this says "judgment seat," which is the bema seat judgment, and one sat on that throne, John says. He saw the glorious one on the throne. The throne was not empty like the tomb was empty. There is one who fills it.

In Revelation 4:3 we see the description of the one on the throne. He was like jasper, later we will see this is seen as clear as crystal, and a sardine stone. No human features are seen, just an image seen in His transcendent brightness, the seal the token of God given to man through Noah that no more would He judge the earth by flood. Here surrounding the throne is the covenant promise Christ made to the church and all His people; an everlasting covenant of our salvation secure in Him. The rainbow looked like an emerald; the most prevailing color was a green, showing the reviving and refreshing nature of the covenant. The emerald was the stone of Judah, and praise is seen in this color. The rainbow pointed to the divine covenant of God; a covenant of Grace, a covenant of promise, which has been given to the church. All who believe in Christ have been saved by grace, and we have a promise of spending eternity with Him.

Revelation 4:4 tells us there are twenty-four seats round about the throne, which signifies the twenty-four divisions (or courses) of the priesthood. Twenty-four elders are seated on these thrones. Notice how they are clothed. They have white raiment on, which, as we have seen, is what the believer is promised for overcoming in this age. Notice too they have crowns on their heads, proof that they have faced the *bema* seat judgment and have received what is due for their works, whether good or evil.

Their sitting represents their honor, rest, and satisfaction. Their sitting around the throne shows their relationship to God, their nearness to Him, the sight and enjoyment of being in His presence; they are in places of honor. When lightning's and thundering's and voices are mentioned, we have a sign of terror in judgment (Rev. 4:5), but the elders are unmoved by this. They remained seated on the thrones and not moved. Theirs is a place of respect in judgment before God. These are signs of the dreadful storm that is about to hit the world below. The seven lampstands of fire burning before the throne, the gifts, the grace, and operations of the Holy Spirit in the churches is seen.

We see these dispensed according to the will and pleasure of Him who sits upon the throne. We saw these in chapter 1 verse 4; we have in these the sevenfold fullness of His power. We see the church now in heaven, clothed in white and rewarded. The twenty-four elders who represent the church seated upon the thrones as judgment is soon to come upon the earth below. We see the Holy Spirit and His seven Spirits burning before the throne in the seven candlesticks. What a beautiful scene in heaven we have, what we have to look forward to for having believed on Christ as our savior.

We see we will gain rewards for our works of intrinsic value, as Scripture has promised, and we see the throne and the one who sits upon it. *Wow*, what a great place we have to look forward to.

7

The Bride before the Throne

In Revelation 4:6, we move from the royal court to the things surrounding it. Up to this point, we have been looking at the royal court. Before the throne is a glassy sea. Thus, it brings to mind the sea of brass seen in Solomon's temple. It contained the water used for priestly cleansing. We are sanctified and cleansed by "the washing of water by the word." The sea here in Revelation is not for cleansing. It is the word of God, but it is not needed for cleansing, for in heaven there is no more sin.

The word of God abides forever, stable and sure forevermore. A glassy sea filled with crystal; it is firm, glorious, and on it the people of God will stand, eternally saved and in His presence. We see what is in the middle of and round about the throne. John is concentrating now on the things seen in and around the throne. We see what we have to look forward to. We saw the glassy sea and now what is in the midst and surrounding the throne of God, round-about are four living ones; they are not beast. There are, however, we are told, full of eyes front and back. These four living ones represent the attributes of the living God. They surround the throne. They show God in His fullness.

In Revelation 4:7 we see each described here. The first beast was like a lion. It is the well-known symbol of divine majesty. The lion is of the tribe of Judah, the root of David, the lion-like courage. The second is like a calf or a young ox. The ox represents power, God as the all-powerful one. It shows the great diligence and labor, the great strength of God seen as the Ox who graciously serves mankind. The third had the face of a man, where we see God's attribute of intelligence and purpose. It shows that deity is no longer a blind force, nor is He simply the "great first cause" or impersonal law. Yes, Jesus is coming again. Praise God! The fourth resembles the eagle; this shows the swiftness of God. As the swiftness of an eagle to his prey, so is the swiftness of God's judgment, which is swiftly coming upon mankind on the earth below. "With the wings" and "full of eyes" show us that with all their meditation, all their ministration, they act in knowledge.

We see in Revelation 4:8–9 their ceaseless activity, seeing everything, as they never rest day or night. Continually they're saying, "Holy, Holy, Holy, Lord God Almighty, which was, and is, and is to come." They ceaselessly adore the one true God the Father. They ceaselessly adore the Son. They ceaselessly adore the Holy Spirit. Their continuous praise, "Holy, Holy, Holy," show us the Triune God in the Trinity.

Revelation 4:10 tells us the elders, as we saw in the beginning, were wearing crowns. We see them now worship the one on the throne; worshipping Him who lives forever, Jesus Christ. Then they throw down those crowns before His throne, more blessed to own His glory than in possessing their own. We see them worshiping the Lord Jesus here, the one who provided their salvation.

Notice it wasn't their works that brought salvation; it was their faith mingled with God's grace that saved them. They gave God the glory, the glory of His holiness with which He had crowned them both on earth and the honor and happiness which He crowns them in heaven. They, just as we, owe all the graces and the glories to Him. They acknowledge Him and that His crown is infinitely more glorious than theirs, that it is their glory to be glorifying God instead of Him glorifying them.

In Revelation 4:11 they say, "Thou art worthy, Christ is Worthy, O Lord of our praise." Christ is worthy to receive glory from us. He is worthy to have honor and power given to Him because He has created all things. The one who created all things is worthy of glory, honor, and praise. That is what we should be giving Him every day of our lives! We should be saying, "Holy, Holy, Holy, Lord God Almighty." He created all things for His pleasure. Notice they didn't say "for man's pleasure." He didn't create all things for our pleasure. Since He created us for His pleasure, we should be giving Him praise, glory, and honor for His daily supplying of our needs. It was His will and pleasure to create all things for His purpose, for His will. He who died upon this earth to be the propitiatory sacrifice for all mankind is worthy of our praise and adoration.

In Revelation 5:1 we now see the Lord Jesus on the throne. We find here in chapter 5 the Lamb of God who is the bridegroom. He is holding in His hand a book. It has writings on both sides and sealed with seven seals. We now see the counsels and decrees of God. We see them sealed and in Christ's hand. We must use verses 1–7 as a springboard in order that we rightly understand the remainder of the book, the remainder of the revelation of Jesus Christ. There will be seen seven sealed books in the coming chapters of the book of Revelation.

It is important to understand this one first in order to interpret the others correctly. Revelation 5 is the key that opens the entire book of Revelation. The right interpretation of the mysterious little book or scroll will therefore give us the correct understanding of the rest of the book. If a mistake occurs here, then we will be wrong all the rest of the way through the study. In following the messages, one must attempt to pull everything together correctly. The entire book or scroll in the hand of Christ will be seen; it was sealed, as verse 1 tells us, and explained a little later in the book.

We look first to setting the scene. In Revelation 1 we have a vision of the glorified Christ all in the majesty of His coming for the bride. In chapters 2 and 3 we have a history of the professing church in all the phases of apostasy in the figure of the seven churches. When the current church seen in Laodicea has finished its course, we then see John as representing the true church that is caught or raptured (Revelation 4:1–3). The bride is snatched away and is caught into heaven. As John faced the bema seat for judgment, first he saw Christ on His throne in all His glory, in all His majesty, followed by heaven's song of praise and adoration by the entire host of glory; then the elders, representing the church and saints of all ages; then the four beasts of living creatures, representing the angelic hosts. Someday we will also face the bema seat of Christ for judgment.

8

The Bride in Heaven

In the King James Version, chapter 5 of Revelation begins with the conjunction *and* therefore linking the closing verse of chapter 4 verse 11 to chapter 5 Verse 1. The scene, as we have seen, is in heaven. We saw John caught up in chapter 4 verse 1. He went to meet the Lord in the air and then on to heaven, just as the bride will be snatched away. Once there, he saw Christ on the throne.

At first, seeing only the Lord, our Savior, he is completely occupied with the vision of His Lord and God. Soon he sees the thrones and the four living creatures. Now John sees something else, something he hadn't been aware of. He sees another sitting on the throne and in His hand is a little book. Everything comes to a standstill in heaven.

In Revelation 5:2 they are searching for one worthy to open the book. Diligently they search for someone, anyone, who can break the seals in order to open the book. Until they find that person, there can be no further revelation a strong angel cried out in a loud voice: "Who is worthy to open the book, to loosen the seals!"

There are many among the church in heaven that you think might be a worthy candidate; just think: Peter and James and John, the big three of the disciples, will be there. Paul will be there. You and I will be there as will Billy Graham. Everything hinges on finding the one who is worthy to open the book, to loosen the seal. The cry was if there be any creature who thinks he is sufficient enough to open the book, to explain or execute the council of God, to come forth as a champion of the faith, then let him stand, approach the throne, and make the attempt.

In this little book is contained the Revelation, the account of all that is to follow, the seven trumpets, the pouring out of the seven vials of the wrath of God; the book of redemption. What is the sealed book? We need to understand the history of the Old Testament. In the numerous laws given to Israel, there was a law that dealt with redemption of three things. God provided that a wife, a slave, and a possession might be redeemed.

In the case of the wife, if her husband died before leaving offspring, in order that his name might not disappear from earth, the dead husband's brother was to take the widow as his wife (if he were able) and perpetuate the name of his departed brother. There was also the redemption of a slave. If a man, because of neglect or misfortune, fell into debt and was legally tried and unable to pay, he was to serve his master whom he owed this debt as a servant, but the law provided that after six years, he could gain his freedom.

In the meantime, however, a near kinsman, some close relative, could choose to redeem him; and if he was able to meet the payment, he could redeem his poor brother or relative and release him before the six years. This is seen in Leviticus 25 among the laws of redemption. Provision was also made for redemption of land that had been lost by its owner. As seen in Leviticus 25:23–25, the method of redemption went like this: When a man had fallen into debt and lost his property, he was taken before the judges. A document was prepared, which stated that the land had passed from the debtor into the possession of the one whom he owed the debt. But this transfer was not a permanent transfer. When the year of Jubilee came, the land was returned to the original owner.

In the meantime, it could be redeemed and returned to him. There were two ways this transaction would work: First, either the man himself could repay the redemption price, which was very unlikely because he was now a servant. Second, it could be purchased back by a near relative such as an uncle or closer kinsman. The terms were written on two different scrolls, or as we see in Revelation books. On both of these were written the terms of the redemption of the lost possession. One scroll was left open in the court of the temple or Tabernacle for all to read. The other was rolled up sealed with seven seals and placed in the temple to be brought out only when the near kinsman redeemer gave evidence that he was willing and able to redeem it. He would go to the court of the Tabernacle, read the terms of redemption found in the open public scroll, and then go to the priest or judge and demand that the sealed document be brought forth and the debtor be freed and the property returned.

If this relative, this near kinsman, was able to prove he could meet the terms able to pay the redemption price, if he could meet all the conditions of the law, the sealed scroll was produced, and he publically opened the seals, thus validating the claim and making invalid the mortgage. The man could return to his possession. Eventually, the practice of one scroll instead of two was adopted. Instead of two, one public scroll and one sealed, these were combined into one. One scroll or book was used.

The terms of the redemption was written on both sides within and without. When the scroll was rolled into a tube and sealed with the seven seals, the inside corresponded to the secret record and the outside containing the terms for the public and especially the near kinsman redeemer. Who might want to know the terms of redemption of the lost possession! That is the picture we see here in Revelation 5.

Here we see the judge of the entire earth sitting on his throne, and in His hand is the scroll with the seven seals. This is, therefore, the book of redemption. This is evident also in Revelation 5:9–10.

We see the church now in heaven, waiting for the Lord to have the book of the redeemed opened, ready to show our redemptive price paid by Him, the title deed complete and our freedom gained.

The Lion of Judah, with the swiftness of the eagle, the majesty of a lion, and the strength of the ox, is the one able to open the seven seals. In verse 3 of chapter 5, we now see the search for the one who is worthy to loosen the seals and open the book. No one in heaven or in earth, not one under the earth, is found that is able to open the book. Remember, the apostles are there, believers of the church age are there, we, as we saw in chapter 4, are there in our redeemed and resurrected bodies.

The search is on for the one, yet no one is worthy to open the book, not even to look thereon. Not one person can accept the challenge and not one will; not one who is only human. None of the angels in heaven can accept that challenge; not the wisest men on earth or the wisest who have passed away, that would include Solomon, is able to accept the challenge. None of God's prophets can accept the challenge. None who even God revealed His mind to can open the book or scroll. None under the earth can open the scroll. Satan isn't worthy and fallen angels aren't worthy. The priest of Christ's time who judged Him aren't worthy.

There is only one who can open the seals and thus open the book. In Revelation 5:4, John begins to weep because no man was found worthy. Not even the apostle John was found worthy. John felt a great concern inside himself for this matter, so he wept in great disappointment. Wouldn't we? John is brokenhearted over this. John is weeping because the redemption terms are found in the book, but whose or what redemption terms? This is what we need to understand concerning this book. In the Levitical law, the scroll had to do with the redemption of land.

We saw the three things that could be redeemed: a wife, a servant, and the land. At this point in chapter 5, the first two have been accomplished. Christ's bride, the church, is now in heaven, as seen in chapter 4. We who are Christ's servants have been fully redeemed. We have, at this point, received our resurrection bodies, for we were changed, just as seen in 1 Corinthians 15:52: "In a moment, in the *twinkling of an eye*, at the last trump: for the trumpet shall sound, and the dead shall be raised incorruptible, and we shall be changed" (emphasis mine). But the earth has yet to be redeemed from the curse.

The animals on this earth are still groaning under the curse. The earth itself is groaning under the curse." Romans 8:22 says, "For we know that the whole creation *groaneth* and travaileth in pain together until now" (emphasis mine.) These too must be redeemed, for Christ is the perfect redeemer. Every realm that came under the curse of Adam's sin must also be redeemed by the Last Adam. Adam was placed in headship over the earth. When Adam fell, he did not fall alone; he fell as the head of this earth. He fell as the head of the animals. Through his sin, the curse fell upon all that had been placed under him. Everything was under his authority.

Adam was created and given dominion over the earth and all that was on it and in it. Being given dominion means he was the leader or head over creation. He was the father of mankind and all nations. Because of his sin, the whole earth fell under the curse. The whole human race fell under the curse. Every human being is born with an old sin nature, therefore all are sinners, and all are condemned until they place their faith in Christ. Through Adam's sin, death passed upon all mankind. The soil of this earth too is under the curse; God said it was. Look at Genesis 3:17–18: And unto Adam he said, "Because thou hast hearkened unto the voice of thy wife, and hast eaten of the tree, of which I commanded thee, saying, 'Thou shalt not eat of it': cursed is the ground for thy sake; in sorrow shalt thou eat of it all the days of thy life; Thorns also and thistles shall it bring forth to thee; and thou shalt eat the herb of the field."

Not only was the ground cursed, deserts, waste, barren lands would appear to be under the curse. All the vegetation is under the same curse. Thorns, thistles, and weeds begin to spring up, all as a result of the corruption of their nature, all of which was brought on by the curse. Not only were the vegetables and minerals affected by the curse, so too were the animals; all were under the curse.

Genesis 3:14 says, "And the Lord God said unto the serpent, 'Because thou hast done this, thou art cursed above all cattle, and above every beast of the field; upon thy belly shalt thou go, and dust shalt thou eat all the days of thy life.'" Look at what God said to the serpent. At the time, the serpent was the most beautiful creature God created, possibly walking upright like man. He has the power to speak to mankind, even to converse with mankind. The serpent in the garden was not ugly, not a crawling reptile, not a slimy creature. If it had been, it would have never come close enough to Eve to make her listen to a word it said.

Instead, we are told in Genesis 3:1: "Now the serpent was more subtil than any beast of the field which the Lord God had made. And he said unto the woman, 'Yea, hath God said, "Ye shall not eat of every tree of the garden"?'" The serpent was more subtle, the term *subtle* shows attractiveness and appeal. We see the curse that God placed on the serpent in Genesis 3:14b: "Upon thy belly shalt thou go, and dust shalt thou eat all the days of thy life." Since God cursed the serpent to crawl upon his belly, that would tell us that before the curse, a serpent didn't crawl. It was beautiful and walked in some form, either upright or on four legs.

Notice in verse 14 the serpent is listed among the cattle and the beast of the field. Adam's sin lost everything; he lost leadership over the earth, the soil, the vegetation, and *Snatching Away of the Bride* all the animals. All came under the curse, all came under the sentence of death, as we see in Romans 8:22: "For we know that the whole creation *groaneth* and travaileth in pain together until now" (emphasis mine).

Christ came to redeem all that Adam lost, and He is a perfect redeemer, a complete redeemer. He is the second and Last Adam. He will bring deliverance to everything that came under Adam's curse. He will redeem the earth. The desert shall blossom like the rose. He will redeem the vegetables. Isaiah 35:7 says, "And the parched ground shall become a pool, and the thirsty land springs of water: in the habitation of dragons, where each lay, shall be grass with reeds and rushes."

Isaiah 11:6–9 also says, the wolf also shall dwell with the lamb, and the leopard shall lie down with the kid; and the calf and the young lion and the fatling together; and a little child shall lead them. And the cow and the bear shall feed; their young ones shall lie down together: and the lion shall eat straw like the ox. And the sucking child shall play on the hole of the asp, and the weaned child shall put his hand on the cockatrice' den. They shall not hurt nor destroy in all my holy mountain: for the earth shall be full of the knowledge of the Lord, as the waters cover the sea.

The redeemer will bring the redemption of creation. When Adam lost dominion over the earth, man must battle the forces of the curse that has affected nature. He must fight the weeds, thistles, insects, storms, droughts, and floods. After the flood, animals begin to prey upon one another. Death, groaning, and destruction are everywhere. Adam lost his inheritance, but God provided a plan of redemption whereby all that Adam lost will be redeemed. All this is contained in the little book that is in the hand of the one on the throne, the little book we see in Revelation chapter 5, the seven-sealed book that contains the terms on which Adam's lost estate may be redeemed.

There is good news! It will be redeemed by the Lion of the tribe of Judah, the Lamb with seven horns and seven eyes. The Last Adam, the Lord Jesus Christ. Therefore, we see the diligent search and we see the reason for John's weeping—no creature is worthy, not in heaven or upon the earth; no one under the earth.

Then in Revelation 5:5, one of the elders tells John, "Weep not!" Understand there will be no weeping after Christ wipes our tears away, when New Jerusalem comes to rest. Then we are told He will wipe all our tears away. Revelation 21:4 says, "And God shall wipe away all tears from their eyes; and there shall be no more death, neither sorrow, nor crying, neither shall there be any more pain: for the former things are passed away." See it here that all their tears will be wiped away and be no more because all the former things are passed away. We see the elder tell John to weep no more.

Why is he not to weep? Because the Lion of the tribe of Judah, who is the root of David, He has prevailed. He is able and worthy to open the book. He can open the seven seals. He has shown proof of His worthiness. Adam had forfeited the right to be in dominion over the earth. He had brought all things under the curse. The earth refused to yield the normal increase. We must today work by the sweat of our brow to make it produce and provide an increase. Man fertilizes and waters to ensure that crops grow. Satan, we are told, is the ruler. Ephesians 2:2 says, "Wherein in time past ye walked according to the course of this world, according to the prince of the *power of the air*, the spirit that now worketh in the children of disobedience" (emphasis mine).

Today Satan is still holding the mortgage on the earth because when he caused Adam's sin, he became the landlord over everything. The earth, when redeemed, is destined to belong to the saints. Jesus said the meek shall inherit the earth. The terms of redemption or mortgage are contained in that little scroll. Jesus is worthy of opening the book, of meeting the terms of redemption. These two chapters (4 and 5) naturally become the most majestic and overwhelming of any portion of Scripture up to this point. They reveal that awesome event in which God the Father has been directing all the events in the history of creation; that the entering of Jesus (who obeyed Him even unto death, yea, the death of the cross), with that inheritance of glory, honor, dominion and power, is bringing to every part of the creation.

John is not to weep any longer, the elder tells him. His attention is drawn to the one and only redeemer. There is no mistaking who this redeemer is; He is described for us. He is the Lion of the tribe of Judah, the root of David. This can be none other than the Lord Jesus Christ. All of mankind should be drawn to Him. Our job is to tell the world about Him in order that the Holy Spirit will draw all men to Christ, the one who was prophesied of in Genesis, the promised one to Israel, who was promised to come out of Judah, who was promised as the Son of David, thus showing his two natures as God and man; as a man the offspring of Judah and David, yet as God, the eternal creator, the root or origin that is the creator of David.

The Lord Jesus is both the root and the offspring of David. This is mentioned to indicate that He is worthy to open the book, to break the seals. To meet the three qualifications, He must be related to David, He must be willing, and He must be able. Two of these conditions have already been mentioned.

First, He was fit to be the kinsman redeemer because He is the offspring of David (as a man, Jesus was a descendant of David, therefore a human being and near relative of the human race).

Second, as the root of David, He was God, omnipotent God, therefore fully able to be the Redeemer and to pay the infinite price of redemption from the curse of sin, which He willingly did on the cross (the third qualification).

There are many in this world who will say Jesus was not fully God but only a mere human. They hurl the charge that we build this doctrine of His deity on vague evidence in Isaiah 7:14: "Therefore the Lord himself shall give you a sign; Behold, a virgin shall conceive, and bear a son, and shall call his name Immanuel." They say this is only biblical references to His virgin birth and deity, but those who have been spiritually born from above, thus given spiritual insight and having their eyes of understanding open, know the entire Bible abounds with statements of His being fully God and fully man. We cannot understand the fact, but we believe that Christ was both perfect God, perfect man. We believe in His supernatural birth.

The Bible is clear about the supernatural birth. The first promise in the Bible after the record of man's fall is a declaration of the virgin birth and the deity of the redeemer. He is called "the seed of woman," and only He is called the "seed of woman." We are told in Revelation that He is both the root and offspring of David, both the one who created and the one born in the line of David. When we study Scripture, we must follow the "spirit of prophecy." From the beginning of Scripture until the end of the book of Revelation, we will find that Jesus is the continual theme found in all Scripture; that will prepare us for the blessed scene of chapter 5.

Because all creation has utterly failed—failed to take on the business of carrying out the required judgment of God as written in the sealed book—it gives the account of everything which is to come. We anticipate with great joy this great public handing over of this book of judgment to our Lord as the Lamb that was slain. Therefore, we see the book and the search for the worthy one.

Christ is seen as the worthy one, the one who is able to redeem all of creation. In verse 6 of chapter 5, we see the Lamb now appear; the one who is worthy to open the book and remove the seals appears. Revelation 5:6 tells us the Lamb who is worthy appears He is none other than the Lord Jesus. The Lion of Judah also appears as the Lamb slain. He is the Lion who is worthy and able to conquer Satan, and He is the Lamb who is worthy to satisfy the justice of God. He appears with the marks of His suffering. This shows that He interceded for us in heaven. He does so by virtue of His satisfaction of God's requirement for our salvation. He appears as a *lamb, having seven horns and seven eyes,* perfect power to execute all the will of God and perfect wisdom to understand it all and to do it in the most efficient manner, *for he hath the seven Spirits of God.*

He has with Him the Holy Spirit without measure, in all completeness of light and life and power by which He is able to teach and rule all parts of the earth, having the seven Spirits of God, and those attributes of the Spirit we see in Galatians 5:22–23, which are called the fruit of the Spirit. John looked up to see the Lion and saw the Lamb slain, the lamb that depicts innocence, meekness, gentleness, and sacrifice. He is the One who will go forth as the mighty conqueror.

He will reclaim this earth as His own, and He will drive all His enemies from before His face. He will open the book of redemption of the earth, and He will meet all the requirements. Remember what we are told about His coming out of the tomb; He still bore the marks of the nails in His hands and his side where the spear was thrust. John saw Him many years after His resurrection in the vision, now as Christ in glory.

He saw a Lamb that looked as though it had once been offered in sacrifice. Christ will be a constant reminder to us of His suffering for our sins. We will never be found worshiping Gabriel instead of Christ. We will not even mistake so loving an apostle as John for his Lord. We will have eyes only for the Lamb because we see on His body that He bore for all eternity the marks that tell of our redemption. Habakkuk 3:4 says, "And his brightness was as the light; he had horns coming out of his hand: and there was the hiding of his power." There, where the cruel spear pierced Him, is the hiding of His power.

It says that the Lamb in the midst of the throne had seven horns. Yet it is not a mighty bull that is seen; it is a lamb, and the small form of the word, "a little lamb," with seven horns! Just as horns speak of power, *seven* speaks of perfection or completion. Perfect power belongs to the Lamb of God. That is what we see in the seven horns, and we are told He had seven eyes, which is interpreted to mean "the seven Spirits of God sent forth into all the earth." We see the connection of this phrase with Isaiah 11:1–2: "And there shall come forth a rod out of the stem of Jesse, and a Branch shall grow out of his roots: And the spirit of the Lord shall rest upon him, the spirit of wisdom and understanding, the spirit of counsel and might, the spirit of knowledge and of the fear of the Lord." This too shows us His being fully God and fully man.

The Holy Spirit is the Spirit of Christ. Colossians 2:9 says, "For in him dwelleth all the fullness of the Godhead bodily." All spiritual favors are His. He is anointed with the oil of gladness, and He gives the Holy Spirit to us. In Revelation 5:7 He is described by his act and deed: He approaches the throne; He takes the book out of the right hand of Him who sat on the throne. It isn't done with violence, neither was it by fraud, but He has prevailed by conquering sin and death on the cross and found worthy to take that book. He prevailed by His merit and worthiness, not by any works we have done. He did it by authority, the authority He has as God and by the Father's will.

God willingly and justly put the book of his eternal counsels into the hand of Christ. Christ, as willingly and gladly, accepted it into his hand, for He delights in reveling and doing the will of His Father, just as we too should be pleased to do the will of the Father. Christ willingly went to the cross for us. He willingly suffered shame and physical torture in order that we might be saved.

In chapter 5, here we are with Him, and He is willing still to do as the Father instructed—to redeem all creation. He came and received the book, taking it out of the right hand of Him who sat on the throne. What right had He, thus, to act? Because He willing went to the cross in infinite grace to pay the great debt of sin, while He too redeem the inheritance forfeited by Adam, freeing it from Satan's domination. He is the near-kinsman redeemer. He is the Lamb that has title to the book, the Lamb who can claim the title deed to this world! When He died on Calvary's cross, He purchased the entire world to be His own; He redeemed all creation.

The glory of God will be displayed in this world for a thousand marvelous years. We aren't to that point in Revelation with this book; the thousand-year reign comes at the end of the book of Revelation. It is His because He created it. He gave it to man, then man Surrendered it through sin. The Lord Jesus Christ bought it all back when He hung on the cross of Calvary, there at Golgotha. For almost two thousand years, He has been waiting patiently in glory for the appointed time in which He can claim His inheritance. The book of the title deeds has been sealed.

In this time in which it is as if God had driven a wedge in time, men have practically had their own way. The devil has been running things to suit his way that is as much as God allows. When Christ comes, it will be swiftly. He is going to make everything right. He will have to act first in judgment so that the order to complete the redemption process is accomplished. The very world in which the Lord Jesus died becomes the means by which God's glory is to be displayed.

This will be true not only in the millennium but also afterward, when the new heaven and earth are brought into being.

Revelation 5:8 tells us when He takes the book, the four living creatures and elders fall down before Him. The golden censers full of the prayers of the saints are seen. The elders which are as we believer priests are seen here. John beholds this book that the Lord Jesus has taken into His hand. It is to be unsealed, opened by Him. Christ is described by his place and position. He is *in the midst of the throne, and of the four beasts, and of the elders.* He was on the same throne with the Father; He was nearer to Him than either the elders or ministers of the churches. Christ, the man and the Mediator, is subordinate to God the Father as the Son. He is nearer to the Father in this scene than all the creatures, *for in Him all the fullness of the Godhead dwells bodily.*

All had fallen down before Him, we see. Having each one a harp, golden bowls full of incense which we are told are the prayers of the saints. Our prayers are poured out before the Lord. To me, I see these as the prayers we have prayed for the lost who have been left behind so that our prayers for their salvation could still be answered even when we are in heaven with Christ.

Revelation 5:9–10 tells us now a new song is sung to celebrate the Lamb. Understand we are going to sing a new song in praise to the Lamb, who is worthy, once we reach heaven and once He has received the book. What seemed to be dishonor and rejection of Him on earth becomes the ground of His worthiness to take the book. He suffered so greatly, and at such a great cost to Himself. He who had glorified everything that God is He was able and worthy to unfold what was made well in the way of government.

It was not the government of Israel but of all the earth, not merely earthly punishments, which we see occurred according to God's revelation of Himself in Israel, but the display of all of God's power that was in the whole earth. He had glorified all in who He was. We are redeemed, by Faith in the gospel of what He was for us through His death. Out of all from the earth, He was the One found worthy to bring forth redemption and salvation for mankind, in power. He does not yet come forth; His work is the worthy way in which the divine reason of God is on display in everything.

With the new song that they sing, they are acknowledging the infinite qualification and worthiness of the Lord Jesus for this great work of opening and executing the counsel and purposes of God. "Thou art worthy to take the book and to open the seals thereof, every way sufficient for the work." Deserving the honor, they mention the grounds and reasons of this worthiness. Though they do not exclude the majesty of His person as God, which without it He could not have been sufficient to carry it out, they primarily insist upon the merit of His sufferings, which He had endured for them as well as the whole world. This is what reached their souls with thankfulness and joy.

There isn't one redeemed person who doesn't want to be in a place of honor, but all see that their redemption was from the great grace of God, that they have been restored to the place of creation, given freedom in which man was created to possess. When we as believers who have become the elect of God by faith and His foreknowledge were born as slaves by Adam's sin and Satan's deception, people in every nation of the world, we see Christ not only purchased the liberty for us, but we as believers have received the highest honor and election, for He *made us kings and priests*; kings to rule over our own spirits, to overcome the world, and the evil one.

Having made us believer priests, He gave us access to Himself and gave us liberty to offer up spiritual sacrifices. We shall reign on the earth, we shall be with Him, and we will judge the world at the great day. They sing not only of themselves but of all the redeemed. The four living ones, the divine attributes, join in it too. Take note of the term "and the great throng" that is indicated by the words of the song. Far more people will be in heaven than will ever be lost in hell, it appears by this phrase. All the babies who died in infancy will be there, even the aborted ones.

How many millions is that? What a throng will fill that eternal throne room, and how joyous the fellowship will be. The gathering of all the pure and holy to this point—all who have been made pure by the blood of Jesus! They sing up there, giving credit for their redemption entirely to the Lamb and His work. Those are the saints of God, the believers by faith in Him by God's grace. That is you and me. That will be the glory of heaven. What a wondrous thing to see and know we are going to be praising and worshipping Him there in heaven. See Revelation 5:11. Wow, just think of all those voices in perfect harmony, singing praise to Christ; joy and thanksgiving that fill heaven.

No sooner had Christ received this book out of the Father's hand, the praises and adorations of angels and men came to Him, we are told, from *every creature.* What a scene of joy for the world to see and for all to know that God does not deal with men by means of complete power and strict justice. He does so by grace and mercy through Christ the Redeemer, he who governs the world not simply as a Creator and Lawgiver; he does so as our God and Savior. For the entire world has reason to rejoice in this.

The song of praise offered up to the Lamb can be broken down into three parts, one part sung by the bride, that is, the church; they are joined by the angels, and finally, every creature joins in. The hymn of praise is begun by the church; this is the bride, continued with the angels, who take the second part, in harmony with the church. The angels are said to be *innumerable*; we see they are the attendants of the throne of God.

They are the guardians of the church but ones who did not need a savior themselves. They rejoice in the redemption and salvation of sinners. They are in total agreement with the bride, that is, the church, in acknowledging the efficacious work of the Lord Jesus in His death on the cross for sinners.

He is *worthy to receive power, and riches, and wisdom, and strength, and honor, and glory, and blessing.* He is worthy of that office and authority; these require the greatest power, wisdom, the greatest deposit, and all the worthiness to properly settle the payment for man's redemption. He is worthy of all honor, glory, and blessing because He is the perfect One for the office and faithful in it.

Revelation 5:13–14 tells us the four living creatures, that is, all the completeness of God's power in creation and providence, all join in the amen. The elders worship God in the greatness of His being, worshiping the one who lives forever and ever. Christ is worthy of all worship and praise. We need to be found worshipping Him even while here on this earth.

CONCLUSION

While many have different views on the church and the Rapture, as it is normally called, this author is a pre-Tribulation, premillennial one. I hold that to be the truth of Scripture. I tried to prove that point with this book. The Lord will soon return and take the bride home. He will snatch her away and then will begin the Tribulation and Great Tribulation. You must be prepared, and you can only be prepared to be snatched out if you have received Christ as your personal savior.

Salvation is by grace through faith plus nothing. Works will not get you to heaven; works bring rewards in heaven after you have been saved, as we saw, but they cannot bring salvation, the Bible is clear on that. Revelation 4 shows the trumpet sound, which, at that point in the writing, represents the snatching away of the church. At that point, the believers in Christ will receive our rewards as we face the judgment seat, aka the bema seat judgment of Christ. There we are rewarded for our works after salvation. Many will receive wood, hay, and stubble; countless others will receive gold, silver, and precious stones.

I happen to believe that the majority will have a bounty of both. Believers can receive a crown for watching for the return of Christ, that is why it is important to be faithful, and that is why it is very important to believe He will come first for the church prior to the Tribulation.

It is important that one has to believe Christ is returning for the church, His bride prior to the beginning of the Tribulation. The crown you will receive for being faithful in that belief cannot and will not be earned without believing that the imminent return of Christ is still to come and is near. Scripture is clear on that. How do you stand today? Have you believed on Jesus as your Lord and Savior? If not, you need to do so right now. Don't miss being snatched away in the Rapture.

"For God So Loved the world that He gave His only begotten son, that whosoever believeth on Him will not perish but have eternal life" (John 3:16). Do you see how God, by grace, gave His Son, Jesus Christ, and you must believe in Him? "For whosoever shall call upon the name of the Lord shall be saved" (Rom. 10:13).

Believe then call is God's order. Look at what Jesus said in John 3:17–21: For God sent not his Son into the world to condemn the world; but that the world through him might be saved. He that believeth on him is not condemned: but he that believeth not is condemned already, because he hath not believed in the name of the only begotten Son of God. And this is the condemnation, that light is come into the world, and men loved darkness rather than light, because their deeds were evil. For every one that doeth evil hateth the light, neither cometh to the light, lest his deeds should be reproved. But he that doeth truth cometh to the light, that his deeds may be made manifest, that they are wrought in God.

Do you see, believe, and call upon Him? Believe you are condemned already because you haven't believed in Jesus Christ. Believe you are sinner in need of salvation, and believe that Jesus died for your sins. Call on the Lord and admit all to Him, even that you believe Jesus died for your sins. You see, it isn't a matter of your sin that you are condemned; it is a matter of your unbelief. Believe and call upon Christ for salvation, and you too can be snatched away at the Rapture.

SECTION 2

Beginning of Earth's Redemption

CONTENTS

INTRODUCTION

John was in the isle called Patmos, exiled there by the Roman emperor Domitian. Of course the Lord had sent him there for a purpose because God always has a purpose for every believer. Having a purpose which was to be revealed by Jesus Christ in the vision given to John. A purpose which would ultimately would become the Revelation of Jesus which came to him in a vision. The Lord came to Him and instructed him to write.

The scene has now changed in Chapter 6 and for this book. Now God's judgment in the redemption of the earth begins. It starts with the opening of the seals one by one. It brings on the four horsemen, each one having a role and a meaning. The Lamb, the only One qualified to open the seals and scroll or book as it is called, is found. The Bride, now in heaven, is gathered around the throne observing closely as the events unfold. We now begin to see what is to occur after *The Snatching Away of the Bride.*

The opening of the seals brings with it the greatest devastation that has ever been seen upon the earth. Each of the horsemen shows the progression of God's judgment upon both mankind and the earth. Yet most of mankind will refuse to believe in God and will reject the Lord Jesus Christ. Let's cover a few things that must happen before you can receive the message which the Holy Spirit's purpose is in you reading this book.

Before you can receive the message and serve God as He commands, before you can walk for him, you must have a personal, intimate relationship with Him. Romans 10:13 states, Whosoever shall call upon the name of the Lord shall be saved." Acts 16:31 says, "And they said, Believe on the Lord Jesus Christ, and thou shalt be saved, and thy house." Of course, John 3:16 is known by almost everyone, but verse 17 and 18 state, "For God sent not his Son into the world to condemn the world; but that the world through him might be saved. He that believeth on him is not condemned:

but he that believeth not is condemned already, because he hath not believed in the name of the only begotten Son of God." You must admit you are a condemned sinner because of not having believed, you also must believe and then call upon Christ for salvation.

Next, if you are a believer, you must practice 1 John 1:9: "If we confess our sins, he is faithful and just to forgive us our sins, and to cleanse us from all unrighteousness." Before you can receive God's message, you need to confess all known sin and God will forgive that sin and all the things which you don't realize are sins, as I like to say unknown sins.

1

The Beginning of Judgment

As John is watching things unfold in heaven, he has just seen the Lamb receive the book with seven seals. Who was the only one who is qualified to redeem all of creation! In Verse 1 of Chapter 6, we now see the Lamb open the seals. The thunder is loud as one of the seals is opened.

Revelation 6:1: "And I saw when the Lamb opened one of the seals, and I heard, as it were the noise of thunder, one of the four beasts saying, come and see." As we begin Chapter 6, let me reemphasize that the Great Tribulation—that is, the seven-year period of time—cannot begin until the redeemed of the Lord are gathered around Him in glory and crowned there. This cannot be emphasized enough. No saint in heaven currently has a crown.

Paul in 2 Timothy 4:8 states, "Henceforth there is laid up for me a crown of righteousness, which the Lord, the righteous judge, shall give me at that day: and not to me only, but unto all them also that love his appearing." That day when the Bride has been gathered home and assembled around the BEMA seat of judgment, is the day we will all receive our crowns!

We saw that day in my previous section *The Snatching Away of the Bride.* After the church is gone, many ask what is going to take place in the world. We need to look at this chapter from the standpoint that we are in heaven, the rapture having already taken place. Look at it as if last night, while things were going their ordinary way, the snatching away (the rapture) took place. The trumpet sounded and we met the Lord in the air. Every redeemed person responded to the trumpet of God. In the twinkling of an eye, the graves were opened, and in every place where the dead were resting, their bodies were raised and the living saints were changed.

We found ourselves snatched away, as 1 Thessalonians tells us. We entered with Him into the Father's house and gathered around the throne, falling down to worship Him. At first, our hearts would just be too full of Christ to think of anything else. He Himself stirs us at last to think of what He is about to do. We ask ourselves,

"What is going to happen next in that world we have left behind?" We look down to that unhappy scene where we lived yesterday. Men are going on much as before, only in great excitement. Look at the streets of the great cities. We can see the headlines: "A Great Number of People Have Disappeared!" There is a rush to get the newspapers to find out all about this strange event. Television news is reporting nonstop.

Throngs are crowding the popular churches to hear the preachers give their explanation of the great disappearance of so many people. Those left alive will be crowding into the churches as never before. Yet the pastors are clueless in most cases. Some will realize that there truly was a rapture of the church. An event they had taught wouldn't occur has occurred.

In heaven, we have Christ the Lamb and He has the book of Redemption in hand. Not mankind's redemption though, for mans' redemption came at the cross and comes by faith in Christ Jesus! He enters upon the work of opening and accomplishing the purposes of God. The purposes directed toward the world and God's final chastening. The period of trial is set to begin, that day of darkness! That day of the vengeance of the Lord is beginning. That time called in the New Testament the Hour of Temptation or Trial is set to begin.

It is divided into two parts: the Tribulation, followed by the Great Tribulation. As the Lamb breaks the first seal, John hears the noise of thunder. Thunder always speaks of a coming storm. The scene is peaceful enough for us. This time of Tribulation, this awful day of the Lord, is found prophesied throughout the Old Testament.

However, the best description of that time is found here in the book of

Revelation. The great picture we are given of this day here in Revelation. Fourteen of its chapters are occupied with a description of that time called in the Old Testament the Day of the Lord.

Then as the prophecy concerning the church was completed in Chapters 2 and 3 as we saw. Chapter 4 showed the church called up hither, the church snatched away to meet the Lord in the air, and Chapter 5 then revealed the church in heaven. The search for the worthy one has begun the one who would redeem all creation.

We now come to the sixth chapter which reveals the events unfolding on the earth with the Tribulation period beginning. This will extend through Chapter 19. The Tribulation will begin immediately when the snatching away of the bride has taken place. The chaos it brings will be devastating! It will end with the Battle of Armageddon! With the coming of the Lord in glory!

We see that the Tribulation period is divided into parts. The first part starts here in Chapter 6 and goes to Chapter 10. This section covers that period of time.

This portion contains the breaking of the seals. The blowing of the first six trumpets. Then we see the coming of three more chapters which describe the chief characters in the Great Tribulation for the reader of Revelation. As Chapter 11 unfolds, we are shown the two witnesses of the Lord. They will prophesy for exactly forty-two months, or 1,260 days, which will be the third book of the series. Three and a half years, the time of the Tribulation will be seen first. Chapter 12 speaks of the chief character of the book, the Lord Jesus Christ. It shows us His relation to His people in the Great Tribulation. Chapter 13 discusses Satan and the other two parts of the unholy trinity—the beast out of the sea and the beast out of the land.

Now we get into the study in full swing. Revelation 6:2: "And I saw, and behold a white horse: and he that sat on him had a bow; and a crown was given unto him: and he went forth conquering, and to conquer."

We see the horsemen come, the first on a white horse. He has a bow in his hand, a crown on his head. He goes forth conquering and to conquer. The white horse symbolizes peace and victory. The rider is the Beast of the Revived Roman Empire. He is not to be confused with the rider of the white horse in Revelation 19:11. The rider in 19:11 is the Lord Jesus Christ.

Chapter 6 brings out the unholy trinity, the trinity of Satan! This trinity seeks to imitate the Lord the Triune God. Therefore, he comes riding a white horse and preaching peace. For just a brief period after the church has been snatched away. Amid all the chaos comes this great man of peace. There will be a short period of peace on earth and he will say he has come to bring peace on earth and good will to all mankind!

The nations will join together in peace. He will not have gained full power over the earth, but he is a great leader working hand in hand with other leaders. No more war will exist, they will say! The people left after the snatching away will be found in the churches that exist. They will unite under the Laodician system. Since all true believers are gone, they will meet no opposition from those they labeled as fanatics or bigots. The dispies, the Premils, and pretriber bunch aren't here to oppose their false teaching anymore. We church believers are at home in glory with the Lord forever.

A period of false peace has come, a false millennial they believe! This will ensue when the beast upon the white horse has convinced the world that the golden age of peace has come. He will unleash his fury upon the unsuspecting nation and plunge the world into war.

Revelation 6:3: "And when he had opened the second seal, I heard the second beast say, Come and see." The lamb now opens the second seal. John is called to come get a little closer. Revelation 6:4: "And there went out another horse that was red: and power was given to him that sat thereon to take peace from the earth, and that they should kill one another: and there was given unto him a great sword."

This second horse is red, which is the color of blood. It is the horse of war. This rider the ungodly ruler is coming to take the peace from the earth. The greatest war of all time will begin. Notice this war is not between the righteous and the wicked. It is among the wicked alone. The wicked slaughter one another. The rider is the same as on the white horse. He now begins to identify himself. He is not the prince of peace he is the old enemy of mankind and God. He is the tool of Satan and thus Satan himself! But what is this war that is taking place?

Do we see it in scripture? It isn't the battle of Armageddon! That battle is between the wicked and He who is to come, Christ with His army in white. We go to Ezekiel 38:1–23, which will show us this war as prophesied by Ezekiel. The Tribulation being a time of the Jews would be the key to Old Testament prophecy revealing to us what is occurring. Gog and Magog will come swooping down upon Israel.

The chief prince of Meshech and Tubal, Meshech, now spelled Moscow. Tubal, now called Tobolsk. Persia, now Iran, Ethiopia, and Libya join in with Russia. Joining too is Gomer (Germany), and all his bands; the house of Togarmah (Slavic people). They are coming into Israel to take a spoil from them. They come like a storm into Israel. Verse 8 of Ezekiel 38 says they come against the mountains of Israel. Verse 9: "Thou shalt ascend and come like a storm, thou shalt be like a cloud to cover the land, thou, and all thy bands, and many people with thee."

Here is our key these will say, "I will go up to the land of unwalled villages; I will go to them that are at rest, that dwell safely." Verse 11, this time of peace at the beginning of the Tribulation is shattered! Israel will feel the brunt of it! We see the purpose of this coalition in verse 2: "To take a spoil, and to take a prey; to turn thine hand upon the desolate places that are now inhabited, and upon the people that are gathered out of the nations, which have gotten cattle and goods, that dwell in the midst of the land."

Verse 15: "And thou shalt come from thy place out of the north parts, thou, and many people with thee, all of them riding upon horses, a great company, and a mighty army:" Verse 16: "And thou shalt come up against my people of Israel, as a cloud to cover the land; it shall be in the latter days, and I will bring thee against my land, that the heathen may know me, when I shall be sanctified in thee, O Gog, before their eyes."

Do you see they come from their place in the north parts! This was not the Roman Army in AD 70 as some want to teach today. This is a massive army sweeping down, riding upon horses. A great company, a mighty army! They are coming upon Israel! They come from a Russian coalition of nations, coming as a cloud. God has a purpose, God shall be sanctified!

Verse 17: "Thus saith the Lord God; Art thou he of whom I have spoken in old time by my servants the prophets of Israel, which prophesied in those days many years that I would bring thee against them?" Verse 18: "And it shall come to pass at the same time when Gog shall come against the land of Israel, saith the Lord God, that my fury shall come up in my face." Verse 19: "For in my jealousy and in the fire of my wrath have I spoken, Surely in that day there shall be a great shaking in the land of Israel." Verse 20: "So that the fishes of the sea, and the fowls of the heaven, and the beasts of the field, and all creeping things that creep upon the earth, and all the men that are upon the face of the earth, shall shake at my presence, and the mountains shall be thrown down, and the steep places shall fall, and every wall shall fall to the ground." God has spoken through His prophets that this nation and its allies would come against Israel. God's fury will come up in His face. In His jealousy and the fire of His wrath, He will deal with Gog and his allies.

An earthquake will occur while Gog is sweeping down. The fish and the fowl, the beast of the field, and the creeping things, all mankind that is upon the face of the earth, all will shake in God's presence! The mountains will be thrown down, steep places fall apart, and every wall will fall to the ground. Remember all this as we get further into Revelation, for we will see these prophecies fulfilled.

Verse 21: "And I will call for a sword against him throughout all my mountains, saith the Lord God: every man's sword shall be against his brother." Verse 22: "And I will plead against him with pestilence and with blood; and I will rain upon him, and upon his bands, and upon the many people that are with him, an overflowing rain, and great hailstones, fire, and brimstone." Verse 23: "Thus will I magnify myself, and sanctify myself; and I will be known in the eyes of many nations, and they shall know that I am the Lord." God will bring a sword against Gog and his allies.

Every man's sword will be against his brother! The great battle will ensue. All the armies of the world will be involved. World War III will begin full force upon this world. Pestilence and blood will destroy this great army, as God rains down fire and brimstone upon them! God will magnify Himself! He will sanctify himself! Many nations will recognize Him as God, they will turn to Him.

Ezekiel 39 continues the prophecy. Verse 1: "Therefore, thou son of man, prophesy against Gog, and say, Thus saith the Lord God; Behold, I am against thee, O Gog, the chief prince of Meshech and Tubal." Verse 2: "And I will turn thee back, and leave but the sixth part of thee, and will cause thee to come up from the north parts, and will bring thee upon the mountains of Israel." Verse 3: "And I will smite thy bow out of thy left hand, and will cause thine arrows to fall out of thy right hand." Verse 4: "Thou shalt fall upon the mountains of Israel, thou, and all thy bands, and the people that is with thee: I will give thee unto the ravenous birds of every sort, and to the beasts of the field to be devoured." God is against Gog, the chief of Meshech, and Tubal. God will turn them back and leave one-sixth of the army.

God will bring them from the northern parts to the mountains of Israel. God will smite the bow from his left hand; his arrows will fall out of his right. They will fall upon the mountains of Israel. All the bands with this people will fall. Their carcasses will be left for the birds and beast of the fields to consume.

Verse 5: "Thou shalt fall upon the open field: for I have spoken it, saith the Lord God." Verse 6: "And I will send a fire on Magog, and among them that dwell carelessly in the isles: and they shall know that I am the Lord." Verse 7: "So will I make my holy name known in the midst of my people Israel; and I will not let them pollute my holy name any more: and the heathen shall know that I am the Lord, the Holy One in Israel." Verse 8: "Behold, it is come, and it is done, saith the Lord God; this is the day whereof I have spoken." Not only upon mountains will they fall but in the fields. God will make His name Holy in Israel again! He will no longer let them pollute His Holy Name. The heathen, the Gentile nations, will also know that He is the Lord God, for He has spoken of this day coming. Verse 9: "And they that dwell in the cities of Israel shall go forth, and shall set on fire and burn the weapons, both the shields and the bucklers, the bows and the arrows, and the handstaves, and the spears, and they shall burn them with fire seven years:"

Notice how long they burn, seven years, the exact length of the Tribulation Period." Verse 10:

"So that they shall take no wood out of the field, neither cut down any out of the forests; for they shall burn the weapons with fire: and they shall spoil those that spoiled them, and rob those that robbed them, saith the Lord God." Verse 11: "And it shall come to pass in that day, that I will give unto Gog a place there of graves in Israel, the valley of the passengers on the east of the sea: and it shall stop the noses of the passengers: and there shall they bury Gog and all his multitude: and they shall call it The valley of Hamongog." Notice this is not the Valley of Megiddo, thus it is not the battle of Armageddon.

Russia will instigate this Conflict; God will win this the battle. Verse 12: "And seven months shall the house of Israel be burying of them, that they may cleanse the land." The people dwelling in Israel will go and set fire to the weapons, the shields and the bucklers, the bows and arrows, hand staves, spears, and they will burn them for seven years. They will take no wood out of the field, nor cut down any forest because they will be burning weapons.

Israel will spoil those who spoiled and robbed them. Israel will rob them, the Lord says. Gog will have a place of burial in Israel. The valley of passengers, there will Gog be buried and his entire multitude. It will be the Valley of Hamangog. Seven months Israel will be burying the dead that the land might be cleansed. Verse 13: "Yea, all the people of the land shall bury them; and it shall be to them a renown the day that I shall be glorified, saith the Lord God." Verse 14: "And they shall sever out men of continual employment, passing through the land to bury with the passengers those that remain upon the face of the earth, to cleanse it: after the end of seven months shall they search." Verse 15: "And the passengers that pass through the land, when any seeth a man's bone, then shall he set up a sign by it, till the buriers have buried it in the valley of Hamongog." Verse 16: "And also the name of the city shall be Hamonah. Thus shall they cleanse the land!" All the people of Israel will bury them, even hiring people for burial details.

Those passing through the land to bury the dead, people who come through the land will mark remains till the burial details can bury them buried in Hamongog. The city of Hamonah, the land will be cleansed. Do you see it? This battle doesn't take place in Megiddo. It is in Hamon or Hamonah. Verse 17: "And, thou son of man, thus saith the Lord God; Speak unto every feathered fowl, and to every beast of the field, Assemble yourselves, and come; gather yourselves on every side to my sacrifice that I do sacrifice for you, even a great sacrifice upon the mountains of Israel, that ye may eat flesh, and drink blood." Verse 18: "Ye shall eat the flesh of the mighty, and drink the blood of the princes of the earth, of rams, of lambs, and of goats, of bullocks, all of them fatlings of Bashan." Verse 19: "And ye shall eat fat till ye be full, and drink blood till ye be drunken, of my sacrifice which I have sacrificed for you." Verse 20: "Thus ye shall be filled at my table with horses and chariots, with mighty men, and with all men of war, saith the Lord God." Verse 21: "And I will set my glory among the heathen, and all the heathen shall see my judgment that I have executed, and my hand that I have laid upon them." Verse 22: "So the house of Israel shall know that I am the Lord their God from that day and forward." Verse 23: "And the heathen shall know that the house of Israel went into captivity for their iniquity: because they trespassed against me, therefore hid I my face from them, and gave them into the hand of their enemies: so fell they all by the sword."

Verse 24: "According to their uncleanness and according to their transgressions have I done unto them, and hid my face from them." Verse 25: "Therefore thus saith the Lord God; Now will I bring again the captivity of Jacob, and have mercy upon the whole house of Israel, and will be jealous for my holy name." Verse 26: "After that they have borne their shame, and all their trespasses whereby they have trespassed against me, when they dwelt safely in their land, and none made them afraid." Verse 27: "When I have brought them again from the people, and gathered them out of their enemies' lands, and am sanctified in them in the sight of many nations." Verse 28: "Then shall they know that I am the Lord their God, which caused them to be led into captivity among the heathen: but I have gathered them unto their own land, and have left none of them anymore there." Verse 29: "Neither will I hide my face any more from them: for I have poured out my spirit upon the house of Israel, saith the Lord God." All this will bring Israel back to God. You see, God is not through with Israel as a nation or a people.

All will prepare the way for Jesus's return as Messiah and King. They and all nations will know that He had placed Israel in captivity and had scattered them, but now He returns them to the land the Feast of Ingathering is taking place. The seals are being broken by the Lamb. The rider on the white horse comes with a great deception of peace. Then the rider on the red horse appears bringing war. I believe this is the war we see in Ezekiel 38 and 39.

Some believe the Ezekiel 38 and 39 war is in fact Armageddon, but that war takes place in the Valley of Megiddo which is hundreds of miles from Hamonah. Ezekiel 38 and 39 show Israel living in peace in unwalled cities, this has yet to happen. The rider on the white horse brings a short time of peace and Israel would relax, and then comes war as never seen before!

2

Chaos on Earth

In verse 5 of Chapter 6, we now see the Lamb open the third seal. Revelation 6:5: "And when he had opened the third seal, I heard the third beast say, Come and see. And I beheld, and lo a black horse; and he that sat on him had a pair of balances in his hand." The third horse comes forth. The color of this horse is black, the color of gloom, mourning, and lamentation. The greatness of the condition is seen in the fact that the balances are held in the rider's hand. Here we the see the scarcity of goods in this time.

The third living creature cries as the others had done before. Come and see what is about to happen he tells John. Goods will be hard to come by. Just as all the book of Revelation reveals prophecy fulfilled, so too does this verse. Leviticus 26:26: "And when I have broken the *staff of your bread*, ten women shall bake your bread in one oven, and they shall deliver you your bread again by weight: and ye shall eat, and not be satisfied." Ezekiel described the torments coming with the siege of Israel. Ezekiel 4:16: "Moreover he said unto me, Son of man, behold, *I will break the staff of bread in Jerusalem*: and they shall eat bread by weight, and with care; and they shall drink water by measure, and with astonishment." To give out corn by weight instead of measure was thus an emblem of scarcity.

The black horse is a sign of famine coming upon the earth. Revelation

6:6: "And I heard a voice in the midst of the four beasts say, A measure of wheat for a penny, and three measures of barley for a penny; and see thou hurt not the oil and the wine." We see in the Black horse the devastation that always follows war. The black horse of famine and inflation is a terrible thought. Everything must be weighed in time because of the scarceness.

Most don't remember the Great Depression and then World War II. Soup kitchens and long lines existed in those days. Rationing goods during World War II was the norm. My dad was a young boy in those days. He told us of the rationing of gasoline and all types of goods. Goods became more and more scarce. While the war raged, the need for goods continued to increase.

Yet the supply is depleted, the famine has hit. As we see today with our gas prices, it is a matter of supply and demand that controls the price at the pump. Increased supply and low demand drives prices down, while low supply and high demand drives the prices up. Once the church has been removed and the Holy Spirit taken with it, the short false peace fails. War comes like no other ever seen on earth. The greatest famine to ever hit the world follows.

A measure of wheat for a penny, a measure of wheat is approximately one quart. Some say this was enough wheat to make one meal in that time. You think, well, a penny for a quart of flour isn't bad, but wait!

Three measures of barley would make three meals or equal three quarts. Understand in that day a penny was one day's wages for most people. That means that the entire daily wage of a working individual will be required to buy a quart of wheat. Prices in Tribulation period will be unprecedentedly high.

The average daily wage in the US currently is $24.78 an hour. If the world average daily wage of a person is say $10 an hour and they work ten hours, that would make a quart of wheat cost $100 in that day. See the famine? The poor will be devastated in the greatest way by this. Just as the poor of the Great Depression and during World War II were hit the hardest so it will be in this time.

Let's look at it like this. Four US cups equal a quart. Let's say a loaf of bread takes 1 cup to make, which means it would cost $25 for just the flour to make the bread. Add the labor, trucking cost, and markup at the store. A loaf of bread would cost almost $100. Let's say a person on social security in that day received $2,000 a month and average thirty days for that month. That would be $66 a day, which would be 1-1/2 days' wages for a loaf of bread or a bag of flour.

Notice though the oil and the wine were not to be touched. Oil and wine in those days will be delicacies of the rich. The rich will scarcely be touched by it, just like the Great Depression. Only the wealthy will have sufficient food, at least for a time. Let's observe this spiritually. When people avoid taking in their spiritual food, God may justly deprive them of their daily bread! One judgment seldom comes alone. The judgment of war naturally draws after that of famine.

Those who will not humble themselves under one judgment must expect another and yet greater. When God deals with people, He will prevail! The famine of bread is a terrible judgment, but the famine of the word is more so, though careless sinners are not sensible of it. The black horse brings famine.

Now look at Revelation 6:7: "And when he had opened the fourth seal, I heard the voice of the fourth beast say, Come and see." We see the fourth seal opened. The fourth beast is saying, "Come and see." You might be thinking, wait! Peace has failed and now there is war that brought famine. What more is God going to do to the people there? Haven't they had enough?

Revelation 6:8: "And I looked, and behold a pale horse: and his name that sat on him was Death, and Hell followed with him. And power was given unto them over the fourth part of the earth, to kill with sword, and with hunger, and with death, and with the beasts of the earth."

Now we see more death. The pale color is that of a corpse corresponding to the rider whose name is Death. Hell follows this horse. We see Death coming to the inhabitants left upon the earth. This death comes to over a quarter of the earth. War, famine, and pestilence bring death to a quarter of humanity. The beasts of the earth are ravenous, searching for food, and they will attack even humans!

The world's population today is thought to have reached seven billion. If we allow for one-third of that being Christians who were removed at Rapture, just for a number, then one-quarter of those left would be 1,166,666,666 people who will die in this devastation. This shows us why it is called the Tribulation period. This is why we as believers need to rejoice in the fact that we shall be *snatched* out prior to this time. The Bride is taken out before this great and terrible day.

This too should motivate us to carry the word to our world—to our community, friends, and family, not wanting them to go through this time of Tribulation upon the earth. That would include witnessing to your enemy or those who despitefully use you! Christ is working to redeem the earth and the Father's judgment is coming. War, famine, and death are coming. These are God's tools used to afflict mankind, giving the general expression of God's judgments on the human race.

Notice too though this says a fourth, not the whole world. The Tribulation saints are those who God is really thinking of. They come in remembrance before other scenes are brought out. Those who had been martyred for the word of God and their testimony demand how long before they were avenged. We aren't told why only one-quarter of the earth is given to death and Hades, when it might have been extended over the whole earth.

The period of the fourth seal is one of great slaughter and devastation, destroying whatever may tend to make life happy, making ruin the spiritual lives of men. The exact times of these four seals cannot be determined, for the changes were gradual. God gave them power that is, those instruments of his anger, or those judgments. All public calamities are at his command. They only go forth when God sends them, and no further than he permits.

Before examining what is written concerning the breaking of the fifth and sixth seals, it is necessary to say something as to God's dispensational dealings with His earthly people Israel. We need now to link this with Daniel's seventy weeks. God dealt with Israel for 1,500 years before the cross. He gave them covenants and the law. Israel was and is in a covenant relationship with God. He has chosen them to be peculiarly His own, in accordance with His promise (covenant) to Abraham, Isaac, and Jacob. He called them out from the Gentile nations starting with Abraham.

He called Abraham out of Ur and sent him to Canaan. Canaan is Israel's inheritance. The covenant given to Abraham was unconditional. His descendants will inherit the land. The law and entering the land brought with it several conditional covenants. He gave them His Holy law and declared that if they obeyed His voice, they would be the head of all nations and His witnesses to the ends of the earth.

On the other hand, He warned them that if they were disobedient to Him, if they did not keep

His testimonies, if they broke His commandments, if they turned to the false gods of the surrounding nations, He would no longer protect them from their enemies. He would give them up to desolation and scattering until they judged themselves and turned from their sins. Then He would remember His covenant with their fathers and would restore them to their own land and fulfill all His promises.

As we know, they completely and utterly failed in following the law and its commands concerning the land. They completely broke down under every test, and in accordance with God's word, ten tribes were carried away by the king of Assyria. A little later, the remaining two tribes were deported to Babylon, where they remained in bondage for seventy years. At the end of this prophetic period, they were permitted to return to their own land, that they might be there to welcome their promised Messiah when He would be revealed!

Only a remnant of the Jews took advantage of this privilege and it was their descendants who were living in Palestine when the Lord Jesus Christ appeared in the fullness of time. He was rejected by the very nation that had waited for Him so long. The time of His coming had been very definitely foretold in the book of Daniel.

In the ninth chapter, we are told that a heavenly messenger brought word to the prophet that God had appointed seventy weeks to His people and their holy city. These are not to be understood as weeks of days, but sevens of years. The term "weeks" might better be simply rendered sevens. Seventy sevens were given to them. Seventy times seven years would be 490 years. It is an appointed period in the course of time and has to do especially with the Jews and Jerusalem.

This period was divided into three parts:

1. Seven weeks, or forty-nine years, in which the streets and the wall of the city were to be rebuilt.
2. From there, an additional sixty-two weeks, or 434 years, were to immediately follow the completion of this work, at which time the appearing and cutting off of Messiah the Prince.
3. 434 plus 49 is 483 years, which would leave

4. One final week, or seven years, to complete the cycle. At the end of this week, the King would be reigning in the holy city and all prophecy fulfilled by the establishment of the kingdom so long foretold.

The starting point is clearly defined as, "The going forth of the commandment to restore and to build Jerusalem" (Daniel 9:25). This is the decree of Artaxerxes as recorded in Nehemiah 2. During the next forty-nine years, the city was rebuilt. Then, 434 years later, our Lord rode into Jerusalem and was acclaimed by the multitudes as King, the Son of David. That would be 483 total years from the decree to the coming of Christ on a colt, the foal of a donkey, as Zechariah
9:9 prophesied.

A few days later, He was rejected and crucified. Thus Messiah was cut off as Daniel had prophesied. What about the last week? Has it been fulfilled? Four hundred and eighty-three years were fulfilled, but from extra biblical history, we see no event where this great devastation hit the world. In AD 70, only Israel was destroyed, not a quarter of the inhabited earth. The Lord has not returned and set up His kingdom on the earth in Jerusalem so that seven-year period has yet to occur. Therefore, the answer is of course no, it has *not* been fulfilled.

When His Son was cast out, God cast off the nation of Israel. It was not forever but for a time. That week would not be fulfilled until a future day. A day in which God will take up Israel again, as a nation in the Promised Land at the end of the Tribulation period with Christ reigning 1000 years.

The messenger said to Daniel, "Unto the end of the war desolations are determined" (Daniel 9:26). This gives the whole history of Palestine for the past almost two thousand years. It has been a great battleground, a scene of almost unparalleled desolation because Israel knew not the time of their visitation. Their times are not in progress now. God is doing another work. While the Jews are blinded, in part He is gathering out the church. We are part of that church and the Body and Bride of Christ that is, those who have placed their faith and trust in Christ as their personal Savior.

A heavenly company, we will reign with Christ when He establishes His kingdom of righteousness on the earth. The last week of seven years cannot begin to run until the Jews are again in the land, which some are very much there today. Jerusalem must become the Jewish capital, which it is today. The church must be caught up to meet the Lord in the air. We are still here so this is yet to be fulfilled. The greater part of the book of the Revelation reveals this last week. It is only when this is seen that all becomes plain. The prophecy becomes intelligible. The church began on the day of Pentecost fifty days after the resurrection and ten after the ascension, when the Holy Spirit, sent by the glorified Christ, came on the disciples, on the church.

Yet the full truth of this wonderful mystery was not made known until Saul of Tarsus became Paul the apostle. The truth of the time of the church was made known to him and through him to us. The true church of Christ is one, though men who take His name and claim to be His followers have become sadly divided. They have formed many systems, often embracing saved and unsaved alike. God's true church exists only of those who are born of the Spirit and baptized by the same Spirit into the body of Christ.

The Baptism of the Spirit occurs immediately at Salvation. 1 Corinthians 12:13: "For by one Spirit are we all baptized into one body, whether we be Jews or Gentiles, whether we be bond or free; and have been all made to drink into one Spirit." Do you see that *we are all baptized*, not by water, but this says *by one Spirit*? When does that occur? At Salvation, otherwise, we are not believers for *we are all baptized*. The "we" are believers. Therefore, Baptism of the Holy Spirit occurs at salvation, not sometime after.

We see too in 1 Corinthians 6:19–20: "What? know ye not that your body is the temple of the Holy Ghost which is in you, which ye have of God, and ye are not your own? For ye are bought with a price: therefore glorify God in your body, and in your spirit, which are God's." God's true church consists only of those who are born of the Spirit and baptized by the same Spirit into the body of Christ. That occurs immediately when you receive the Lord Jesus as your Lord and Savior, by grace through faith. This special work will cease at the return of the Lord in the air, which is the first part of His return.

The second part—that is, the Second Advent—will be when He comes to earth to reign in glory. The seventieth, or last, week of Daniel comes in between these two momentous events. The Lord spoke of this period as the *end of the age* in Matthew 24.

He divided it into two parts.

1. The beginning of sorrows
2. The Great Tribulation

As I wrote in first section, *The Snatching Way of the Bride*, we will meet Him in the air someday. A careful comparison of our Lord's great prophecy with Revelation 6 will make it plain that the first six seals correspond to the first half of the week, *the beginning of sorrows.*

From the opening of the seventh seal (Revelation 8), we are introduced to the Great Tribulation itself with all its momentous terrors. Jesus's warning as to false Christ's, implying that there will be false hopes of a lasting peace (Matthew 24:5), corresponds to the first seal. His declaration that wars and rumors of wars will follow (Matthew 24:6) perfectly aligns with the second seal. As the pattern continues, we see His solemn warnings of famine and pestilence (Matthew 24:7).

Here we see the parallels in the third and fourth seals. The Lord then goes on to prophesy of a time when His followers will be mercilessly killed (Matthew 24:9). This brings us to the breaking of the fifth seal. It will cost the believer's life to confess Christ's name. The seals are being broken by the Lamb. The riders upon the horses show the time of the Tribulation period, the seventieth week of Daniel's prophecy and the time of Jacob's trouble.

We need to allow this whole portion of prophecy to drive us to witness to our friends, family, and neighbors, even those who are our enemies, before it is everlasting too late.

In verse 9 of Chapter 6, we see the Lamb open yet another seal. The horses now complete, we swing to greater things. Revelation 6:9: "And when he had opened the fifth seal, I saw under the altar the souls of them that were slain for the word of God, and for the testimony which they held." The fifth seal is opened on the book of redemption. Souls are seen under the altar. No fifth rider. We now pass from material to the spiritual, from visible to the invisible world.

The transition is intentional. The point of division is seen in Revelation 9 and the trumpets. The point of the bowls in Revelation 16:10. More significant, I believe, is the numbers.

1. Four is the number of elements that make it the earth.
    a. Earth

    b. Air
    c. Fire
    d. Water
2. Four shows the regions of the earth.
    a. North
    b. South
    c. East
    d. West
3. Four shows the division of the day.
    a. Morning
    b. Noon
    c. Evening
    d. Midnight
4. Four, therefore, shows His creative work.

Five is the number of grace. Now we have a further revelation of a people called out from mankind, redeemed and saved, to walk with God from earth to heaven. We therefore see the number seven divided into three and four. Seven, the number of spiritual perfection or completion is prominent throughout Revelation. Three is the number of Divine Perfection. Then with four, we see the coming judgment upon the earth and it is of more consequence we see. The souls are seen under the altar, which shows there is a temple in heaven.

John sees the souls of those martyred. Not in our present age but in the age of the Tribulation. The altar is like the brazen altar of sacrifice. It stood in the outer court of both the tabernacle and the temple. The Jews would offer their sacrifices there. The souls or lives seen here are therefore significant.

They are seen under it as covered with the blood. Blood always represents life. The Law of Moses commanded that the blood be poured out. "At the bottom of the Alter of burnt offering which is before the tabernacle of the congregation." These had been slain for the word of God and for their testimony. Do you see there will be people saved during the Tribulation! We see that from this, many will be from the House of Israel. They will be martyred for their faith.

The fifth seal shows they have not died in vain. They are to be patient and wait until the indignation of the Lord is completed. Understand that believers in our age were slain too. But in this age they are slain for the testimony of Jesus—the testimony of Him as their Savior in this present age—while the martyrs of the Tribulation are said to have been martyred for their faith and testimony. One thing is very clear here. The soul doesn't sleep. Persecutors can only kill the body. After that, there is no more they can do to the souls of those killed, they live on!

The next thing we see is that God has provided a good place in the better world. Those who are faithful in the Tribulation, faithful to death, are no longer on earth but immediately in heaven. Revelation 6:10: "And they cried with a loud voice, saying, How long, O Lord, holy and true, dost thou not judge and avenge our blood on them that dwell on the earth?" The souls ask how long before they are avenged. The cry heard is a loud cry. A humble admonition about the long delay of avenging justice for their lives is sent forth. Even the spirits of men who have been made perfect still retain a proper resentment of the wrong they sustained by their cruel enemies, though they were slain for the word and their testimony.

In charity, praying as Christ did, that God would forgive them. They still desire that for the honor of God, Christ, and the gospel, for the terror and conviction of others, God will repay the sin of persecution, even though He pardons and saves the persecutor. They commit their cause to Him of whom vengeance belongs. They leave it in His hands. They don't try to avenge themselves, but leave it all in God's hands! This shows us that we too should not try to avenge ourselves. We should leave it to God for "He will repay!" There will be joy in heaven at the merciless adversaries of Christ and Christianity! As well as the joy over one soul that is saved.

Revelation 18:20 tells us when Babylon falls, "rejoice over her O heaven and you holy apostles and prophets, for God hath avenged you on her." Rev. 6:11: "And white robes were given unto every one of them; and it was said unto them, that they should rest yet for a little season, until their fellow servants also and their brethren, that should be killed as they were, should be fulfilled." They are given white robes. The white robes are witness of their righteousness, God's declared approval of them. Notice though they don't receive crowns as the church does, they don't receive the rewards of 1 Corinthians 3. Those come to the church when she is snatched away and all believers in this present age face the Bema seat judgment!

The time of their avenging was not quite here. They have not yet been resurrected they have been given the white robes. The Church has had her resurrection, but this is still a time of the Jews, the final week of the seventy weeks of Daniel. Christ's sacrifice has cleansed their robes. These white robes are robes of victory, robes of honor. Their present happiness was an abundant honor of their past suffering. Great was their martyrdom. They are told they should be satisfied. It would not be long that the number of believers martyred would be fulfilled.

In heaven, there is no imperfect state as here on earth. There is a world of perfection, no impatience, no uneasiness, and no need for admonition. There is great patience! We see from this that God has appointed a number of believers to be as sheep for slaughter, set apart to be God's witnesses. He has chosen and appointed them to this purpose. The extent of the sin of persecution is getting full. So too is the number of the persecuted martyred for Christ. When is the number going to be fulfilled? God will take a just and glorious revenge upon the cruel persecutors. He will bring payment in the form of Tribulation and eternal damnation to those who trouble them.

He will bring to those who are troubled and persecuted peaceful, continual rest. These souls must wait. Wait until the Tribulation has ended. The time of Jacob's trouble comes to pass. They will be joined by their brethren who will be martyred. The hatred to God and Christ continues, rising ever higher on the earth. It continues until the Lord Jesus will be revealed from heaven in a flaming fire. Then He will invoke the vengeance on those who do not know Him (2 Thessalonians 8).

Revelation 6:12: "And I beheld when he had opened the sixth seal, and, lo, there was a great earthquake; and the sun became black as sackcloth of hair, and the moon became as blood." The sixth seal brings a great earthquake. The pace and intensity of the judgments increases. All the judgment is falling upon the earth after the removal of the true Church, the Body of Christ which is the Bride having been snatched away. The Holy Spirit has been removed too. Men are doing evil continually. Notice this earthquake is different from others.

Most commentators don't see it as a literal earthquake. The actual islands, mountains, and seas, along with the cities of all the nations, are still in existence long after this vision has had its fulfillment. Does this represent the complete breaking of society? The destruction of the boasted civilization of today! This is not a literal earthquake most believe. Look at the description with this earthquake. The sun became black as sackcloth of hair, and the moon became as blood.

This may have been hard to understand prior to World War II. That war came to an end with a great nuclear explosion with the atom bombs dropped on Hiroshima and Nagasaki! When these were dropped, the earth shook for miles around. It almost dislodged the crews of the airplanes that dropped them. The sun became dark by a pillar of smoke and several nights later the moon still could not be seen through the smoke. The moon appeared to be a blood red disc. The billowing clouds of smoke made the heavens appear to be rolled away like a scroll. Fear that had never gripped mankind seized the Japanese. They surrendered unconditionally and speedily, even though the nation had not been invaded and seven million men were still ready and able to fight. They sought shelter in caves, dens, and underground, and many committed suicide.

This event in history is a mild description of the havoc seen in Revelation 6 and also in Revelation 16. At the surrender of Japan, General MacArthur spoke from that country very prophetically. In his speech, he said, "Military alliances, balances of power, leagues of nations, all in turn failed, leaving the only path to be by way of the crucible of war. We have had our last chance. If we do not now devise some greater and more equitable system, Armageddon will be at our door." Where did MacArthur get the word *Armageddon*? The term is only found in the Bible.

It is the final battle of the Tribulation. Christ comes back as the conqueror in that battle. That terrible day will spare no one who stands against Christ. Christ will win that battle. Today the nations we see in Ezekiel 38 and 39 have nuclear capability. Iran wants to develop one to drop on Israel so this strike could very well happen.

The sun, we are told in Revelation 6:12, becomes "black as sackcloth of hair." The sun, the source of light and life for this planet, symbolizes supreme authority. Many times the Lord Jesus is referred to in scripture by using the sun. Malachi 4:2 is an example. At His coming, Malachi describes him as the "sun of righteousness who arises with healing in His wings." With this great nuclear war, all the authority which had been in place is destroyed.

The moon became as if it were blood. The moon gets it light from the sun. The powers ordained by God and are appointed for man's blessings are being overthrown, anarchy reigns, for a time at least. Revelation 6:13: "And the stars of heaven fell unto the earth, even as a fig tree casteth her untimely figs, when she is shaken of a mighty wind." We see in this fulfillment of prophecy. Isaiah 13:10: "For the stars of heaven and the constellations thereof shall not give their light: the sun shall be darkened in his going forth, and the moon shall not cause her light to shine." Isaiah 34:2: "For the *indignation* of the Lord is upon all nations, and his fury upon all their armies: he hath utterly destroyed them, he hath delivered them to the slaughter." Isaiah 2:19: "And they shall go into the holes of the rocks, and into the caves of the earth, for fear of the Lord, and for the glory of his majesty, when he ariseth to shake terribly the earth."

The stars falling from heaven indicate the downfall and apostasy of great religious leaders, the bright lights in the ecclesiastical heavens, at least in man's eyes. Daniel 12:3: "And they that be wise shall shine as the brightness of the firmament; and they that *turn many to righteousness* as the stars for ever and ever."

Remember, as Revelation began, stars were referred to as messengers of the church. When the Church is snatched out there will be a vast host of unconverted pastors left in the wake. Thousands of Protestant and Catholic dignitaries looked on as spiritual guides will be revealed as utterly wanting of divine life. These professional clergymen, despite their deceptions and supposed high calling, are merely natural men assumed to know spiritual things.

These are the stars that will be hurled from their places of power and importance in that awful day of the wrath of the Lamb. Apostatizing from the last remnants of Christianity, they will soon become leaders in the worship of the antichrist. Keep in mind too that as war is raging, bombs are falling from heaven. These too could be symbolized by the stars falling to earth, bringing with them destruction. A scene of almost unparalleled desolation, we see this great time of destruction. Wars are raging, disease and famine running rampant.

Revelation 6:14–17: And the heaven departed as a scroll when it is rolled together; and every mountain and island were moved out of their places. And the kings of the earth, and the great men, and the rich men, and the chief captains, and the mighty men, and every bondman, and every free man, hid themselves in the dens and in the rocks of the mountains; And said to the mountains and rocks, Fall on us, and hide us from the face of him that sitteth on the throne, and from the wrath of the Lamb: For the great day of his wrath is come; and who shall be able to stand?

God's word is rejected. "Every mountain and island were moved out of their places." Israel has taken the full brunt of these attacks. All nations are now living in fear. Those who were held in high honor, seeming to be secure, fall under God's judgment. Dread and terror would seize upon all sorts of men on that great and awful day (Revelation 6:15). No authority, nor greatness, no riches, no valor, no strength, will be able to support men at that time. The very poor slaves, who, one would think, had nothing to fear, because they had nothing to lose, would be all in amazement at that day.

Notice the degree of their terror and astonishment. They are like troubled and divided men. What is the cause of this terror? The angry countenance *of him that sits on the throne and the wrath of the Lamb* is the cause. They want the mountains and rocks to fall upon them. They call for them to fall upon them in their despair and desperate situation. Yet they still refuse to call upon Christ. No repentance, no true turning to God! Just an awful realization that they have to face the rejected Lamb, they cannot escape His wrath we see in (Jeremiah 8:20). They are not saved.

Verse 17 tells us they know it is God's wrath. "The wrath of the Lamb has come." This they acknowledge. Yet they refuse to turn to Him. God is pouring His wrath upon them. The seals are being broken by the Lamb. God's wrath is being poured out upon the earth; all nations are being troubled now. We need to allow this whole portion of prophecy to drive us to be a witness to our friends, family, and neighbors before it is ever lasting too late.

3

Sealing the 144,000 Witnesses

We come to the scene on earth where the judgment stops for a short period. God has to identify those who can't be touched by death in the Tribulation, a protected remnant. There is a remnant not of Gentiles, not of the church, but a remnant of the nation Israel. In verse 1 of Chapter 7, we now see four angels on the four corners of the earth. The Tribulation period is in full swing, but we now see God intervening for a short period. These angels are ready to unleash God's fury upon the earth.

Revelation 7:1: "And after these things I saw four angels standing on the four corners of the earth, holding the four winds of the earth, that the wind should not blow on the earth, nor on the sea, nor on any tree." The wind is controlled by God. The wind is the judgment of God. Judgment is paused. It isn't touching the earth or the sea or the trees. This being in the number four, which is a representation of the earth. Held back by four angels who are stationed at the four corners of the Earth!

When the judgment is inflicted, it will be over all the earth now. There will be nowhere the ungodly can hide from God's judgment. They can't find a place to escape Gods judgment. Ezekiel 9:9–11: "Then said he unto me, The iniquity of the house of Israel and Judah is exceeding great, and the land is full of blood, and the city full of perverseness: for they say, The Lord hath forsaken the earth, and the Lord seeth not. And as for me also, mine eye shall not spare, neither will I have pity, but I will recompense their way upon their head. And, behold, the man clothed with linen, which had the inkhorn by his side, reported the matter, saying, I have done as thou hast commanded me."

We see too in Amos 9:1–3: "I saw the Lord standing upon the altar: and he said, Smite the lintel of the door, that the posts may shake: and cut them in the head, all of them; and I will slay the last of them with the sword: he that fleeth of them shall not flee away, and he that escapeth of them shall not be delivered. Though they dig into hell, thence shall mine hand take them; though they climb up to heaven, thence will I bring them down. And though they hide themselves in the top of Carmel, I will search and take them out thence; and though they be hid from my sight in the bottom of the sea, thence will I command the serpent, and he shall bite them."

God has servants ever ready to work! These winds are being restrained until all of God's people were safely sealed. Nothing will happen that will destroy God's chosen to be witnesses for Him in the Tribulation, that is, of the 144,000 Jews. Before the seventh seal is opened, He stops and gives us two prophetic visions found here in Chapter 7. First John sees the 144,000 Israelites sealed by an angel.

In the second, he beholds a great multitude of Gentiles led in triumph by the Lamb, taking a possession of the millennial earth. We are told these come out of the Great Tribulation. Thus they are Tribulation saints and a great multitude that will be saved. Let's make sure it is understood exactly what the book of Revelation contains. Chapter 1 gives us a vision of Christ in the Glory of His coming again. He is the center of the book. We must never lose sight of Him.

Many get so occupied with His second coming and the Tribulation that they lose sight of Him! Prophecy doesn't deal with future events it deals more with the future of a person, the person of the Lord Jesus Christ. Therefore, Chapter 1 is devoted to Him, for He is the beginning and end in our study of Revelation.

Chapters 2 and 3 describe the professing church which is the Church in the dispensation of the age of grace or the Church age. In the midst of this age is the true church, the body of Christ. Chapter 3 concludes with the Church of Laodecia, the lukewarm church. Then in Chapter 4, we see the snatching away of the Bride that is the Church, which is the Rapture. The remainder of Chapter 4 and all of Chapter 5 show what John representing the raptured church is seeing from Heaven!

With the beginning of Chapter 6, the scene returns to earth and what follows in the remainder of the book to the return of Christ at His Second coming concerns God's judgments upon the earth during the Tribulation. The true church as the Bride of Christ is with Jesus Christ, the Bridegroom in heaven. Chapter 19 shows the Lord's return, followed by Chapters 20 to 22, which show the millennial reign, the last judgment, and then finally the eternal state.

We now have the outline of the book. Keep this clear as we continue through the study, and as we continue, you can then have a clear picture of the details of the study of Revelation, not only instructive and interesting but exceedingly easy.

As we said earlier, we have a pause in judgment here in Chapter 7. The Lord put a hold on His judgment, but the writing of the book continued, right between the sixth and seventh seal. As we will see, the seventh seal will usher in judgments so terrible, with destruction so complete, that except those days will be shortened no flesh would be saved (Matthew 24:2).

The seventh chapter deals with the Lord and how He will keep and protect His people. In the midst of the Tribulation, He will keep and protect a remnant of Israel. Thus the approaching day of Jacob's trouble, Judgment will be suspended for a brief period of time. The Tribulation will be in a brief recess until these faithful ones have been sealed, so that is the meaning of the opening verses of Chapter 7.

Revelation 7:2–3: "And I saw another angel ascending from the east, having the seal of the living God: and he cried with a loud voice to the four angels, to whom it was given to hurt the earth and the sea, Saying, Hurt not the earth, neither the sea, nor the trees, till we have sealed the servants of our God in their foreheads." Can you picture this in your mind? The true church has been snatched out. As seen in Chapter 4 verse 1, Satan is loose upon the earth. The Beast and false prophet, the unholy trinity, have not yet come to power. The unbelievers are doing their best to defeat God and anyone who believes.

This is the Tribulation period, the last week of Daniel's seventy weeks as prophesied. Satan's unholy trinity will have their hatred directed against Israel, God's chosen people. Understand Satan has his hatred directed toward the church in this time we are living. Once the church has been removed, Satan knows that Israel is God's covenant nation. Although Israel now rejects God's Son Jesus, there is coming a day when Israel will be converted and all the promises of the kingdom and their reestablishment in the land of Palestine will be fulfilled.

Satan seeks to thwart God's program, as he sets out to destroy all Israel and thus defeat God's program. He has tried this in the past through Pharaoh, Nebuchadnezzar, the Assyrians, the Greeks, the Romans, Mussolini, Hitler, and today the Iranian leader. Satan failed to destroy Israel in the past with God's intervention and He will fail again.

In the past, God raised up Moses, Nehemiah, and Mordecai, so again in the Tribulation, He will protect His faithful remnant. We see ascending out of the east an angel which had the seal of God. This may be the Lord Jesus himself. With his great voice he cries out, "Hurt not the earth, neither the sea, nor the trees." Don't bring the full brunt of judgment just yet.

He has a mission to accomplish. He must place God's seal upon the servants of God. It will go in their forehead. This seal is similar to that which Christ was sealed. The seal which in the Song of Solomon the Bride desires as the token of the Bridegroom's love for her alone. Song of Solomon 8:6: "Set me as a seal upon thine heart, as a seal upon thine arm: for love is strong as death; jealousy is cruel as the grave: the coals thereof are coals of fire, which hath a most vehement flame." This seal expresses the thought, "Nevertheless the foundation of God standeth sure, having this seal, *The Lord knoweth them that are his.* And, let everyone that nameth the name of Christ depart from iniquity" (2 Timothy 2:19).

Revelation 7:4: "And I heard the number of them which were sealed: and there were sealed an hundred and forty and four thousand of all the tribes of the children of Israel." We now see the number of the sealed from Israel. Understand these are Israelites! This number is thrown about by several religious sects. Many people are perplexed by the conflicting stories regarding the number 144,000. The Seventh-Day Adventists apply it to the faithful of their religion, those they say who will be found observing the Jewish Sabbath at the Lord's return.

Then we have the followers of Charles Russell (Jehovah's Witnesses) who teach that the 144,000 include only the "overcomers" of their following who continue faithful to the end. They are following the teaching of the system commonly called *Millennial Darwinism*. Another sect also claims that the 144,000 are those who will have their blood so cleansed that they cannot die, but will have immortal life on this earth!

There are many other sects whose leaders claim that their own followers will be the 144,000 sealed ones at the time of the end. All of these, however, overlook a very simple fact that, if observed, would save them from their error. The 144,000 are composed of twelve thousand from each tribe of the children of Israel. There is not a Gentile among them, nor is there confusion as to the tribe.

When you have someone tell you they are one of the 144,000, ask them which tribe. How clear can the record be here? Verse 4 says the 144,000 are of all the tribes of the children of Israel! Verses 4 to 8 make it very clear they leave no doubt as to the identity of the sealed ones. As you go through the list you may not notice something. First look at Genesis 49:1–33, note the tribal list as they were in Egypt.

Now look in Revelation 7:5–8 at the list.

Of the tribe of Juda were sealed twelve thousand. Of the tribe of Reuben were sealed twelve thousand. Of the tribe of Gad were sealed twelve thousand. Of the tribe of Aser were sealed twelve thousand. Of the tribe of Nephthalim were sealed twelve thousand. Of the tribe of Manasses were sealed twelve thousand. Of the tribe of Simeon were sealed twelve thousand. Of the tribe of Levi were sealed twelve thousand. Of the tribe of Issachar were sealed twelve thousand. Of the tribe of Zabulon were sealed twelve thousand. Of the tribe of Joseph were sealed twelve thousand. Of the tribe of Benjamin were sealed twelve thousand.

We see in Genesis these tribes listed:

- Rueben
- Simeon
- Levi
- Judah
- Zebulun
- Issachar
- Dan
- Gad

- Asher
- Naphtali
- Of Joseph
    - Ephraim
    - Mannesseh
- Benjamin

The list from Revelation 7 goes like this:

- Judah
- Reuben
- Gad
- Asher
- Naphtali
- Manasseseh
- Simeon
- Levi
- Issachar
- Zebulon
- Joseph
- Benjamin

One tribe from Genesis 49 is totally left out. That tribe is Dan. Also, there is no mention of Ephraim. So why is Dan omitted, you might wonder? One of Joseph's sons is added along with Joseph, so Joseph gets the double portion. The rabbis used to say that the false messiah (the antichrist) would arise from Dan. They based the supposition on Jacob's words in Genesis 49:17: "Dan shall be a serpent by the way, an adder in the path, that biteth the horse heels, so that his rider shall fall backward."

Note the historical record in the book of Judges; Dan was the first tribe to go into idolatry. It would not be surprising if Dan would be the leader in the last great idolatry that is the worship of the antichrist. The Bible doesn't give clear indication. Anything we do look to is clearly speculation. Maybe it is best if we leave it in the infinite wisdom of God. This, we know, He will reveal to us what He wants us to know in this present age. Notice we have in this the number twelve. Twelve is the number of governmental perfection: 12,000 for each of the twelve tribes, thus we have 144,000. We have governmental perfection for Israel. The church is in heaven having been snatched out, so who is the great multitude seen in the rest of the chapter?

In verse 9 of Chapter 7, we now see a multitude of souls. The number is too great to number. Who are they? Revelation 7:9: "After this I beheld, and, lo, a great multitude, which no man could number, of all nations, and kindreds, and people, and tongues, stood before the throne, and before the Lamb, clothed with white robes, and palms in their hands." This multitude is from the Gentile nations.

This is a great gathering of the Gentile multitude. Redeemed by the blood and numbered by God, never by men. Being like the sand on the seashore, innumerable. They are from all races, all nations. All souls will be alike in the kingdom of God. The color of their flesh will not matter, just as God saves people today from all nations and peoples and tribes and tongues.

Notice they are carrying palms in their hands, just as the Jews did on what is referred to as Palm Sunday. It seems strange that some people have taught that in this great multitude we have the raptured church. Some believe that the Lord will not return for His church until the middle of the Tribulation period. However, in a careful study of the passage, it becomes very clear what we are seeing here, what is occurring on earth.

It is not a scene in heaven, not a heavenly company. This great multitude is made up of the Gentile nations, those who will enter into millennial blessing. It is the great ingathering of the coming kingdom. From all nations, and kindreds, and peoples, and tongues, a vast multitude from all parts of the earth will be redeemed to God. Redeemed by the blood of the Lamb and will enter into the physical earthly kingdom of our Lord. During these dark days of the Great Tribulation, they will heed the testimony which will be carried to the ends of the earth by 144,000 Jewish missionaries. These who are noted as wise come from the core of the nations of people and they will instruct many in righteousness. We see here in Daniel 12:3: "And they that be wise shall shine as the brightness of the firmament; and they that turn many to righteousness as the stars for ever and ever." They are identical with the "sheep" of Matthew 25, who are placed on the right hand of the Son of man when He comes in His glory and all His holy angels with Him. These will inherit the kingdom prepared for them from the foundation of the earth.

Matthew 25:31–33: "When the Son of man shall come in his glory, and all the holy angels with him, then shall he sit upon the throne of his glory. And before him shall be gathered all nations: and he shall separate them one from another, as a shepherd divideth his sheep from the goats. And he shall set the sheep on his right hand, but the goats on the left."

The 144,000 Israelites, the physical descendants of Abraham through Isaac and Jacob, will become God's missionaries during the Tribulation period. As a result of their preaching and testimony, there will be great numbers saved. Many Gentiles will come from all nations and kindreds and people and tongues. Many believe that these will have never heard the gospel. Others interpret this as a mid-Tribulation rapture.

Many believe that the great masses in the world who have never heard the Gospel of God's grace will hear the message in the Tribulation from the lips of the 144,000 Israelites. As a result, a great number will be saved, most of whom will be martyred and will be raised at the close of the Tribulation period.

The final gleaning of the First Resurrection in verses 13 to 14 bear this out:

"And one of the elders answered, saying unto me, What are these which are arrayed in white robes? and whence came they? And I said unto him, Sir, thou knowest. And he said to me, These are they which came out of great tribulation, and have washed their robes, and made them white in the blood of the Lamb."

I happen to believe that God is a God of second chances. I believe that many who have heard the Gospel will be saved in the Tribulation. 2 Thessalonians 2:10: "And with all deceivableness of unrighteousness in them that perish; because they received not the love of the truth, that they might be saved." Those who will not receive the love of the truth will be deceived and continue to reject Christ.

When the beast and false prophet come, these will follow after them. But when did they reject the truth? That is what we need to see in 2 Thessalonians 2:3–4: "Let no man deceive you by any means: for that day shall not come, except there come a falling away first, and that man of sin be revealed, the son of perdition; Who opposeth and exalteth himself above all that is called God, or that is worshipped; so that he as God sitteth in the temple of God, shewing himself that he is God."

In our age, there will be a falling away that is happening today. People who are believers are falling away and following false teaching. Many are saved but have turned from the truth. They received the truth and accepted Christ, but they are falling away from following the truth. But that is not the only thing we see in the passage. We see that when the Tribulation comes in 2 Thessalonians 2:7–9, the mystery of iniquity was at work even in Paul's time.

In our age, the Holy Spirit is referred to as "he who now letteth will let, until he be taken out of the way."

The Holy Spirit is taken with the Church. Once He has been taken away, then the Wicked One is to be revealed. Those who rejected the truth will follow him. God will give them over, those who did not receive the love of the truth. Could they at the beginning of the Tribulation believe? Or is it as some teach if they reject the truth of the Gospel on this side of the Tribulation they will then in fact be doomed? Or do many reject the truth after the Tribulation and are then deceived and doomed? The ones doomed in the Tribulation are those who do one specific thing.

They take the mark of the beast, either in the forehead or the back of the hand. Then they cannot be saved! The great multitude before the throne, we are told, are those from the Great Tribulation. Revelation 7:14: "And I said unto him, Sir, thou knowest. And he said to me, These are they which came out of Great Tribulation, and have washed their robes, and made them white in the blood of the Lamb." This is not the church raptured at this point.

These are from the Tribulation. These are those saved after the church age has ended and the church has been snatched away. These received the gospel of Christ after the church had been taken out. This occurs after the one that *letteth* was removed, that being the Holy Spirit.

When did they hear the gospel? When did the 144,000 hear the gospel? Was it in this church age? Once the church is gone and the Tribulation begins with only the lost, who will be the witness to the 144,000 whom we saw sealed? When will they believe Jesus is the true Messiah and Savior? To me they must have heard the gospel on this side of the Tribulation and were saved after the church was snatched away. Of the multitude of Gentiles, many may hear on this side and trust during the Tribulation. The rest who rejected the truth will be deceived, take the mark of the beast, and perish!

Let's look closer at 2 Thessalonians 2. Paul wrote this to keep error from spreading and confusion for continuing over what he had written in the first letter. In verses 1 to 3, we see they had mistaken his meaning in the first letter concerning the Lord's return. They thought as one group teaches that the coming was near at hand in that day. That Christ was just about ready to appear and come in judgment. Two events had to occur before the Lord's return. Paul said, "Except there be a falling away first." The second, "And that man of sin be revealed, the son of perdition" Paul's words from then ring ever so true today.

There are many who are lurking about teaching a conflicting doctrine and seeking to deceive, and they have many ways of deceiving people. We need to be careful and stand on guard. Some false teachers will profess the Holy Spirit has revealed to them new revelations, others simply misinterpret scripture, and others will be guilty of blatant alterations by saying they have a different method. Changing the method is fine as long as it doesn't change the message. They are teaching a false or mistaken interpretation, and it is used to lead people astray.

Therefore, we must be careful that no man deceives us by any means. Let's center on verse 10 though. Who are those who didn't love the truth and will be deceived? Their sin is "they believed not the truth, but had pleasure in unrighteousness." They did not love the truth, and therefore they did not believe it. Because they did not believe the truth, therefore they had pleasure in unrighteousness, or in wicked actions, and were pleased with false notions.

Note, an inaccurate belief and malicious life will most often go together and help give courage to one another. Their loss is expressed in the fact that "God shall send them strong delusions, to believe a lie." Thus, God will punish men for their unbelief, and for their rejection of the truth. That, coupled with a love to commit sin and wickedness, leads to destruction.

God is not the author of sin. In righteousness He may at times withdraw His grace from this type of sinner mentioned here. He will give them over to Satan, or He will leave them to be deceived by the instruments of the false teacher and Satan. He gives them up to their own hearts' lusts, and leaves them to themselves, and then sin will follow of course! The worst wickedness, it shall end at last in eternal punishment that will be their fate. God is just when he carries out spiritual judgments here and eternal punishments in the hereafter. This upon those who have no love of the truth of the gospel, those who will not believe them but who will indulge in false teachings in their minds, performing wicked practices in their lives and conversations.

"That they all might be damned" (verse 12) or judged, separated, and isolated from true Christians and real believers is clear. Realistically, we can note that they might be condemned and punished with everlasting destruction. They will die the second death—that is, they are not believers and will be eternally separated from the presence of the Lord. They will have their portion in the lake which burns with fire and brimstone. Where the devil, the false prophet, and the beast, whose followers they are, will be cast and it is a just declaration that God will give them up to such delusion, that they may be damned, since they received not the love of the truth that they might be saved.

Their character justifies God's divine judgment. To interpret this as those of this age doesn't seem to ring true at least not to me what about you? Those who reject the truth in the Tribulation will be given over to all these things, just as those in this age are condemned to the second death. These people followed after false religion and have rejected the truth. Many may be told about the false Christ, the beast, and the Tribulation and rejected it in this age, and when the church is taken out and the man of perdition is revealed, they again reject the truth.

Do you see that is what Paul is telling the Thessalonian believers? This is what will happen in that age and that is the sign of the second coming of Christ. Revelation 7:15–17: "Therefore are they before the throne of God, and serve him day and night in his temple: and he that sitteth on the throne shall dwell among them. They shall hunger no more, neither thirst any more; neither shall the sun light on them, nor any heat. For the Lamb which is in the midst of the throne shall feed them, and shall lead them unto living fountains of waters: and God shall wipe away all tears from their eyes." What a picture of peace, joy, and quietness.

This is the short interval of God sealing His 144,000 witnesses. This is short–lived, as we will see in Chapter 8. The one that sits on the throne will dwell with them forever. That is great news. When the millennial kingdom comes, Christ will be on the throne in Israel reigning with them. When New Jerusalem comes down, He will be on the throne there forever. There will be no need for the sun or moon because He gives off the light. Christ will cover His people as He did when

He led Israel out of Egypt. No more will they hunger or thirst. Those with Him will have all their needs supplied. For the Lamb will be in the midst of the throne. He shall feed them. He shall lead them to fountains of living water. In the end, He will wipe away all tears from their eyes, but for now the judgment must continue.

The judgment is delayed until the 144,000 can be sealed, twelve thousand from each of the twelve tribes of Israel with Dan omitted and Manasseh added. God has a plan for Israel in the future. The church is in heaven having been snatched away. There is, however, a great multitude of Gentiles saved during the Tribulation. That we see here!

4

Seventh Seal Opened, Trumpets Sound

We come to the seventh seal where the judgment will begin afresh. John says there was silence in heaven for about half an hour as Chapter 8 verse 1 opens. The final part of the title deed redemption of the earth. This begins the next phase, the blowing of the seven trumpets. After the parenthetical matter of Chapter 7 has been completed with the sealing of the 144,000 and the multitude from Gentile nations,

We come to the opening of the seventh and final seal. Christ forms a pattern that John will be following from this point on. For the remainder of the book of Revelation, John follows this same pattern, so that we can't be led astray or shouldn't be led astray. There will be a series of sevens, as well as a series of fours which relate to the Great Tribulation. John gives the first six of the series, then a parenthetical subject which adds to our understanding of that specific series of events.

Then he will follow that as he open's the seventh of the series, which shows us that the series is interrelated. They are tied together and actually belong to the same event. Revelation 8:1: "And when he had opened the seventh seal, there was silence in heaven about the space of half an hour."

The seventh seal brings a period of silence. This silence may perhaps include a pause even of the songs which rise before the throne of God from the redeemed creation, the voice of whose praise rests not either day or night. A brief suspension of judgment is thereby indicated, a pause by and during which the Lord would call attention to the appearance of His wrath which is about to follow. The exact length of this silence, "about the space of half an hour," has never been adequately explained. The general thought of John's language does not imply an idea of a literal interpretation. Perhaps to make a more synchronized method in the spirit in which the Revelation is written.

We might consider some things: First, in the book the half of anything suggests not an actual half but a broken and interruption of a whole, five a broken ten, six a broken twelve, three and a half a broken seven. A "half-hour" may simply mean that the sequence of events has been interrupted and that the restart of judgment has been delayed. The Lamb opened the seventh seal. The Lord is still in command. He opens the seventh seal. He directs the action from heaven. We need to remember this through the entire book. Never losing sight of the fact that Revelation shows us Christ. The Lord Jesus Christ in His glory as the judge of all the earth.

This is the same Jesus who in His earthly ministry went about doing good. He is the Lamb we also see bringing the wrath of God. In John 1:29, we see what John the Baptist said: "Behold the

Lamb of God which taketh away the sins of the world." Remember that people are not lost because they are sinners. They are lost because they have rejected Christ. It is a Son issue, not a sin issue, that sends them to hell. Christ died for all! He is the propitiation for us and them. 1 John 2:2: "And he is the propitiation for our sins: and not for ours only, but also for the sins of the whole world."

It makes it very clear he is the *propitiation* (satisfaction) for *us* (believers). Then it goes further. He is the *propitiation* "for the sins of the whole world." That is the unbelievers. Jesus paid the price for their sins too on that cross. It is a matter of salvation by grace—that is, by grace He became the propitiation for sins. It is by our placing our *faith in Him*, accepting Him as the payment for our sins, that makes the difference. Reject and be lost and in the Lake of Fire forever, accept His payment and be saved and with Him for *all* eternity.

So we have a very solemn scene here. Nothing can move without His permission. He had already said to the angels to hold the judgment. They are ready to release judgment on the four corners of the earth! Now there is a brief pause in judgment. There is a heavenly hush, calm before the storm! Why this strange silence? God's patience is not exhausted. When the sixth seal was opened, nature responded with a violent convulsion. Brave men weakened for a moment.

Christ gave them an opportunity to repent! Many will be like Pharaoh when the intensity is removed, then they allow their stubborn heart to resume and guide them back to their ungodly ways. Everything can be explained by a natural cause, man says. The seventh seal broken makes it clear where God stands in all the concerns of the earth. He will judge according to His holiness with the holiness of His character, the righteousness of His throne.

The seventh seal introduces the final drama of the Great Tribulation. Is it no wonder there is silence in heaven for about half an hour! It is as though all heaven is waiting in breathless expectation! We seem to hear the questions. What will the Lamb do next? What will be God's next move toward judging and reclaiming that rebellious world?

Verses 2 to 5 give the answer. Revelation 8:2–5: "And I saw the seven angels which stood before God; and to them were given seven trumpets. And another angel came and stood at the altar, having a golden censer; and there was given unto him much incense, that he should offer it with the prayers of all saints upon the golden altar which was before the throne. And the smoke of the incense, which came with the prayers of the saints, ascended up before God out of the angel's hand. And the angel took the censer, and filled it with fire of the altar, and cast it into the earth: and there were voices, and thunderings, and lightnings, and an earthquake."

We now see seven angels appear and stand before God. The angels are employed as the wise and willing instruments of divine purpose from God's providence. They are supplied with all the materials and instructions from God our Savior. As the angels of the churches are to sound the trumpet of the gospel, the angels of heaven are to sound the trumpet of Divine Providence.

Everyone has his part given him or her as believers. The seal is broken, the book is fully unrolled, and the seven angels appear and are given seven trumpets. These angels are messengers standing, waiting one after the other for their instructions. The seven trumpets have a special meaning.

We have seven special angels and seven trumpets. Where else do we find Scripture mention seven trumpets?

We see trumpets mentioned in several places in Scripture, so what too is their significance? First in the book of Numbers, Moses was given instruction from God. We see in Numbers 10:2–6: "Make thee two trumpets of silver; of a whole piece shalt thou make them: that thou mayest use them for the calling of the assembly, and for the journeying of the camps. And when they shall blow with them, all the assembly shall assemble themselves to thee at the door of the tabernacle of the congregation. And if they blow but with one trumpet, then the princes, which are heads of the thousands of Israel, shall gather themselves unto thee. When ye blow an alarm, then the camps that lie on the east parts shall go forward. When ye blow an alarm the second time, then the camps that lie on the south side shall take their journey: they shall blow an alarm for their journeys."

Two is the number of division, but also God said on several occasions that in the mouth of two witnesses, a matter would be established. More important is to see Joshua 6. Center in on verse 13: "And seven priests bearing seven trumpets of rams' horns before the ark of the Lord went on continually, and blew with the trumpets: and the armed men went before them; but the reward came after the ark of the Lord, the priests going on, and blowing with the trumpets." We see the fall of Jericho connected to seven trumpets. This is the great city just across the Jordan that barred the progress of the people of Israel into the Promised Land, Jericho. It fell with the blast of God alone! The priests of Israel were given the trumpets of judgment. For seven days they marched around the city blowing the trumpets.

Seven times on the seventh day they did so. At the seventh blast the walls fell down flat. Jericho is a type of this present world in its estrangement from God, its hatred of God's people. Jericho fell at the sound of seven trumpets. The world, as you and I know it, is going to fall at the sound of the seven trumpets of doom. The Trumpets are blown by these angels of judgment. The seven trumpets of Revelation will have the positive effect of moving the nation of Israel into the land of Palestine. This will be in masses. In a move of God's judgment, swiftly it comes.

These seven trumpets will get Israel back into her land. The current nation is not complete and was manmade, not God-made. Fulfillment of prophecy for Israel begins here in the return to the land. As the seven trumpets were used in the battle of Jericho, the walls of this world's opposition to God will crumble and fall during the Great Tribulation. He will put down the next to last trace of rebellion against Himself and against God the Father.

He will establish His kingdom here upon the earth. This is the book of triumph, of victory for our God. At the end it has the hallelujah chorus that you and I may join in on!

In Verse 5, we see: "The angel took the censer, and filled it with fire of the altar." In Israel, the high priest took a censer with him as he carried the blood into the Holy of Holies. Here the ritual was reversed; the angel has a golden censer. We are told that the smoke of the incense is the prayers of the saints, those suffering saints on the earth. The angel took the censer, filled it with the fire of the altar. As yet the seven trumpets have only been given to the seven angels. More has to pass before they put them to their lips and sound. At the opening of the fifth seal, we read of a great brazen "altar" which was impossible not to identify. The altar of burnt-offering, in the outer court of the sanctuary was a type of this.

Such identification is not so obvious here. Some commentators agree in thinking that the altar now spoken of is rather the golden or incense altar which had its place within the tabernacle immediately in front of the second veil. To this altar, the priest on ordinary occasions, and more particularly the high priest on the great Day of Atonement, brought a censer with burning frankincense, that the smoke of the incense, as it rose into the air, might be a symbol to the congregation of Israel that its prayers, offered according to the Divine will, ascended as a sweet savor to God.

Incense speaks of the value of Christ's name. He has told us, "If you ask in My Name." Here they are offering incense. Sweet smelling incense! The smoke of the incense came up with the prayers of the saints! The smoke of the incense, with the prayers of the saints, went up before God out of the angel's hand we see in verse 4. Prayer is going to be answered because of Christ.

The prayers of the saints, ascended before God out of the angel's hand. Alluding to the incense like that of the Levitical priest taking it in his hand he Cast it upon the burning coals, and shows how that by the smoke of the incense, the imperfections of the prayers of the saints are covered. It shows how they are perfumed and made acceptable to God. These are said to ascend up before Him, and to be regarded by Him.

We then see something that didn't occur in the Old Testament with the censer. Cast it into the earth. Here the ritual is reversed. The censer is hurled out of heaven to the earth. In other words, the prayers ascended as incense. Now the answer was coming, the Tribulation saints had prayed,

"Oh, God, Avenge us." The people of earth having rejected the death of Christ for the judgment of their sins, they must now bear the brunt of judgment. Judgment for their having rejected Christ! The Great Tribulation is set to begin! Casting the censer to the earth has the effect of where there were voices, thunders, lightings, and an earthquake. Thunders always denote the approach of the coming storm of God's judgment. Voices reveal that this is intelligent direction of God and not a purposeless working of natural forces. God is in charge.

Lightning follow the thunder, a reversal of natural order. We see the lightning before we hear the thunder due to light moving faster than sound waves. Actually, the thunder comes first. We do not hear it until after we have already seen the lightning. The earthquake is the earth's response to severe pressure which is placed upon it during the judgment of the Great Tribulation.

These prayers were accepted in heaven and they produced great changes upon the earth. In return to them the same angel that in his censer offered up the prayers of the saints. Now in the same censer took off the fire of the altar, and cast it into the earth, and this began to cause a set of devastating events. These were the answers God gave to the prayers of the saints! Tokens of his anger against the world, that He would do great things to avenge Himself and his people of their enemies. Now, all things being prepared, the angels discharge their duty.

We now come to verse 6 of Chapter 8: "And the seven angels which had the seven trumpets prepared themselves to sound." The *Solemn Moment*, the half hour of silence, is over. The interruption of judgment is complete. The prayers of the saints have been heard. The orders to these trumpeters have been issued. Prepare to blow! The angels come to attention. At the signal the blowing of the trumpets will begin and so too divine wrath will begin for those rebellious people.

The blowing of the trumpets does not introduce symbols or secrets. Just as Egypt experienced the plagues from God, so too the world will have literal plagues brought upon them. Many today want to disallow the literal meaning. They want to deny the inspiration of scripture. Many want to say God really wouldn't bring this upon mankind. Not if He is a God of love! This has to mean something else, they say. It must be some type of symbolism.

Revelation 8:7: "The first angel sounded, and there followed hail and fire mingled with blood, and they were cast upon the earth: and the third part of trees was burnt up, and all green grass was burnt up."

God's judgment is coming full force on mankind. The first thing we see is hail and fire mingled with blood. They are cast upon the earth. A third of the trees are burnt up. All the grass was burnt up. Botanical life is affected. The process of photosynthesis is affected. This process is a plant's way of making food. Oxygen is a byproduct of that process. Fire, the great enemy of plants, is the tool God uses to begin the judgment process in order to begin the removal of the curse.

Isaiah 40:6: "The voice said, Cry. And he said, What shall I cry? All flesh is grass, and all the goodliness thereof is as the flower of the field." Grass is the symbol of mankind. In Isaiah 40:6, man being trampled beneath the foot is a picture of human frailty and weakness. The flood was the first judgment on mankind. We have the rainbow as the symbol that God would not judge mankind by means of a flood. The earth is purified by fire.

Today, people burn grass and fields to purify and kill bugs and weeds. God is bringing this fire to purify the earth. The forest and prairies are covered with grass. All the grass is burnt but only a third of the trees. The first day God created light, the second day He created the firmament in heaven.

We see in Genesis 1 the creation chronology. The third day God moved the waters and created dry land. And He called the dry land earth. Look at Genesis 1:11: "And God said, Let the earth bring forth grass, the herb yielding seed, and the fruit tree yielding fruit after his kind, whose seed is in itself, upon the earth: and it was so."

The third day the earth brought forth grass, as well as the Herb yielding seed, the tree yielding fruit. We see God destroy a third of the trees here in Revelation. Before man was created, God supplied the green vegetation for man's sustenance. In this last judgment, He begins with destroying life-sustaining vegetation. God created plant life after order. Once the earth had been brought into place with light and firmament in order, God brought the plants that make oxygen into being.

We see God bring a literal judgment upon plant life just as He did in Exodus 9:18–26 in Egypt. The plagues of Egypt and the Judgment here are similar. That is not a mistake! When you go back to Exodus, you find that the plagues there are literal also. We must acknowledge this fact! Revelation needs to be dealt with in that fashion.

We see that the first trumpet brings a fiery judgment upon the life-sustaining needs of mankind. It may be a horrifying picture, but the reality of it will be much worse. When the hail came down in Egypt, we see the hail smote every herb of the field, and break every tree of the field (verse 25). There was one hundred percent destruction in Egypt. Except in the land of Goshen, here we see a third of the trees are destroyed.

We now come to verses 8 and 9 of Revelation 8: "And the second angel sounded, and as it were a great mountain burning with fire was cast into the sea: and the third part of the sea became blood; And the third part of the creatures which were in the sea, and had life, died; and the third part of the ships were destroyed."

We see in Jeremiah 51:25 the second trumpet affecting the sea. God first destroys the life-giving vegetation that supplies both food and oxygen. Now we see He brings judgment upon the seas. Remember, we are dealing in threes here, three being the number of divine perfection. God separated the water and the earth on the third day (Genesis 1:9–10). A great force causes the mountain to be burning. We know how a volcano has this great burning lava that comes with it, but notice this doesn't say it is a mountain or a volcano.

Scripture states, "As it were a great mountain burning with fire was cast into the sea." Notice the trumpet sound as if it were a great mountain. The mountain represents something tangible, something great. As we see in Jeremiah 51:25, the Lord is speaking of Babylon. Here we see a literal mass fall into the sea. One-third becomes blood. One-third of all literal sea creatures die a literal death!

This can't be any plainer than that. One-third of the literal ships of all literal nations are literally destroyed. John makes it clear a great force, a massive force, is put into the ocean. Thus God brings judgment upon the waters of the earth. This should make our heart fear sorrowfully. It should do more than that—it should not only affect our hearts, it should also affect our wills as well as our feet that we should get moving to get the word of God to a lost and dying world. That is our responsibility.

We cannot keep this judgment from coming. We can get the word out. When we do get the word out and bring souls into the kingdom of God, we reduce the population that will be left behind to go through this terrible time.

Now we come to the third trumpet seen in verses 10 to 11 of Revelation 8: "And the third angel sounded, and there fell a great star from heaven, burning as it were a lamp, and it fell upon the third part of the rivers, and upon the fountains of waters; And the name of the star is called Wormwood: and the third part of the waters became wormwood; and many men died of the waters, because they were made bitter." A star falls from the heavens with the blowing of the third trumpet. Almost sounds like a comet! It falls on a third part of the rivers. Again, we see the third day of creation being judged. One-third of the drinking water is affected.

Notice we have in the past twenty-five to thirty years seen many laws that deal with the environment. Man had to clean up the drinking water or we wouldn't have water to sustain us. But God will pollute the rivers in judgment. Not just the rivers are affected, but also the fountains of water. The underground rivers of water are affected. The sweet waters are made bitter. A meteor or comet, or it could even be from a nuclear attack, will make the waters bitter.

Both rivers and fountains beneath the earth the name of the star is "Wormwood." In many Old Testament verses, wormwood is considered in the following ways:

- Idolatry of Israel (Deuteronomy 29:18)
- Calamity and sorrow (Jeremiah 9:15; 23:15;

Lamentation 3:15, 19)

- False judgment (Amos 5:7)
- All have to do with God's judgment

The star here is a literal thing:

- It could be a meteor
- It could be a manmade satellite
- It could be nuclear in nature
- It makes the waters bitter, whatever it may be

It brings with it poison and contaminants. It contaminates one-third of the fresh water supply. The star's name suggests it is a judgment upon mankind, for idolatry, injustice, calamity, and sorrow come with it. We are told "many men died of the waters, because they were made bitter." With this comes death.

We see the finish of Chapter 8 with the fourth trumpet in verses 12 and 13: "And the fourth angel sounded, and the third part of the sun was smitten, and the third part of the moon and the third part of the stars; so as the third part of them was darkened, and the day shone not for a third part of it, and the night likewise. And I beheld, and heard an angel flying through the midst of heaven, saying with a loud voice, Woe, woe, woe, to the inhabiters of the earth by reason of the other voices of the trumpet of the three angels, which are yet to sound!"

We see here another phase of creation. In Genesis 1:14–19, we see the fourth day of creation. Man is dependent upon the sun, moon, and stars. The sun gives light for photosynthesis to occur, which again affects oxygen creation. The moon and stars control tides and other things. Now a part of the light, a third of the sun's light, is put out. Remember, we talked a few chapters ago about how the sun was darkened and the moon turned red. We need to look at what Jesus said in Matthew 24:29: "Immediately after the Tribulation of those days shall the sun be darkened, and the moon shall not give her light, and the stars shall fall from heaven, and the powers of the heavens shall be shaken." The laws of nature are radically altered by these disturbances. Only a third of the light is affected, only a third of the day. The intensity of the light is reduced by one-third. We see an energy shortage in this time. We see one is coming, greater than any we have seen. "Woe, woe, woe," we hear from an angel! The warning to the inhabitants of the earth is clear. When the fourth trumpet blows, the announcement of the intensity of woe goes forth. Judgment is coming and it is going to be greater than all others have been! The last three trumpets are separated from the other four. They each are mentioned by the angel, "Woe, woe, woe." The warning is to those who inhabit the earth, because of the next three trumpets, which are yet to sound! This shows a greater time of Tribulation is coming, a greater time of judgment! We have now seen the first four trumpets sound and great judgment begins on the earth. The worst is yet to come with the last three trumpets.

5

The Fifth and Sixth Trumpets

The first four trumpets have sounded and judgment has restarted after a brief pause. The angel shouted in verse 13 of Revelation 8: "Woe, woe, woe, to those who inhabit the earth by reason of the other voices of the trumpet of the three angels, which are yet to sound!" The final portion of the title deed redemption of the world has begun! The blowing of the last three trumpets begins the next phase of judgment upon mankind.

We now come to Chapter 9, verse 1: "And the fifth angel sounded, and I saw a star fall from heaven unto the earth: and to him was given the key of the bottomless pit." The fifth trumpet blows. In this case, the star seen in context is an angel. Notice the terminology given to him. This star, as it says acts, with intelligence. Therefore, it is not to be interpreted as a literal star. He is given a key. That key is to the bottomless pit.

Many have interpreted this star as being Christ. Others have him as the antichrist. Some have taken it as the eminent bishop in the Christian church. Another view is that he is Satan. If it is the antichrist that would mean Satan would become incarnate like Christ did. The antichrist is a man, not Satan and man. Antichrist is exactly that. He is everything Christ isn't! He is possessed by a demon and motivated by Satan.

There are many reasons to interpret the star as Satan. Isaiah 14:12: "How art thou fallen from heaven, O Lucifer, son of the morning! how art thou cut down to the ground, which didst weaken the nations!" Luke 10:18: "And he said unto them, I beheld Satan as lightning fall from heaven." This would be like a falling star. Paul states in 2 Corinthians 11:14: "And no marvel; for Satan himself is transformed into an angel of light." These scriptures should help us confirm the position that Satan is the star of verse 1.

We will see later in Revelation 12:7–9 that Satan was put out of heaven. He was cast to the earth. If this is indeed Satan we see in these scriptures, what does he do? We see he takes the key to the Abyss, aka the bottomless pit! God gives him permission to take the key. A key denotes authority and power it is given to him by God. This is God's permissive will taking place. The bottomless pit is what we see in the King James Version.

Where is this pit located? Many believe it is the abode called Tartarus which is believed to be located in the center of the earth. The bottomless pit, the Abyss, is believed by many to be a long shaft leading to the bottomless pit. We will see it again in Chapter 20 verse 3. It is a part of Hades.

Christ gave some hints to us about Hades at the time He was on the earth. Matthew 12:40: "For as Jonas was three days and three nights in the whale's belly; so shall the Son of man be three days and three nights in the heart of the earth." Christ speaks of his descent into the heart of the earth. Christ's body was in the tomb for three literal days and nights. He went to Sheol or Hades for three days and nights.

But understand what He told the thief on the cross in Luke 23:43: "And Jesus said unto him, Verily I say unto thee, Today shalt thou be with me in paradise." In Ephesians 4:8–10, Paul made it clear. "Wherefore he saith, When he ascended up on high, he led captivity captive, and gave gifts unto men. (Now that he ascended, what is it but that he also descended first into the lower parts of the earth? He that descended is the same also that ascended up far above all heavens, that he might fill all things.)" Understand paradise was once in Hades as part of the three compartments there.

The Lord confirmed this in Luke 16:22–26. The Abyss is a literal place; it is a part of Hades. The great gulf fixed between paradise and torments leads to the bottomless pit. The people who say heaven and hell are myths are proven wrong by Christ and by scripture. Understand once Christ completed mankind's salvation He emptied paradise. How do we know, Paul tells us in 2 Corinthians 5:6–8 and in Romans 8:34? Do you see it? When we die, we are *absent from the body and present with the Lord*!

The Lord is in heaven seated at the Father's right hand. It is said and believed by many that in the three days Christ's body was in the grave, paradise was emptied of the captives and he led captivity captive and preached to those in torments.

Revelation 9:2: "And he opened the bottomless pit; and there arose a smoke out of the pit, as the smoke of a great furnace; and the sun and the air were darkened by reason of the smoke of the pit." God's judgment is coming full force on mankind. The bottomless pit is opened. Out of the shaft, the great gulf, like a great volcanic eruption, a plume of smoke comes out of that pit! So massive it blots out the sun and the air is filled with it! The smoke covers the earth! That is a massive plume of smoke.

It is vicious, as we see in Revelation 9:3–4: "And there came out of the smoke locusts upon the earth: and unto them was given power, as the scorpions of the earth have power. And it was commanded them that they should not hurt the grass of the earth, neither any green thing, neither any tree; but only those men which have not the seal of God in their foreheads."

Now we see supernatural spirits called locust, creatures so frightful that this is the only way John could speak of them. They are locusts of a very unusual character. This too is like the plague of locusts in Egypt when God was judging Pharaoh and Egypt in order that they let His people go. Joel the prophet (Joel 1) prophesied of a coming plague of locust. We see in all this just how we must connect the dots of New Testament to Old Testament in order to understand what Revelation is dealing with. The difference between the locust in Joel and these seen in Revelation is the character of the locust and the object of their destruction.

They sting like scorpions! Their objects are evil men! We see God bring a literal torment upon evil mankind in Revelation 9:5: "And to them it was given that they should not kill them, but that they should be tormented five months: and their torment was as the torment of a scorpion, when he striketh a man." These locusts seem to have a stinger like a scorpion. The scorpion's sting is in his tail. This is the picture we are given, the sting is not fatal. It is, however, very painful.

They torment men for five months, we are told. Notice they are only allowed to touch those who are not sealed by God. Satan's power is limited by God. These are demonic creatures. We will see the description of them shortly. We need to understand who these demons are! They are a class of especially wicked demons, who because of their vicious nature are not permitted to be at large until this time. There is a reason! These are fallen angels but not just any fallen angels.

Jude 1:6 tells us who they are: "And the angels which kept not their first estate, but left their own habitation, he hath reserved in everlasting chains under darkness unto the judgment of the great day." Isn't the Tribulation the *Great Day of Judgment* they were reserved for? What does it mean they left their first estate?

Another look back to the Old Testament is in order. In Genesis 6:1–2, we see: "And it came to pass, when men began to multiply on the face of the earth, and daughters were born unto them, that the sons of God saw the daughters of men that they were fair; and they took them wives of all which they chose." Do you see it? Angels, demon angels, the sons of God as created, have become tools of Satan. Angels took wives of human females as they chose thus *Leaving their first estate*. To do that which was evil and to corrupt mankind's race.

We see the result of this comingling in verse 4 to 5: "There were giants in the earth in those days; and also after that, when the sons of God came in unto the daughters of men, and they bare children to them, the same became mighty men which were of old, men of renown. And God saw that the wickedness of man was great in the earth, and that every imagination of the thoughts of his heart was only evil continually.

These were as the original text, states Nephelim, giants, believed by many to be the result of the cohabitation of angels and women. These were like the mule that in most cases is unable to reproduce it is believed these Nephilim could not reproduce. But were strong, mighty beings. You say yes, but aren't angels referred to as sexless beings? How can these be angels who kept not their first estate?

Again the Old Testament must be sought look at Job 1:6, where we see: "Now there was a day when the sons of God came to present themselves before the Lord, and Satan came also among them." The *sons of God* came to represent themselves before the Lord. Satan came also among them, *these are angels*. In Job 2:1, again we see: "Again there was a day when the sons of God came to present themselves before the Lord, and Satan came also among them to present himself before the Lord." *Sons of God* came to present themselves and Satan came also to present himself.

Finally, in Job 38:7, we see: "When the morning stars sang together, and all the sons of God shouted for joy?" The *sons of God*, the angels shouted for joy. So the sons of God in Noah's time who took wives of the daughters of men were angels. Jude describes them as *angels who left their first estate.* Reserved until the time of judgment! Reserved in chains until the Tribulation! Now they are loosed upon mankind.

We now come to verse 6 of Revelation 9: "And in those days shall men seek death, and shall not find it; and shall desire to die, and death shall flee from them." What a terrible time this will be! No exaggeration is seen here. We are only seeing what God's word says is coming, judgment upon evil mankind! In Noah's day, as they did evil continually, God judged them by flood.

Now we see Him judging with torments, *Tribulation.* Men during this time seek to commit suicide. We are told they won't be able to accomplish that goal. God will not permit them to find death. Satan wants them here because there is a battle being waged. A battle between light and dark! God is letting mankind face the consequences of their rebellion. There is no escape!

We now come to Chapter 9, verse 7: "And the shapes of the locusts were like unto horses prepared unto battle; and on their heads were as it were crowns like gold, and their faces were as the faces of men." The description of these locusts as John called them.

The description is seen in parts.

- heads
- face
- hair
- teeth
- breastplates
- wings
- tails

It is said they have a king over them. This king's name is seen in verse 11. These locusts are prepared to do battle. They seem to be monstrous in size and shape. They are equipped for their work, like horses prepared for battle. This is a frightful, weird, and unnatural description! Since they come out of the bottomless pit, then we know them to be demons. As we saw earlier, these are the angels which kept not their first estate as described by Jude in verse 6.

We now come to the descriptions. Their heads had crowns like gold, counterfeiting authority. Their faces are like that of men, thus showing they have wisdom. Revelation 9:8: "And they had hair as the hair of women, and their teeth were as the teeth of lions." Their hair as that of women, The Bible says a woman's hair is her glory. 1 Corinthians 11:15: "But if a woman have long hair, it is a glory to her: for her hair is given her for a covering." Thus we see that they have intense seductiveness and attractiveness. Solomon 7:5: "Thine head upon thee is like Carmel, and the hair of thine head like purple; the king is held in the galleries." We see from Solomon that the king was spellbound by the woman's hair.

Their teeth are like the teeth of a lion. This shows how cruel they truly are. They are vicious! Tearing the flesh of men, like lions. They were ready to rush into battle. Revelation 9:9: "And they had breastplates, as it were breastplates of iron; and the sound of their wings was as the sound of chariots of many horses running to battle."

Their skin is hard and tough! These locusts had protection from death, the hardness of their heart, their consciences seared. Their wings sound like chariots. This shows they come charging upon mankind. They made a mighty noise in the world. They flew about from one country to the other. The noise of their motion was as if it were chariots and horses racing to battle.

We see God bring a literal torment upon evil mankind in Revelation 9:10: "And they had tails like unto scorpions, and there were stings in their tails: and their power was to hurt men five months." They have a stinger, like a scorpion. The scorpion's sting is in his tail. This is the picture we are given. As earlier stated, the sting is not fatal. It is, however, very painful and they torment men for five months!

Their torment is the torment of scorpions, which gives great pain and is very distressing. These demonic creatures are troublesome and afflict mankind. Vicious, not caring who is in their path, but they can't touch those sealed by God! For five months they afflict mankind. Five is the number of *grace.* Even in judgment, God's grace is shown to these evil men. Even in this time of Tribulation!

We now come to verse 11 of Revelation 9: "And they had a king over them, which is the angel of the bottomless pit, whose name in the Hebrew tongue is Abaddon, but in the Greek tongue hath his name Apollyon." These demons have a leader over them. This shows them differentiated from a normal locust. Proverbs 30:27: "The locusts have no king, yet go they forth all of them by bands." We are told the name of this king: Abaddon in Hebrew and Apollyon in Greek. Some believe this to be Satan, others that it is a chief angel of Satan.

He is able to lead an invasion of the earth for the first time. The thought of these locusts and their attack seems frightening. Abaddon in Hebrew means "destruction." Apollyon in Greek means "the destroyer." This would reinforce what Paul says about the demon world of fallen angels. It is divided into ranks. Ephesians 6:12: "For we wrestle not against flesh and blood, but against principalities, against powers, against the rulers of the darkness of this world, against spiritual wickedness in high places." Just as Satan was an archangel and in charge of one-third of the angels, so too are the angels divided up into rankings:

1. Generals
2. Majors
3. Lieutenants
4. Sergeants
5. Privates

He was their leader in the bottomless pit, we are told. Even there he was their leader and therefore would not be Satan. We are told he was the angel of the bottomless pit. The ruling angel there, of whom Satan has loosed with the key to the bottomless pit leads the others. The end of the fifth woe is seen here and we are told this in Revelation 9:12: "One woe is past; and, behold, there come two woes more hereafter."

The first woe is past from John's vision and would last five months, the first woe of the Great Tribulation. The last two woes will deal with the second and third part of the Great Tribulation. The warning indicates there are worse things to follow! The next woe will be much more providential.

It will be directed to a generalized kingdom. The instruments are let loose upon the earth and mankind.

The fifth trumpet has sounded and judgment has begun. We saw this in Revelation 9:12. This one woe brought the demons out of the bottomless pit and for five months they tormented men. The final part of the title deed redemption of the world has begun.

We see in Revelation 9:13: "And the sixth angel sounded, and I heard a voice from the four horns of the golden altar which is before God." The sixth angel blows his trumpet, and a voice is heard from the horns of the altar. The golden altar is a figure of the intercession of Christ! It represents or speaks of prayer. In the tabernacle of Israel, it showed prayer.

Revelation 8:3 told us the angel offered prayer at the beginning of the trumpets blowing. With this voice, we will see what the results are when Satan worship becomes prevalent. Many believe the four horns represent four evangelists sent to the four corners of the earth. Many see this as the gospel sent to the four corners of the earth. The power of God's salvation offered to mankind! Christ interceding for them to be saved! God makes one of the enemies of the gospel the scourge of another, yet men do not turn to Christ.

Revelation 9:14: "Saying to the sixth angel which had the trumpet, Loose the four angels which are bound in the great river Euphrates." The sixth trumpet not only sounds but is given a command. Loose the four angels which are bound in the great Euphrates River. The orders from a voice which as we are told came from the four horns on the golden altar are given. It is the voice of Christ!

The seventh seal, now removed, led to the trumpet judgments beginning. This leads to seven personalities and the seven bowls of wrath. These angels are restraining the hordes from the east! These are not the same angels we saw in Revelation 7. Those were upon the four corners of the earth. They held back the four winds. They were restraining evil from occurring. These are bound, we are told, bound in the great river Euphrates. What their crime is we are not told, but they are bound here. Why this specific river?

Why the Euphrates, you might ask. We get our first glimpse of the Euphrates in Genesis 2. Look at verses 10 to 14 to see the river. It was part of the four coming out of Eden. The sin of man began here. The first murder occurred here in this region. The first war was fought here. It was here that Noah lived and the flood began in this region. Here is where the Tower of Babel was built. Here we see the Israelites and the southern kingdom of Judah brought into captivity under the Babylonians. Babylon is considered the center of idolatry. The river actually marks for man where east and west begin.

When man was evicted from Eden, we are told in Genesis 3:24: "So he drove out the man; and he placed at the east of the garden of Eden Cherubims, and a flaming sword which turned every way, to keep the way of the tree of life." God has kept angels there to protect the way of the tree of life, to keep man from reentering the Garden.

We see He has bound four angels in the great river. The Euphrates was the eastern boundary of the Roman Empire. There is great significance for this river. They have been bound for a purpose! Releasing them will release a flood of destruction. Again judgment is coming into that same region where the flood began!

Revelation 9:15–16: "And the four angels were loosed, which were prepared for an hour, and a day, and a month, and a year, for to slay the third part of men. And the number of the army of the horsemen were two hundred thousand thousand: and I heard the number of them." These four angels were specifically prepared for this time.

They were prepared for.

- An hour
- A day
- A month
- A year

There was a definite moment in the plan of God for these angels to be loosed. The very hour was marked for their release! Remember the locusts were loosed for a specific period of five months. We see here one month plus a year with a day and hour. This shows the specifics and gives us one year, six months, one day, and one hour of the Great Tribulation. The time of their release was planned out by God!

The time of this military operation and execution is limited to:

- An hour
- A day

- A month
- And a year

God fixed the time right down to the hour! When it shall all begin, God fixed the time right down to its end! When it shall begin and when it shall end! And how long it will last, how many it will affect how many would die! Just before the Lord's second coming to earth, the greatest concentration of military power will be assembled. They will be commanded by the leader of the Revived Roman Empire (the Beast) of Revelation 13. The religious leader of that time, the antichrist will sanction it. This army is being prepared here, in the middle of the Tribulation. Their number is seen here in verse 16. The number of horsemen, we are told, is two hundred thousand thousand, which equates to a staggering number!

Two hundred million! Here we have a full scale world war! With every nation in the world involved. Most commentaries believe this is an army of demon angels. A third of the remaining population will be killed. Remember back to Revelation 6, we said after the Rapture a third of mankind would be killed. That number seemed to be great. We saw in Revelation 6 death coming to the inhabitants left upon the earth. This death comes over a quarter of the earth. War, famine, and pestilence bring death to one-fourth of humanity. The beasts of the earth are ravenous searching for food, and they will attack even humans. The world's population today is thought to have reached seven billion. As we said earlier, if we allow for a third of that being Christians who were removed at the Rapture, then a quarter of those left would be 1,166,666,666 people who will die.

Now we see yet another one-third of mankind will be killed here. We now see another 1,244,444,444 people killed. That would be so far 2,411,111,110 total killed by wars and famine in the Tribulation period. Now remember, these are just estimates from what is believed today not dogmatic numbers.

We see God bring a literal judgment upon the world in verse 17 to 18 of Revelation 9: "And thus I saw the horses in the vision, and them that sat on them, having breastplates of fire, and of jacinth, and brimstone: and the heads of the horses were as the heads of lions; and out of their mouths issued fire and smoke and brimstone. By these three was the third part of men killed, by the fire, and by the smoke, and by the brimstone, which issued out of their mouths." The description of this army is hideous. Their arsenal is deadly! Breastplates are fire, judgment from God. Jacinth is a blue color, like the middle of a flame is sometimes blue. Brimstone is yellow, like the yellow tip of a flame. The horse was the war animal of John's time. The underworld is now making war on mankind!

These are unnatural creatures. We know that the nations of Asia could muster such an army.

We see these as something other than men; these riders of the horses have an unusual arsenal:

- Vicious
- Out of their mouths issued fire, smoke, and brimstone

The same thing occurred at the destruction of Sodom and Gomorrah. This time of the Great Tribulation will be worse than Sodom and Gomorrah! Homosexuality is an accepted alternate lifestyle in many nations today, especially ours. Even in the NFL now and NBA we have openly gay men playing with no repercussion. President Obama sent the Olympic delegation to Russia with many gay-lesbian people in the group. So this will be very prominent during the Tribulation. Now the recent Supreme Court ruling for same sex marriage has brought this blight upon our nation while taking another step toward fulfillment of God's prophecy.

We now come to verses 19 to 21 of Revelation 9: "For their power is in their mouth, and in their tails: for their tails were like unto serpents, and had heads, and with them they do hurt. And the rest of the men which were not killed by these plagues yet repented not of the works of their hands, that they should not worship devils, and idols of gold, and silver, and brass, and stone, and of wood: which neither can see, nor hear, nor walk: Neither repented they of their murders, nor of their sorceries, nor of their fornication, nor of their thefts."

Their power is in their mouth and tails, we are told, similar to the locust of the fifth seal. Here we see their description:

- Their tails were like serpents
- They had heads
- With their heads they hurt.

The two-thirds who are not killed repented not under this great judgment. Punishment or judgment doesn't in itself lead men to repentance.

The greatest judgment God brings on evil men doesn't soften their hard heart! Like Pharaoh of old, they harden it even more. More blasphemous, God-defiant, when judgment is being poured out upon them, they will not repent. We are told they repented not of their sinful ways. They didn't repent of the works of their hands. Works of any type will not save you! They would not stop worshiping devils. They have idols of gold, silver, brass, stone, and wood, dumb idols that don't see, hear, nor walk.

They are guilty of crimes to mankind Murders, sorceries, this from the Greek word *pharmakeion* where we get our word pharmacy. So the Tribulation will be a great time of drug abuse! Today we have states making marijuana legal and many pushing for it in many other states. Drug use will be a big part in the lives of these unsaved people. Drugs help them to bear the judgment. They will utilize drugs in worship, having a regular drug culture. Aren't we seeing a whole lot of this today?

They are guilty of fornication, illicit sexual behavior, men with men and women with women. We see this in 2 Timothy 3:1–7. The Tribulation is the last days for earth as we know it! Notice it says "without natural affection." Romans 1:25–28 makes it clear how they are in the Great Tribulation just as today. The Tribulation will have these characteristics. It will be a time of great sinfulness and God's judgment! It is not a laughing matter to reject Jesus Christ. People say there are more important things in this life. Accepting Him as savior is the most important.

6
A Second Pause in Judgment

The sixth trumpet has sounded and a great war is begun. We see that two hundred million-strong army is coming once the four angels who were bound in the Euphrates River are released. One-third of the remainder of the inhabitants of the world will be killed by these warriors. The final part of the title deed redemption of the earth has begun!

We now come to Chapter 10 with a description of even more to occur. Another angel comes to our attention as the chapter opens! We see in Revelation 10:1: "And I saw another mighty angel come down from heaven, clothed with a cloud: and a rainbow was upon his head, and his face was as it were the sun, and his feet as pillars of fire." Yet another part of the vision is seen here by John. This angel comes down from heaven, clothed with a cloud, a rainbow upon his head, his face like the sun, his feet like pillars of fire.

An interlude is what we have here! The interlude between the sixth and seventh trumpet sounding comes. Like the break we had between the sixth and seventh chapters, a break in the judgment and the pause to seal the 144,000. Here we will have an interlude with three personalities introduced. God is showing John a new prophecy. Many a debate has come about who this angel is, seven men including DeHaan and Ironside say this is Christ. Christ was my first thought too! Newell and others consider it an angel of great power and authority, but not Christ.

We can go with either crowd, but I also thought of Michael the Great Archangel or Gabriel the proclaiming Archangel. We see first and foremost he is identified as a mighty angel. The original Greek text says this for Revelation 10:1 "mighty ischyrós, (is-khoo-ros)'of living beings, strong either in body or in mind, of one who has strength of soul to sustain the attacks of satan, strong and therefore exhibiting many excellences, on inanimate things, strong, violent, forcibly uttered, firm, sure."

Called *ángelos*, a messenger, envoy, one who is sent, an angel, a messenger from God the same word is used in Luke 1:26 ("The angel Gabriel was sent.") about the annunciation. Another strong messenger is sent, we see here. He is described as clothed with a cloud. This is his uniform as the mighty envoy of God. The clouds of glory are associated with Christ's second coming at the end of the Tribulation.

This angel is clothed with a single cloud and is not coming in clouds of glory! Christ is not coming at this time for there is still more judgment to come! This angel announces Christ is coming soon. Gabriel announced to Mary and Joseph that Christ was the baby Mary would have and that the Messiah was being born through her. Angels announced to the shepherds in the fields the birth of Christ. They will announce His second coming too.

There was a rainbow upon his head. This is the cap of his uniform. It brings to mind God's covenant with man not to bring judgment by flood again and given as a sign to Noah. The judgments here have come thick and fast, weird and wild. It lets us know God will not send a flood as He did in Noah's time. He will not send a flood to destroy men again.

His face like the sun this is his identification badge the signature of the Glorified Christ. From that can we conclude that this mighty angel is just that, an angel, not the Son of God! Moses's face, we are told, shone after he had been in presence of God (Exodus 34:29). This angel's face is shining because he has just come out of the presence of Christ. Look too at Luke 24:4. The angels at the annunciation of Christ resurrection also shone brightly.

This Angel's feet are as pillars of fire. Still part of the angel's uniform. He has come to make a special and solemn announcement. One of coming judgment, these are the identification of his credentials. They connect him to the person of Jesus Christ as His special envoy. Christ is in charge of everything right now, He is the Judge of all the earth.

Revelation 10:2: "And he had in his hand a little book open: and he set his right foot upon the sea, and his left foot on the earth." He has a little book opened. This is the book we have seen before, the book of the title deed redemption. With all the seals broken, it is now opened. The seventh seal now removed had led to the trumpet judgments beginning. This leads to seven personalities and the seven bowls of wrath!

The seventh trumpet is yet to blow! The angel standing with one foot in the sea and one on the earth ready to carry out God's will. The angel has the title deed to the earth now in hand. It contains all the judgments that will befall the earth and mankind during the Tribulation. By these judgments, Christ is coming with power. With this book, the angel shows the whole earth will be redeemed. All the oceans and seas and rivers, every part of the dry land, will be redeemed.

We see in Leviticus 25:23: "The land shall not be sold for ever: for the land is mine, for ye are strangers and sojourners with me." The Lord gave instruction to Israel concerning the land here. This lets us know that even the real estate we own is not our own, we have a title deed to it. But that title deed has been passed down through generations. Remember at some point back about 1492 someone came upon this land and claimed it for a European nation. They took it away from the American Indians. The American Indians walked over and took possession of it. But to whom does it really belong? It belongs to God, and always has.

We haven't paid Him for it. Psalms 24:1: "The earth is the Lord's, and the fulness thereof; the world, and they that dwell therein!" Yes, the Bible says it all belongs to Him! We see here in Revelation He is reclaiming it for Himself. God is reclaiming the land, He is reclaiming the sea.

Look at Psalms 8:6–8 and we see God says He owns everything. He only gave us dominion over it. We are the tenants here on earth for just a short time. Most of us haven't paid our rent lately. We are in this little world God created. God owns it and we haven't paid for it yet!

Revelation 10:3: "And cried with a loud voice, as when a lion roareth: and when he had cried, seven thunders uttered their voices." The angel now speaks. He claims the earth and sea for the Lord, with title deed of the earth in hand. As a lion roars, so did his voice. He places his right foot in the sea and his left upon the earth. With a great voice, he claims it all for Christ! The kingdoms of the earth will become kingdoms for the Lord!

It will happen through His judgment upon the nations of the world. As creator and redeemer, the world belongs to Him! The little book as it is described shows that the length of the Tribulation is short. The halfway point has been reached. We will hear there is not much time left till it has been accomplished. Not much more to be written.

Look at Romans 9:28 to see what the Lord promised. The Great Tribulation is really a short time! For those who will go through it, though, I believe it will feel like an eternity! Daniel labeled it with the length we see in Daniel 9:24. We see there seventy weeks of seven years. Verse 27 tell us: "And he shall confirm the covenant with many for one week: and in the midst of the week he shall cause the sacrifice and the oblation to cease, and for the overspreading of abominations he shall make it desolate, even until the consummation, and that determined shall be poured upon the desolate."

Seven years is not a long period of time. Not a long period in comparison with man's time on earth. The seven thunders are God saying amen to the angel's reclaiming the earth. We see now Psalms 29:3. God's voice is seen as His glory that thunders. Then Job 37:5 gives us yet more on the thunder. The thunderings are such that we can't comprehend them. These seven thunders are the voice of God. Christ is coming shortly and He is confirming what the angel has claimed because He is coming in power upon the earth. We see God as the voices have sounded and John is preparing to write.

Look what happens in Revelation 10:4: "And when the seven thunders had uttered their voices, I was about to write: and I heard a voice from heaven saying unto me, Seal up those things which the seven thunders uttered, and write them not." He is told he can't write what was uttered! God doesn't want us to know. Even though the thunders were intelligible, God says to seal it up and not to reveal it to us!

John the scribe was doing what scribes do, taking notes and preparing to write down what was said. He had heard it and heard it clearly! The words were audible! But God says he was not to write that part down! This book's name is the Revelation of Jesus. So why is this specific Revelation sealed up? This is the only place in Revelation where anything said is sealed. Nothing else is. God makes it very clear at the end of Revelation; He has revealed and told us everything.

We see this in Revelation 22:10. "And he saith unto me, Seal not the sayings of the prophecy of this book: for the time is at hand." Yet right here we see seven thunderings John is not permitted to write down. Seems quite interesting, doesn't it? If this angel was Christ, then John would very well have probably fallen down and worshipped him. He did just that when he saw Him in Chapter 1.

Evidently John did not fall down and worship him because this is only an angel. Revelation 10:5: "And the angel which I saw stand upon the sea and upon the earth lifted up his hand to heaven." The angel lifts up his right hand to take an oath, still standing one foot on earth, the other in the sea. We then hear the oath in Revelation 10:6: "And sware by him that liveth for ever and ever, who created heaven, and the things that therein are, and the earth, and the things that therein are, and the sea, and the things which are therein, that there should be time no longer:" If there was any question as to this being an angel or the Lord Himself, this answers that question!

With the little book open in one hand, he lifts up his right hand to heaven, and announces a solemn oath by Jehovah the Creator. It is plain here again that this angel is not the Lord Himself, for when God took an oath, "since he could swear by none greater, he sware by himself" Hebrews 6:13). For when God made a promise to Abraham, because he could swear by no greater, he swore by himself, the Lord Jesus is the creator of all things. That we must understand!

John 1:3 as well as Colossians 1:16. This angel takes the oath by other than himself. There will be no more delay of the time of judgment. The Greek word translated here is *chromos*, which means "time either long or short." This is not saying the end of time for man but the end of the delay in judgment coming. The angel is letting those who are believes in the Tribulation and are being persecuted and troubled know that Christ is soon to come. That it is but a short time and Jesus will be coming back to the earth to rule and reign.

The fulfillment of Matthew 24:22: "And except those days should be shortened, there should no flesh be saved: but for the elect's sake those days shall be shortened." The angel is virtually saying, "Don't worry. He that endures to the end, the same shall be saved." Why is that? Because they are sealed! They are going to make it through the Tribulation period. The hour of accomplishment has almost arrived. God will no longer delay the completion of His plan. The fulfillment of His promise is near.

We see this in Romans 9:28. This is also the answer to prayers of the martyred saints! As seen in Revelation 6:10: "And they cried with a loud voice, saying, How long, O Lord, holy and true, dost thou not judge and avenge our blood on them that dwell on the earth?" In this we also see the fulfillment of what the world calls the Lord's Prayer in Matthew 6:10, "Thy Kingdom Come." Revelation 10:7: "But in the days of the voice of the seventh angel, when he shall begin to sound, the mystery of God should be finished, as he hath declared to his servants the prophets." There is only one more trumpet judgment.

The seventh trumpet will bring the end of the Tribulation period. At this time the mystery of God is made clear. Many parts of the mystery of God have already occurred. This will be the greatest of the others the total sum of all together. The seventh trumpet is ready to be blown. The seventh covers the last phase of judgment. During this final stage, God will accomplish His plan.

The millennial kingdom will be set up when the final judgment is completed. By these judgments Christ is coming with power.

Note what is said to start verse 7: "In the days of the voice of the seventh angel." As he begins to sound the trumpet, there will be no more delay. God's plan will gain momentum and intensity finally reaching fulfillment without delay. We are in Chapter 10; there are still a lot of things to cover. The last part of the Tribulation is seen in Chapters 15 to 19. The next four chapters after this one will introduce to us the six principle characters of the Tribulation and the Great Tribulation.

We will see in Chapter 11 the two witnesses. In Chapter 13, we will see the woman clothed with the sun and her man-child. In Chapter 13 we also see the dragon, as well as his two beasts. In Chapter 14 we see the 144,000 again along with prophecy against Babylon. We see in verse 7: "The mystery of God should be finished, as he hath declared to his servants the prophets." This connection seems to indicate all those counsels and dealings of God made known by Him to and through the Old Testament prophets. They are concerning His governmental proceedings with men on earth.

We are to be looking always toward the establishment of the kingdom in the hands of Christ. When Christ comes to take the kingdom, there will be no mystery all will have been made known to mankind. Isaiah 11: 9 shows that it is important for us to remember that we ourselves are still in the days of "mystery."

If a man would walk godly, there is "the mystery of Godliness" by which he walks unknown to the world. 1 Timothy 3:16: "And without controversy great is the mystery of godliness: God was manifest in the flesh, justified in the Spirit, seen of angels, preached unto the Gentiles, believed on in the world, received up into glory." Those who would walk "lawless," must at present walk in "the mystery of lawlessness," for God is not yet allowing "the lawless one" to be revealed, but restrains him, as we see in 1 Thessalonians 2:1–17.

When the seventh angel sounds, all this will be finished, and there will it be made known to all. We shall expect the antichrist to be brought forth, Israel to be hated and persecuted by all nations, Satan universally worshipped as he is the god of the Tribulation age. We shall expect God to manifest His anger. He will do so, and fully: "In the days of the voice of the seventh angel." Not much more to be written. "Delay no longer." Then the word that governs things let us hold this fact in mind, from this seventh angel onward.

We see a strange thing occur in Revelation 10:8: "And I took the little book out of the angel's hand, and ate it up; and it was in my mouth sweet as honey: and as soon as I had eaten it, my belly was bitter." It is appropriate that the servants of God digest in their own souls the messages they bring to others in his name. To be suitably affected by it themselves! It implores them to deliver every message with which they are charged whether pleasing or unpleasing to men. That which is least pleasing may be most profitable.

However, God's messengers must not keep back any part of the counsel of God. The apostle is made to know that this book of prophecy, which he had now taken in, was not given him merely to gratify his own curiosity. Neither was it to affect him with pleasure or pain. It was to be communicated by him to the world. Here his prophetical commission seems to be renewed. Thus he took the book and ate it.

We see a similar thing in Ezekiel 3:1–3. This is not a bread roll it was the scroll of that time. Ezekiel said he ate it and it was like cake. That is what the word of God is to be to us. The word of God is to be sweet to us. We see in Proverbs 16:24: "Pleasant words are as an honeycomb, sweet to the soul, and health to the bones." Psalms 119:103: "How sweet are thy words unto my taste! yea, sweeter than honey to my mouth!" John eating the book was eating God's judgment.

It was sweet to John because the future is sweet. "It is sweet to know as I onward the way of the cross leads home," but judgment brings bitterness. We see in Genesis 18:17 the judgment that came upon Sodom and Gomorrah was bitter! John eagerly received God's word. When he saw that more judgment followed, it became bitter to his soul! It caused him to become nauseated.

For us, if we can delight in reading and studying this portion of God's word, with the judgments that are to fall upon the earth, then we need a great deal of prayer in order to get the mind of God! It is sweet to know the book of Revelation, seeing what God intends to do, but when we see the judgment is coming to those who reject Christ, we cannot rejoice in that. The prophecy is bitter!

We conclude Chapter 10 with verse 11: "And he said unto me, Thou must prophesy again before many peoples, and nations, and tongues, and kings." Now this is exactly what John goes on to do, ending up with the ten kings allied with the beast, their career and doom, in Chapters 13, 17, and 19. "They," who told John he must thus prophesy, we may surmise were heavenly "watchers." Look at Daniel 4:13 and 17: "I saw in the visions of my head upon my bed, and, behold, a watcher and a holy one came down from heaven. This matter is by the decree of the watchers, and the demand by the word of the holy ones: to the intent that the living may know that the most High ruleth in the kingdom of men, and giveth it to whomsoever he will, and setteth up over it the basest of men. The mind of God as to earthly judgments, prophetic programs are well known by those dwelling in the light of heaven."

John's mission is to prophesy in regard to the nations of the world to the same servants of God to whom he is already writing. The point is that, when the seventh trumpet sounds, which we will see in Chapter 11, the current account of prophecy closes. The seventh trumpet takes us right to the great "Day of Judgment" at the end of the Tribulation period. The last verse of Chapter 11 John will begin prophecy yet again.

He prophesies concerning nations, tongues, people! This prophecy will culminate in the new heaven and new earth. The roll or book was seen in the hand of Him that sat upon the throne. The seals had to be broken by the Lamb of God, Jesus. The scroll had writing on both sides of it. The inside is what we have seen so far. Beginning in Chapter 12, the scroll is reversed. We begin to see what was written on the other side. The rest of the story, as Paul Harvey would say.

God confirms the prophecy we have seen, He fills in the details that are omitted in the first eleven. We will have a clearer view, a fuller understanding of the great events that are to take place in this old sinful world where Christ was crucified. This makes the book clearer as we see it more plainly. Let me say again, it is not a laughing matter to reject Jesus Christ! People say there are more important things in this life. Accepting Him as savior is the most important! It is important for us to see what is going to happen when we have left this earth because it should make us to be a better witness to others here on earth after all it is for eternity.

CONCLUSION

While my previous section the *Snatching Away of the Bride* showed the church being taken to heaven, this book began to show the judgment that is coming upon mankind. To avoid going through these judgments, one must only receive Christ as their personal savior, which I covered the way in the introduction and in the following portion of this conclusion. It is that important that you know how you stand and how to receive so great a salvation! How do you stand today? Have you believed on Jesus as your Lord and Savior? If not you need to do so right now don't miss being snatched away in the rapture. Don't be one of those who will end up in the Tribulation facing the judgment of God! "For God So Loved the Word that He gave His only begotten son, that whosoever believeth on Him will not perish but have eternal life" (John 3:16). Do you see God by grace gave His Son, Jesus Christ, and you must believe on Him? "For whosoever shall call upon the name of the Lord shall be saved" (Romans 10:13). Believe then call, is God's order. Look at what Jesus said in John 3:17–21: "For God sent not his Son into the world to condemn the world; but that the world through him might be saved. He that believeth on him is not condemned: but he that believeth not is condemned already, because he hath not believed in the name of the only begotten Son of God. And this is the condemnation, that light is come into the world, and men loved darkness rather than light, because their deeds were evil. For every one that doeth evil hateth the light, neither cometh to the light, lest his deeds should be reproved. But he that doeth truth cometh to the light, that his deeds may be made manifest, that they are wrought in God.

Do you see, believe, and call upon Him? Believe you are condemned already because you haven't believed on Jesus Christ. Believe you are sinner in need of salvation and believe that Jesus died for your sins. Call on the

Lord and admit all to Him, even that you believe Jesus died for your sins. You see, it isn't a matter of your sin that you are condemned, but rather it is a matter of your unbelief. Believe and call upon Christ for salvation and you too can be snatched away at the Rapture and you won't go through these judgments!

SECTION 3

Tribulations Final Judgment

CONTENTS

INTRODUCTION

John was in the isle called Patmos, exiled there by the Roman emperor. The Lord was in control as always having sent him there for a purpose. God always has a purpose, which is revealed to us, just as it was revealed to John. It came to John by messengers who showed him visions, which ultimately are seen in the book of the Revelation of Jesus that came to him. God's purpose is shown to us by Scripture and the divine leadership of the Holy Spirit.

John had been instructed by Christ to write. The scene has now changed in chapter 11. The change of scene is for a brief period just prior to the unholy trinity being revealed and greater judgment that is to come. It starts with the measuring of the temple and moves forward from that point. We now begin to see what is occurring as Tribulation's Final Judgment is starting here in chapters 11–18.

Let's cover a few things that must happen before you can receive the message, which the Holy Spirit's purpose is in you reading this book. Before you can receive the message and serve God as He commands, before you can walk for Him, you must have a personal, intimate relationship with Him. Romans 10:13 states, "Whosoever shall call upon the name of the Lord shall be saved." Acts 16:31 says, "And they said, Believe on the Lord Jesus Christ, and thou shalt be saved, and thy house." Of course, John 3:16 is known by almost everyone, but verse 17 and 18 states, "For God sent not his Son into the world to condemn the world; but that the world through him might be saved. He that believeth on him is not condemned: but he that believeth not is condemned already, because he hath not believed in the name of the only begotten Son of God."

You must admit you are a condemned sinner because of not having believed; you also must believe and then call upon Christ for salvation.

Next if you are a believer, you must practice 1 John 1:9, which states, “If we confess our sins, he is faithful and just to forgive us our sins, and to cleanse us from all unrighteousness.” Before you can receive God’s message, you need to confess all known sin, and God will forgive that sin and all the things that you don’t realize are sins, as I like to say unknown sins.

1

Center of Prophecy

The scene is in heaven as we see the book of Revelation chapter 11 opening. Another angel comes to John. John again wonders about all the things happening. Yet he is following the messenger's instruction as we now see verse 1 of Revelation chapter 11. Revelation 11:1 says, "And there was given me a reed like unto a rod: and the angel stood, saying, Rise, and measure the temple of God, and the altar, and them that worship therein." We are at the center of prophetic subjects here in verse 1.

Those subjects include prophecy for Jerusalem, the temple, the altar, and those who worship. The worshippers and the altar are recognized and accepted by God; John says he is given a reed like a rod. One very important key to a sign, which we must understand in studying prophecy, is that there is a key portion. This lets us know the time is very close.

The key here is the fact that John is told to take the reed and measure the temple of God. Where is this temple of God? We must turn to the Old Testament in order to answer this question. Zechariah 2:1–2 states, "I lifted up mine eyes again, and looked, and behold a man with a measuring line in his hand. Then said I, Whither goest thou? And he said unto me, To measure Jerusalem, to see what is the breadth thereof, and what is the length thereof." When we go to verses 3–5 of Zechariah 2, it says, "And, behold, the angel that talked with me went forth, and another angel went out to meet him, And said unto him, Run, speak to this young man, saying, Jerusalem shall be inhabited as towns without walls for the multitude of men and cattle therein: For I, saith the Lord, will be unto her a wall of fire round about, and will be the glory in the midst of her." Zechariah then goes on, and we see a very distinct prophecy of the future deliverance of Israel. God's earthly people delivered from all their enemies.

They will be brought from the lands of the North and from all parts of the world where they had been carried into captivity in the dispersion of ad 70. The regathering or the ingathering, we might say, is not fulfilled in its entirety until Christ returns to set up His millennial kingdom. We see in Zechariah 2:8–9 that, "For thus saith the Lord of hosts; After the glory hath he sent me unto the nations which spoiled you: for he that toucheth you toucheth the apple of his eye. For, behold, I will shake mine hand upon them, and they shall be a spoil to their servants: and ye shall know that the Lord of hosts hath sent me." The daughter of Zion is called upon to rejoice because Jehovah Himself will dwell with them.

Then we go to Zechariah 2:10–11 where we see that, "Sing and rejoice, O daughter of Zion: for, lo, I come, and I will dwell in the midst of thee, saith the Lord. And many nations shall be joined to the Lord in that day, and shall be my people: and I will dwell in the midst of thee, and thou shalt know that the Lord of hosts hath sent me unto thee." This is followed by verse 12 that says, "And the Lord shall inherit Judah his portion in the holy land, and shall choose Jerusalem again."

We see a similar measuring in the prophecy of Ezekiel chapter 40. This is seen first in Ezekiel 40:1–2 that says, "In the five and twentieth year of our captivity, in the beginning of the year, in the tenth day of the month, in the fourteenth year after that the city was smitten, in the selfsame day the hand of the Lord was upon me, and brought me thither. In the visions of God brought he me into the land of Israel, and set me upon a very high mountain, by which was as the frame of a city on the south. The city and temple to be measured is in Jerusalem." We see Ezekiel 40:3–5 that states, "And he brought me thither, and, behold, there was a man, whose appearance was like the appearance of brass, with a line of flax in his hand, and a measuring reed; and he stood in the gate. And the man said unto me, Son of man, behold with thine eyes, and hear with thine ears, and set thine heart upon all that I shall shew thee; for to the intent that I might shew them unto thee art thou brought hither: declare all that thou seest to the house of Israel. And behold a wall on the outside of the house round about, and in the man's hand a measuring reed of six cubits long by the cubit and an hand breadth: so he measured the breadth of the building, one reed; and the height, one reed." Here in Ezekiel 40, we see the measuring with a reed. So where is the temple that John is to measure? It will be in Israel or Jerusalem on the Temple Mount.

The Prophecy is that we should see the beginnings of before the snatching away of the bride, which as it appears, the temple will be rebuilt and exists in the tribulation. I believe that we, as believers, will see the beginning of it before we are snatched out and taken home in the rapture. In fact, Israel—from all indication—has control of that Temple Mount but hasn't made any attempts to begin rebuilding the temple.

The angel calls upon John to rise and measure. The Jews will be worshipping in a temple in Jerusalem. God will have witnesses there! God will have worshippers there! The great tribulation will occur before all Zechariah's prophecy is fulfilled completely. That is why we see John's instruction in verse 2 to "leave out the outer court." Thus Israel hasn't been fully restored by God's hand at this time. We see today that some of the Jews have returned and Israel is a recognized nation in the world we live in. During the tribulation, the Jews will have a temple! I believe it will stand right where the original temple, built by Solomon, stood!

The altar of sacrifice is in place. I believe we need to be watching for the temple rebuilding to start! The mount has come under the control of the Jews! Thus God will begin fulfillment of prophecy by Ezekiel and Zechariah! As well as Daniel, for the things we see in chapter 11 of Revelation are occurring during the seventieth week of Daniel's prophecy.

Verse 2 of Revelation 11 says, "But the court which is without the temple leave out, and measure it not; for it is given unto the Gentiles: and the holy city shall they tread under foot forty and two months." We see yet more prophecy fulfilled, look at Luke 21:24. "And they shall fall by the edge of the sword, and shall be led away captive into all nations: and Jerusalem shall be trodden down of the Gentiles, until the times of the Gentiles be fulfilled." Jerusalem is still being trodden down by the Gentiles.

Remember the age we live in is a Gentile age with Gentile powers in charge. The tribulation is that last seven years of Daniel's seventy weeks of years and is a Jewish time. Yet it is still dominated by the Gentiles, as all seventy weeks were to be. The church has been removed as we saw in a previous section, The Snatching Away of the Bride. Gentile nations are still the dominant force!

Notice too that the court is left out because it currently belongs to the Gentiles.

From this point in the prophecy of Revelation, we are told the Gentiles have a short time to be in power. They have forty-two months left to trod over the court! That is three and one half years. The Lord is setting the stage for the end! We see that as the next four chapters are dealing with the great tribulation, for we see the forty two months spoken of in Revelation 13:5. "And there was given unto him a mouth speaking great things and blasphemies; and power was given unto him to continue forty and two months." The beast who will be the dictator over ten countries most often referred to as the revived Roman Empire is given forty-two months to speak over most of the known world. He will speak great things.

Great blasphemies will come out of his mouth! In chapter 13, we also see the dragon gives him his power. Eventually, we are introduced to a second beast. We see from the book of Daniel 7:25 this same beast and the forty-two months of his reign. "And he shall speak great words against the most High, and shall wear out the saints of the most High, and think to change times and laws: and they shall be given into his hand until a time and times and the dividing of time." In other words, that is three and one half years. We see also in Daniel 12:11 the time given again, which says, "And from the time that the daily sacrifice shall be taken away, and the abomination that maketh desolate set up, there shall be a thousand two hundred and ninety days." Three and one half years is equal to 1,290 days.

One last comparison from Daniel in chapter 9 verse 27 states, "And he shall confirm the covenant with many for one week: and in the midst of the week he shall cause the sacrifice and the oblation to cease, and for the overspreading of abominations he shall make it desolate, even until the consummation, and that determined shall be poured upon the desolate." Daniel's week equals seven years, which is the complete period of the tribulation.

Verse 27 states clearly that in the middle of the week, at the three-and-one-half year point, the beast will cause the oblation or offering to cease and set up an abomination, which causes desolation. That would mean there must be a temple in Jerusalem the first three and one half years of the tribulation.

Here in chapter 11, we see the beginning point. When we get to chapter 13, we will see the beast in all his evil. We see even more at what point in the tribulation we have reached as Revelation 11:3 begins. "And I will give power unto my two witnesses, and they shall prophesy a thousand two hundred and threescore days, clothed in sackcloth." The witnesses will testify for 1,260 days. These two witnesses are introduced to us here, at this point.

Who they are has been debated by many for centuries! Some say Enoch and Elijah, others say Moses and Elijah. While some believe they are unknown witnesses, who have no previous existence! I was taught growing up that these were Moses and Elijah. Dr. M.R. DeHaan believed it to be them also. Can we prove it and be dogmatic? I don't think so, but I think we can find scripture that would help us to believe it to be Moses and Elijah and not Enoch and Elijah or two unknowns!

First, look to Malachi 4:1–6, centering on verses 5 and 6. It states, "Behold, I will send you Elijah the prophet before the coming of the great and dreadful day of the Lord: And he shall turn the heart of the fathers to the children, and the heart of the children to their fathers, lest I come and smite the earth with a curse." This says Elijah is coming and he will turn hearts that is witnessing! He hasn't come yet, but prophecy says he will!

We see an occurrence in the New Testament that leads people to speculate and conclude that the two witnesses are Moses and Elijah or Elias, as the New Testament calls him. We see Matthew 17:1–6 but center in on verse 3. "And, behold, there appeared unto them Moses and Elias talking with him." We see next Mark 9:1–8 centering in on verse 4. "And there appeared unto them Elias with Moses: and they were talking with Jesus." We see the same story in Luke 9:28–36. Here we center in on verse 30. "And, behold, there talked with him two men, which were Moses and Elias."

From these passages, many believe these two witnesses are in fact Moses and Elijah. Something that helps in believing these to be Moses and Elijah, we can see in the miracles they will perform later in the book of Revelation. They have similarities to Moses and Elijah! Elijah called fire down from heaven. Moses too can be seen in the miracles! The signs and miracles mirror the ones that Moses performed in Egypt when he delivered the children of Israel from bondage. Turning water to blood brought all types of plagues to the earth.

Not to beleaguer the subject, but let's look too at what Israel believed at the time of Christ coming. The Jews were looking for three men to come. They were looking for the Messiah first and foremost. They also believed that Elijah would return. They were looking for that prophet. Moses and Elijah stand out as the two greatest men in Israel's history! Moses came and delivered the people out of bondage from pharaoh. He did it with many plagues, plagues he called down from heaven. Moses, the deliverer of Israel from material and physical bondage, led them out of Egypt. Lead them toward victory in Canaan. He appeared in one of the darkest moments in Israel's history and performed many signs and wonders.

Elijah, the great prophet, came to Israel. When they were under spiritual bondage, the evil queen Jezebel and her husband King Ahab had led the people away from God to Baal. God sent Elijah, the prophet of fire! Through Elijah, Israel was delivered from spiritual bondage. We see these two deliverers of Israel spoken in the Old Testament scripture and New Testament.

These two men represent the salvation of the Lord! They brought deliverance to Israel from bondage—physical bondage as well as spiritual bondage. So with all these things seen in scripture, why would the two witnesses not be Moses and Elijah?

Revelation 11:4 says, "These are the two olive trees, and the two candlesticks standing before the God of the earth." These two witnesses are referred to as two olive trees and two candlesticks. Again, we must track back to the Old Testament prophecy coming in the vision we have here.

Zechariah 4:2 states, "And said unto me, What seest thou? And I said, I have looked, and behold a candlestick all of gold, with a bowl upon the top of it, and his seven lamps thereon, and seven pipes to the seven lamps, which are upon the top thereof." God has given them the power to witness in Jerusalem! These witnesses were under God's protection.

These two olives trees are two anointed ones. They stand by the Lord upon the whole earth. They stand together as God's witnesses. As the light shines in the world, God's light shines through them. Revelation 11:5 says, "And if any man will hurt them, fire proceedeth out of their mouth, and devoureth their enemies: and if any man will hurt them, he must in this manner be killed." Their enemies are killed by the manifestation of God's judgment! Even though God is righteous in judgment, the fire came out of the mouths of these two prophets.

We see fire in the Old Testament: first, the fire of Elijah; second, Daniel's three companions not being consumed by fire. These two prophets have protection, which is fire. Their prayer and preaching, their courage in suffering, and they can consume all who oppose them! They have free access to God. At their prayers, God will inflict plagues and judgments upon their enemies.

Just as He did at the pharaoh of old with Moses, just as He did at the prayers of Elijah in 1 Kings 17:1. Notice here, these witnesses will finish their testimony! From this, we can take courage because every one of God's witnesses, everyone who has received Christ as their Savior "is immortal until his work is done." No servant of God ever encountered such fear and opposition! Such odds as these two witnesses face. Yet they finish their testimony.

Satan can do nothing without God's permission. He can't take your life or mine without God's permission, and God knows when our course is complete. Verse 6 of Revelation 11 shows even greater power by these two witnesses. "These have power to shut heaven that it rain not in the days of their prophecy: and have power over waters to turn them to blood, and to smite the earth with all plagues, as often as they will."

They can control the weather! They have power to turn water into blood! They have power to bring plagues! Just as Elijah had that power, he kept it from raining on Israel for three and one half years according to scripture. If anyone wants to hurt them, God has them under His protection.

Their time is limited, and we see in Revelation 11:7, "And when they shall have finished their testimony, the beast that ascendeth out of the bottomless pit shall make war against them, and shall overcome them, and kill them." When their time is complete, the beast becomes the leader of the locust—the beast that came out of the bottomless pit—and comes to make war with these witnesses.

These two men stand before God as His witnesses, not as preachers of the gospel. But as witnesses of God's title deed to the earth, witnesses of His love to His people in connection with His return, the beast hour comes when God allows them to come upon the witnesses. He slays these two men of God! Witnesses of God killed for the sake of Christ! Would you stand fast as they will for Christ?

Would you remain faithful to the cause of Christ as these two witnesses will? We see even more in verse 8 of Revelation 11 that states, "And their dead bodies shall lie in the street of the great city, which spiritually is called Sodom and Egypt, where also our Lord was crucified."

Their bodies are treated with the utmost contempt. These two Witnesses bodies lie in the street, the broad open street of the great city. We see degenerate Jerusalem, as it becomes like Sodom in wickedness. We see it as Egypt for its oppression of the Israel of God. It is a wicked and oppressed city. These evil people of this time are so wicked they don't allow a grave for their bodies! They were left in the streets to rot, as the morals of that day have rotted into nothing.

We see the beginnings today of this type of attitude. The city of Jerusalem in the time of the tribulation is called Sodom. This is because of their spiritual wickedness. It is called Egypt because of its idolatry. In its tyranny, here Christ, in His earthly body, suffered greatly. We then see verse 9 of Revelation 11 that says, "And they of the people and kindreds and tongues and nations shall see their dead bodies three days and an half, and shall not suffer their dead bodies to be put in graves."

Their bodies lie in the street for three and one half days. There is no quiet grave for these two prophets of God. In verse 10 of chapter 11, we see, "And they that dwell upon the earth shall rejoice over them, and make merry, and shall send gifts one to another; because these two prophets tormented them that dwelt on the earth." Those of the nation rejoice over their dead bodies, the dwellers upon the earth who want the earth as theirs.

Who want not to hear of God, they are delighted by their death! These two prophets had tormented them! So they made merry over their bodies. They send gifts to one another to celebrate the death of these two witnesses. How did these witnesses torment them? By preaching the Gospel of Christ to them, that's how! Even in judgment, God still performs miracles.

We see in verse 11 of Revelation 11 this very thing. "And after three days and an half the spirit of life from God entered into them, and they stood upon their feet; and great fear fell upon them which saw them." If God can make dry bones come to life and if He could raise Jesus from the dead, He can perform the same even in a time of great trouble!

God breathes the Spirit of life back into them, just as He does for us at the rapture. The Spirit of God makes souls alive. He made their bodies alive! God's work and witness cannot be stopped! These two witnesses rose to their feet, great fear came to the people! Keep in mind, the whole world has seen them laying in the streets three and one half days. News reports on television networks show their dead bodies. It shows the people celebrating. These people who were rejoicing now see a great miracle, which they cannot deny! God revived His work and His witnesses! When believers truly get on fire for God, the souls of God's enemies will melt. Those enemies of God had great fear come upon them. Where there is guilt, there is fear! A persecuting spirit, though cruel, is not courageous. They are cowards! Remember how King Herod feared

John the Baptist even after he had him beheaded? God brings conviction through miracles as well as joy. They feared because they were convinced of their sin. They were convinced of their superstitions and convinced of their idolatry, as well as spiritual bondage. The Holy Spirit brought conviction to them. They were afraid, but more was to come! Revelation 11:12 says, "And they heard a great voice from heaven saying unto them, Come up hither. And they ascended up to heaven in a cloud; and their enemies beheld them." These two witnesses, after coming to life, are now summoned to heaven.

We see yet another snatching away. God, knowing they now have completed their task, calls them home. We have here a picture of the resurrection of saints seen in three forms. If we look at verse 23 of 1 Corinthians 15, it says, "But every man in his own order: Christ the first fruits; afterward they that are Christ's at his coming." If we look to the Feast of Harvest, we see it consisted of three distinct phases.

Three Distinct Phases of the Harvest

1. The first fruits.
2. This was when the first fruits of the harvest, which was just a handful, was gathered and brought to the priest.
3. The harvest itself followed the limitlessness of the harvest.

4. The gleanings the ears, which had been crushed underfoot and left after the great harvest, were gathered and added to the others.
5. This constituted the completed harvest
6. So that is what we see here in Revelation 11:12.

In the first resurrection, we see similarities to the Feast of Harvest. In verses 52 and 53 of Matthew 27, we read, "And the graves were opened; and many bodies of the saints which slept rose, And came out of the graves after his resurrection, and went into the holy city, and appeared unto many." We see a company of Old Testament saints raised from the grave on the day Christ arose. These were the first fruits. When Christ comes for the church and snatches her out, the believing dead will be raised first—this is the harvest.

The remainder of the believing dead will be raised at His second coming, after the tribulation has ended. These will be the gleanings of the harvest, those martyred for the sake of Christ in the tribulation. Do you see the Feast of First Fruits in this? The Lord brings validity to these two faithful witnesses!

Because He is the same today as He was in the past. Since God has not changed, we should not change the message. God still brings judgment to the sinner. The gospel is about Christ's bloodshed for those who are sinners. The church today is in apostasy—gross apostasy. Many people don't want to hear about a God of justice who will bring judgment, they don't want to hear of God who required a bloody sacrifice, or do they want to hear of their immorality and worldliness that will bring judgment.

When we preach that in many churches, we will be hated and persecuted. Many today don't want to hear of judgment, hell, and eternal punishment! Those of us who preach that are condemned by the world. They say we are old-fashioned, not in touch with the times. God hasn't changed the message! We can change the method of reaching folks but never the message.

Soon the Lord will return; God will vindicate those who preach and teach the truth. When Christ does return, the important questions will not be, "How popular have we been with men? What did the world think of us? Were we successful?"

The only important questions will be: "Have we been faithful in the proclamation of the Gospel of God's grace? Have we taken His command seriously?" Mark 16:15 states, "And he said unto them, Go ye into all the world, and preach the gospel to every creature."

We see here a second rapture of sorts another piece of the first resurrection. These martyrs who had sealed their testimony with their blood are raised in power and caught up to be with their still rejected Lord. Like Him, they have ascended to heaven in a cloud. Unlike Christ, their enemies will see them going up. Remember all the news cameras have been on them, for all nations saw them lying in the streets. They go to heaven leaving their enemies behind! God called them home, and then He speaks to the world. Look at verse 13 of Revelation 11. It says, "And the same hour was there a great earthquake, and the tenth part of the city fell, and in the earthquake were slain of men seven thousand: and the remnant were affrighted, and gave glory to the God of heaven."

The same hour, a great earthquake occurs. God is still the God of heaven. If you remember, an earthquake occurred at Jesus's resurrection. We see that in Matthew 28:2. "And, behold, there was a great earthquake: for the angel of the Lord descended from heaven, and came and rolled back the stone from the door, and sat upon it."

The time is short now for Him to come to rule and reign upon the earth as the God of the earth. We see for the first time since the tribulation began that glory is given to God. Whether this implies a true repentance or whether they haven't truly repented, we can't even really know. All that we see is that scripture says, "The remnant was affrighted!" This doesn't necessarily imply repentance, they are afraid that is what we see.

Now we see with this earthquake, yet more souls perish. A tenth part of the city fell! Seven thousand more people lose their lives—this on top of the nearly three billion who had already lost their lives in this awful tribulation! Keep in mind, the number 7 is spiritual perfection, as the number 10 is ordinal perfection.

We have here both of those numbers in the seven thousand. Most commentators feel this is an inference to this being prominent men, the ones who were in league with the beast and false prophet whose names were in the headlines, when the beast and false prophet came into prominence. Remember when we began chapter 10 we saw the three woes? We are still at woe number 2. As we come to verse 14 of Revelation 11, we now see, "The second woe is past; and, behold, the third woe cometh quickly."

The third woe is coming, and it will occur speedily. Remember the witnesses would be prophesying for 1,260 days. The beast and false prophet's power would be 1,290 days. We see here the third woe will be for these last twenty some odd days.

The third woe is not the seventh and last trumpet. The second woe is ending at this point, and it has been a bad one. Yet we were told the last would be worse than the first two! We see this woe in 2 Thessalonians 2:1–17. Centering in on verses 10–13, it states, "And with all deceivableness of unrighteousness in them that perish; because they received not the love of the truth, that they might be saved. And for this cause God shall send them strong delusion, that they should believe a lie: That they all might be damned who believed not the truth, but had pleasure in unrighteousness." But we are bound to give thanks always to God for you, brethren beloved of the Lord, because God hath from the beginning chosen you to salvation through sanctification of the Spirit and belief of the truth."

Those who followed the beast and false prophet are given over to strong delusion, they believed the lie. You remember where we said in this chapter that some equate these verses to those in the church age and go into the tribulation. I believe we see now when they reject and are therefore given strong delusion and are damned or condemned because of their unbelief. That has always been true. Remember what Jesus said in John 3:18, "Those who believe not are condemned already."

This holds true for these people during the tribulation period, just as much as it holds true in our age. People are condemned to hell not because of their sin but because of their rejection of the Lord Jesus Christ as their personal savior. With the killing of the two witnesses, their bodies in the streets three and a half days, we then see their resurrection and ascension. We see God judge with a great earthquake and are told the end of the second woe has occurred. We see in verse 15 of Revelation 11 the seventh angel sounding his trumpet. "And the seventh angel sounded; and there were great voices in heaven, saying, The kingdoms of this world are become the kingdoms of our Lord, and of his Christ; and he shall reign for ever and ever."

The seventh trumpet sounding is of great significance. It becomes relevant as we study the remainder of the book. Here is the breaking forth of the order God has placed upon mankind. Judgment has been taking place! Now we are on the threshold of Christ's kingdom, and God finally revealing the mystery of that kingdom.

We see God's program coming into chapter 21 where eternity begins. Great voices sound from heaven where the bride the church has been during this whole time that is since the fourth chapter. We are at the transition of the whole of events. This is what we will see in the next chapters. We have been in an overview. The next chapters go into the details themselves of what has already been occurring. We will again see the events unfold on earth that we have seen with the overview.

We see in Revelation 11:19 the close of chapter 11, of which is really the beginning of chapter 12. So now Revelation 11:19 says, "And the temple of God was opened in heaven, and there was seen in his temple the ark of his testament: and there were lightnings, and voices, and thunderings, and an earthquake, and great hail." From this point on, we don't see the church again until chapter 19. There is no temple in New Jerusalem. Here we are told there is a temple in heaven. Verse 19 of Revelation 11 will be picked up in our next chapter.

2
Woman with Child

We ended the previous chapter without looking to Revelation 11:19 because it actually should begin chapter 12. Revelation 11:19 says, "And the temple of God was opened in heaven, and there was seen in his temple the ark of his testament: and there were lightnings, and voices, and thunderings, and an earthquake, and great hail." John sees the holy of holies the inner most part of the earthly temple, yet this is a heavenly temple.

The thing we need to see is that this is the representative of the earthly temple. The ark, which was called the Ark of the Covenant, represented God's covenant with Israel. God will remember His covenant with Israel. He will and has already preserved a remnant safely through the judgment of the tribulation. The ark on earth was a symbol of God's presence with Israel. The earthly ark disappeared when God began to deal with the church.

When God begins to deal with Israel once again in all their governmental affairs, the real ark will again appear. The ark of old was the place in which God dwelt, in the holy of holies, with His people! Here we see the ark connected with judgment coming, for there were lightnings, voices, thunderings, an earthquake, and great hail. Judgment is coming! God said He would make a covenant with Israel.

We see what He told Moses after Israel sinned in the wilderness with the calf worship in Exodus 32:34. "Therefore now go, lead the people unto the place of which I have spoken unto thee: behold, mine Angel shall go before thee: nevertheless in the day when I visit I will visit their sin upon them." Exodus 34:10 states, "And he said, Behold, I make a covenant: before all thy people I will do marvels, such as have not been done in all the earth, nor in any nation: and all the people among which thou art shall see the work of the Lord: for it is a terrible thing that I will do!" God is showing here that He will do as He said.

Therefore, His temple opened, and the ark, which is a symbol of His keeping the covenant, is now revealed. The judgment—God's action—will be seen, and this time, it will encompass all the earth, just as He said in verse 10 of Exodus 34. For Israel will be established as God's elect royal nation, she has been punished! God will bring all nations up against Israel to battle just as we saw in Ezekiel 38 and 39 earlier in the section, Beginning of Earth's Redemption.

God is acting in judgment from His temple in heaven. He is acting according to His covenant arrangements, that covenant was given so that God would restore the kingdom to Israel! All by means of severe bitter judgment, just as prophecy has foretold! Now we go from the overview that we have been seeing to the actual events as occurring on earth. We see verse 1 of Revelation 12 that says, "And there appeared a great wonder in heaven; a woman clothed with the sun, and the moon under her feet, and upon her head a crown of twelve stars:" Who the woman is, is the first thing we must determine. According to the Catholic Church, she is the Virgin Mary.

There have been many Protestant teachers who have also been just as far incorrect on their theology. Many other Protestant interpreters see her as the church. They too are far off in that teaching as well! Quite a few of several denominational pieces of literature, you will find, also follow that teaching. So how can she be identified or at least the symbolism she represents be identified?

Notice first she has several distinct things, which identify her. Three distinct things about the woman with child:

1. She is clothed with the sun.
2. The moon under her feet.

3. Upon her head twelve stars.

With the sun, it is the supreme light for the earth, and therefore, she has supreme authority. The moon is later light, but it too controls or administers the tides and other things, so she administers the perfect administration for mankind and shows forth the glory of the old covenant under her feet.

Therefore, with the twelve crowns, we have perfect governmental representation. This is seen in the crown upon her head and it having the twelve stars. These all belong to Israel, as they are seen in Joseph's dream. We see Genesis 37:9–10 that says, "And he dreamed yet another dream, and told it his brethren, and said, Behold, I have dreamed a dream more; and, behold, the sun and the moon and the eleven stars made obeisance to me. And he told it to his father, and to his brethren: and his father rebuked him, and said unto him, What is this dream that thou hast dreamed? Shall I and thy mother and thy brethren indeed come to bow down ourselves to thee to the earth?" Jacob interpreted the sun, moon, and stars to mean himself—Rachel and Joseph's brothers.

They bow down before Joseph. Before everything was said and done, that is exactly what happened with the exception that Rachel had died. This is Israel with Jerusalem as its center as in the purpose of God we see more Old Testament prophecy fulfilled here. Isaiah 9:6 states, "For unto us a child is born, unto us a son is given: and the government shall be upon his shoulder: and his name shall be called Wonderful, Counsellor, The mighty God, The everlasting Father, The Prince of Peace." Psalm 87:6 says, "The Lord shall count, when he writeth up the people, that this man was born there. Selah."

The woman is a wonder in heaven! She symbolizes the events occurring upon the earth or those that are soon to happen. It was Israel who gave birth to Christ. He was the child born. We now see verse 2 of Revelation 12 that says, "And she being with child cried, travailing in birth, and pained to be delivered." She is travailing in child birth, distressed and in pain. Ready to deliver, we go back to a verse we just read. Here is a familiar verse in Isaiah 9:6. Who is the "us" Isaiah is referring to? It is Israel as a complete nation! Isaiah makes it clear who it was that would see a child born. He wasn't speaking of a savior but of the one who would be the Governor, a Ruler, and a King—one who has come to rule over them. "And the government shall be upon His shoulders," Isaiah said. The child who will be delivered of her is that one promised to Adam and Eve.

We see Genesis 3:15. Satan bruised Christ's heel with the crucifixion. This time, Christ is coming to crush Satan's head. This woman is travailing in birth, which is a symbol of Israel. Look at Isaiah 66:7–8. Israel will go through the tribulation after Christ's birth we see from this passage. "Before her pain came, she was delivered of a man child"—that was Christ's first advent. Therefore, we can identify this woman as nation Israel. No woman on earth, including the Virgin Mary, fits this description. It is Israel not the church, for the church has not brought forth a man-child. She has been persecuted, but Christ is not the Child of the church! Quite the opposite is true, the church is the bride of Christ, and we are her children!

Clearing our heads in order to understand this is the beginning of the great tribulation! This is the beginning of the last three and a half years of the tribulation. That is what is being seen here in chapter 12 and following up to chapter 19. Since this is the great tribulation, we know by previous teaching that the church is in heaven at this time. This woman cannot be the church!

She is nation Israel, the one that God is not finished with. The twelve stars representing the twelve tribes sealed. She can represent nothing else! We see another wonder appear in heaven in Revelation 12:3–4; we see the wonder and the mission. "And there appeared another wonder in heaven; and behold a great red dragon, having seven heads and ten horns, and seven crowns upon his heads. And his tail drew the third part of the stars of heaven, and did cast them to the earth: and the dragon stood before the woman which was ready to be delivered, for to devour her child as soon as it was born." Understand these are signs, not literal things. They are symbolisms. John makes clear what is symbolism and what is not.

A great red dragon appears. Who is this red dragon? Revelation 12:9 tells us exactly who it is as well as the stars of heaven. "And the great dragon was cast out, that old serpent, called the Devil, and Satan, which deceiveth the whole world: he was cast out into the earth, and his angels were cast out with him." No speculation needed for this one. In this second sign, all of Satan's character is revealed. First, he is called great because of his vast power. He controls the nations of the world. Remember in his temptation of Jesus, he offered Jesus all the kingdoms of the world if Jesus would worship him. This is seen in Matthew 4:8–9 that states, "Again, the devil taketh him up into an exceeding high mountain, and sheweth him all the kingdoms of the world, and the glory of them; And saith unto him, All these things will I give thee, if thou wilt fall down and worship me." Satan's ultimate goal is to have everyone worshipping him!

The kingdoms of the world are his, and he controls them today! In that day, it was Rome, but he is in control of every nation. Second, we see he is called red because he is a murderer and he was a murderer from the beginning. We are told in John 8:44, "Ye are of your father the devil, and the lusts of your father ye will do. He was a murderer from the beginning, and abode not in the truth, because there is no truth in him. When he speaketh a lie, he speaketh of his own: for he is a liar, and the father of it." He has no regard for human life. Many people chose to serve him, though. Look at the abortion clinics today. Millions of children are killed so woman don't have to be bothered raising them. Satan drives that, he is a murderer.

Third, he is called a dragon because he has a cruel nature. We know he was originally called Lucifer, son of the morning Ezekiel 28:12–19. And we see him in Isaiah 14:12. He is the essence of evil! He shows the depth of disgrace! He has become the most dangerous being that God ever created! He is my enemy as well as he is yours that is if you are a child of God! Understand here that he seeks to defeat the Lord Jesus Christ. Even in our time, it seems he is winning.

However, we can be assured Christ will prevail in the end! Revelation 12:4 says, "And his tail drew the third part of the stars of heaven, and did cast them to the earth: and the dragon stood before the woman which was ready to be delivered, for to devour her child as soon as it was born." We see in this verse, he is ready to devour the child as it is born. Look at Isaiah 66:7–8. It states, "Before she travailed, she brought forth; before her pain came, she was delivered of a man child. Who hath heard such a thing? who hath seen such things? Shall the earth be made to bring forth in one day? or shall a nation be born at once? for as soon as Zion travailed, she brought forth her children." Israel, as a nation and people, will go through the tribulation. It will be after Christ's birth that is what we see from this passage. "Before her pain came, she was delivered of a man child"—that was Christ's first advent!

Therefore, we can identify this woman as nation Israel. It is Israel, not the church the church has not brought forth a man-child. She has been persecuted. Let me reiterate what I said just a few paragraphs back: Christ is not the Child of the church. Quite the opposite is true, the church is the bride of Christ, and we are her children! Please let that absorb into your memory!

Satan, as the open enemy of God and God's power in Christ, seeks to devour the child as soon as he is born—the child who was to have the rule of the earth from God! As Isaiah says, the child was delivered before her pain came. Christ was born, and His heel was bruised at His first advent. As this event in verse 4 is occurring, Christ and the church, His bride, are in heaven. What or, should I say, who is Satan seeking to devour? It is not the church here! The fact that the woman represents Israel must be clearly understood! We have a place here in the prophecy of Jesus. Here is for Israel and from her are the two witnesses seen in chapter 11. They had been placed in Jerusalem, and there we see the fact that temple worship had begun afresh.

As we see the words sun, moon, and stars, what is immediately brought to your mind? Could it be, for many of us, Joseph's dream seen in Genesis 37:9: "Behold, the sun and the moon and eleven stars made obeisance to me?" We see in the dream a prophecy concerning Israel, in these last days. The church cannot be spoken of in this language. Why, because she was chosen "before the foundation of the world." The glory of the church is not describable in terms of this present age. She is in union with Christ who has gone "far above all the heavens." This vision of the woman can be viewed plainly in connection with the solar system, as we view it from earth. We are told that she is clothed with the sun, has the moon under her feet, and on her head a twelve-star crown.

All this indicates the subjection of earth to her administrative glory, seen in "the splendor and fullness of governmental authority on earth," belong, by God's sovereign appointment, to Israel.

The restoring of the kingdom to Israel, under Christ authority, can be seen right here in this portion of scripture. Going back to Revelation 5:1–14, you may recall where Christ began to redeem the earth from the curse, the curse she is currently under. Israel is described by the prophets of the Old Testament as travailing in birth. The church was never seen by the prophets in the Old Testament. As seen in Micah 5:2–3, it says, "But thou, Bethlehem Ephratah, though thou be little among the thousands of Judah, yet out of thee shall he come forth unto me that is to be ruler in Israel; whose goings forth have been from of old, from everlasting. Therefore will he give them up, until the time that she which travaileth hath brought forth: then the remnant of his brethren shall return unto the children of Israel."

We see too in Isaiah 7:14, which states, "Therefore the Lord himself shall give you a sign; Behold, a virgin shall conceive, and bear a son, and shall call his name Immanuel." Again, in Isaiah 9:6, it says, "For unto us a child is born, unto us a son is given: and the government shall be upon his shoulder: and his name shall be called Wonderful, Counsellor, The mighty God, The everlasting Father, The Prince of Peace." Can you see Israel will travail in childbirth, not the Church? Israel, not the church, gave birth to Christ (Romans 9:1–33; Micah 5:1–15; Isaiah 9:6; Hebrews 7:14). In no possible viewpoint can be seen the church travailing with the child here in Revelation. It is very obvious and is of the extreme importance that all believers recognize that this woman's precise history is on earth.

She is persecuted by the enemy. Revelation 12:13–16 give us a sign, which is seen in heaven, her experience progresses on earth. Seeing this as a sign, we can conclude that God's glorious purposes, in regard to her, are heavenly purposes! She is seen experiencing the process of earthly persecution. The earthly history (Revelation 12:1–17) of the woman is in direct correspondence with what Old Testament prophets show us concerning the trouble of Israel in the last days. The period of that trouble, which we see in Revelation 12:6, agrees exactly with the last week of Daniel's seventy weeks—the great tribulation lasting three and one-half years.

The dragon desires to devour the child. Satan seems to know his destiny. He knows that Christ is intended to shepherd all the nations with a rod of iron. Satan has always known God's plan! He has always known that the seed of the woman is to bruise his (the serpents) head, as Christ foretold in Genesis 3:15. All Satan's activities in the tribulation, the time of Jacob's trouble, will be carried on with a greater urgency than he is using currently in this the church age. Because as we have been told earlier in scripture, the Holy Spirit is holding back those forces (2 Thess. 2:7–10) until the time of the Tribulation. When the church is snatched away, so too is "He who letteth," we see verse 7, which tells us, "He that letteth will let, until He be taken out of the way." He will be taken away, we are told, and when He is removed, then the wicked will be revealed—the one who is coming with Satan's power, the one who will deceive those who are unrighteous and will not receive Christ!

Satan has a double purpose in everything here. He has an ambition to rule and to be worshipped! He is filled with hatred toward the one whom God has chosen to redeem the earth and set up the kingdom—the earth and dominion over it, which Satan by deception, snatched away in the garden. We see here the beginning of the end, the end of the great warfare between God and His adversary—the war that began before Eden! In Eden, here the serpent beguiled the woman, and God declared that He would put enmity between the serpent and the woman, and between her seed and his seed the battle for the earth truly began. We know that her (woman's) seed is Christ and no other! This, of course, is the exact subject before us.

Satan's enmity and jealousy is and always has been against Christ. Christ, which scripture says, is to "rule all the nations" because Satan himself had been their prince and god. The scene here in Revelation 12:1–17 is exactly like Zechariah 9:9–10. It looks only at Christ who is the coming Ruler, and it skips all the other history seen in Zechariah 9:9–10. "Rejoice greatly, O daughter of Zion; shout, O daughter of Jerusalem: behold, thy King cometh unto thee: he is just, and having salvation; lowly, and riding upon an ass, and upon a colt the foal of an ass. And I will cut off the chariot from Ephraim, and the horse from Jerusalem, and the battle bow shall be cut off: and he shall speak peace unto the heathen: and his dominion shall be from sea even to sea, and from the river even to the ends of the earth." We see exactly what has already occurred in Revelation 12:5 that says, "And she brought forth a man child, who was to rule all nations with a rod of iron: and her child was caught up unto God, and to his throne."

Do you see her child was caught up unto God, and do you see Zechariah 9 showing Christ's first advent? John is here looking back at that first advent. In Isaiah, Christ is born of a virgin and called Immanuel. That Child was to be born and is said that He is the one who "will have the government on His shoulder." Zechariah saw Him ride into Jerusalem upon the lowly donkey but doesn't see His rejection. John sees Him born and in Israel! Yet despite the dragon's efforts through Herod, the chief priests, and Rome, He rose from the grave and ascended, which as Old Testament prophecy states He is caught up to God and to His throne.

Christ is the One who shall rule all the nations with an iron rod! There is no consideration given to exactly how long He will be in heaven before He "receives the kingdom." The book 1 Peter 3:22 says, "Who is gone into heaven, and is on the right hand of God; angels and authorities and powers being made subject unto him." We see three scenes here in chapter 12. First understand Christ was born to Israel and ascended, despite the efforts of the dragon, there to await His foreordained rule of the nations which has yet to occur. Next we see Satan cast out with his angels from all of heaven. Cast out of the joy of the heavenly multitude. Lastly the vengeful persecution of the woman (Israel) and her seed is seen. Her divine protection we see is for 1,260 days during which the great tribulation is occurring! Here in verse 5 is seen the first and second portions. Now verse 6 of Revelation 12 states, "And the woman fled into the wilderness, where she hath a place prepared of God, that they should feed her there a thousand two hundred and threescore days." The remnant of Israel will be protected! This must be understood!

God has a place prepared for them! In that place, God will supply their every need for 1,260 days. Christ is safely in heaven. Satan's rule on earth is reaching its zenith. If God can feed, clothe, and protect this remnant of Israel for 1,260 days, just think of how much He can supply our needs as we are promised in Philippians 4:19. "But my God shall supply all your need according to his riches in glory by Christ Jesus." There, Israel is protected.

The dragon, as great yet murderousness in his magnificent form, is seen as the prince of the world. Him seen as having perfect wisdom (seven heads) and almost perfect governmental power (ten horns). He will soon develop the power of the beast of chapter 13 that comes forth as his minion, his fatal influence in drawing to people to their ruin just as he did with a third of the angels. His consuming hostility directed toward the child of the woman continues to grow! We see next a war in heaven, a battle between angel leaders in Revelation 12:7 that says, "And there was war in heaven: Michael and his angels fought against the dragon; and the dragon fought and his angels." Michael, God's warrior angel, with his one-third of God's angels, here is seen fighting against the dragon, Satan and his one-third of the angels who are fallen.

Michael is the leader of heavenly host! The meaning of the name Michael, which is of Hebrew origin, is "who is like God." Michael is the great angelic prince, the archangel! He was given charge of the protection of Daniel's people we see in Daniel 12:1 that says, "And at that time shall Michael stand up, the great prince which standeth for the children of thy people: and there shall be a time of trouble, such as never was since there was a nation even to that same time: and at that time thy people shall be delivered, every one that shall be found written in the book." We see Michael here in Revelation in fulfillment of Daniel's prophecy. Here he is protecting Israel and battling Satan!

The battle between Satan and God has been raging since before the world was created. Satan sinned, and God condemned him! This is not the final battle, but it is the decisive one, the turning point, which will lead to Satan's final destiny! The final victory will be won by the seed of the woman, the seed of Israel, Jesus Christ! He will utterly defeat Satan! He will judge him who is the enemy of God and all mankind. Satan then turns his attention to the woman, Israel the nation. If he can defeat her, then he will defeat Christ because Christ has promised to redeem Israel. He has been promised to come to power as her king and establish his kingdom on the throne of David. That is why Satan has attacked Israel with such hatred and fury in the past, why he used the third Reich and Hitler to euphonize millions of Jews, seeking to make God's Word a lie, making God a god that is liar! All his attempts have failed! Think about it. Out of the great attacks on the Jews by Satan, there was a nation reborn in 1947.

It was the same God who saved Israel from Egypt; from the bondage they were in there—the same God who brought them out from under the oppression of Nebuchadnezzar, the dominion of the Persians, the iron rule, which was Rome. The scheming of Haman, the torture of

Hitler, this same God will deliver His people once again from the wiles of Satan—the one who seeks to devour them. Revelation 12:8 says, "And prevailed not; neither was their place found any more in heaven." The dragon and his angels fought. They could not prevail against Michael and his angels. There was a great struggle occurring. Both sides were fighting and struggling. The victory fell to Christ. There was no place found for Satan in heaven.

3
Satan Cast Down

We see Revelation 12:9 that states, "And the great dragon was cast out, that old serpent, called the Devil, and Satan, which deceiveth the whole world: he was cast out into the earth, and his angels were cast out with him." Satan is cast out of heaven at this point. You say, "Well I thought he is already residing in hell," understand that is a myth of the world. Satan has and does, at this present time, have access to God the Father! Job 1:6–8 says, "Now there was a day when the sons of God came to present themselves before the Lord, and Satan came also among them. And the Lord said unto Satan, Whence comest thou? Then Satan answered the Lord, and said, From going to and fro in the earth, and from walking up and down in it. And the Lord said unto Satan, Hast thou considered my servant Job, that there is none like him in the earth, a perfect and an upright man, one that feareth God, and escheweth evil?"

We see also Job 2:1–3 says, "Again there was a day when the sons of God came to present themselves before the Lord, and Satan came also among them to present himself before the Lord. And the Lord said unto Satan, From whence comest thou? And Satan answered the Lord, and said, From going to and fro in the earth, and from walking up and down in it. And the Lord said unto Satan, Hast thou considered my servant Job, that there is none like him in the earth, a perfect and an upright man, one that feareth God, and escheweth evil? and still he holdeth fast his integrity, although thou movedst me against him, to destroy him without cause." As the angels reported to God, we see Satan was right there with them, just as if he had every right to be there, right there with the angels who had not rebelled. We see as the battle is raging and Satan has been in heaven.

That as seen in Zechariah 3:1–2, it says, "And he shewed me Joshua the high priest standing before the angel of the Lord, and Satan standing at his right hand to resist him. And the Lord said unto Satan, The Lord rebuke thee, O Satan; even the Lord that hath chosen Jerusalem rebuke thee: is not this a brand plucked out of the fire?" Do you see Satan has access to God? What does he question or accuse you about when he appears before God? He is able to carry on communication with God. See Luke 22:31. It states, "And the Lord said, Simon, Simon, behold, Satan hath desired to have you, that he may sift you as wheat." Satan was able to come before God and request to test Peter. God gave him permission just as He permitted Job to be tested. What would God say to Satan about believers today and testing them?

We see Michael and Satan have been in conflict before Jude 1:9 that says, "Yet Michael the archangel, when contending with the devil he disputed about the body of Moses, durst not bring against him a railing accusation, but said, The Lord rebuke thee." He is seeking whom he may devour we are told by Peter. Here we see there will be a fierce struggle. We see Michael and his host prevail! Satan and his angels will be cast out of heaven for good at this point of the tribulation. We see Jesus referred to this in Luke 10:18 that states, "And he said unto them, I beheld Satan as lightning fall from heaven." There is no mistaking that the great red dragon is Satan here in Revelation 12. His fingerprints are seen here in Revelation.

We have many who preach that Satan doesn't really exist and that hell is not a real place. God knew that this teaching would be propagated in our time. Therefore, He made it so clear. It can't be missed here in Revelation. Think about it if your enemy can get you to believe he doesn't exist or that he is no longer your enemy he will have a great advantage over you. He will be able to attack you and sweep you off your feet. Satan moved in fresh and new during the twentieth century! Many believed that he didn't really exist!

We are now seeing his influence on our world—murders, rapes, and robberies are on an upswing. He is seeking whom he may devour. Is he seeking permission from God to sift you as he did Peter? Let's see how God identifies Satan for us. We see him called the "old serpent," which takes us back to Eden. Jesus said in John 8:44, "Ye are of your father the devil, and the lusts of your father ye will do. He was a murderer from the beginning, and abode not in the truth, because there is no truth in him. When he speaketh a lie, he speaketh of his own: for he is a liar, and the father of it."

The words old and beginning are like each other. Satan is that old serpent who was in the beginning in Eden. He is called devil, a word that comes from the Greek diabolos, which means "slanderer or accuser." He is labeled that in verse 10 of Revelation 12. It says, "And I heard a loud voice saying in heaven, Now is come salvation, and strength, and the kingdom of our God, and the power of his Christ: for the accuser of our brethren is cast down, which accused them before our God day and night." This is the reason we need an advocate with the Father, one who we know! That is what we have in the Lord Jesus Christ! Our enemy is called Satan, which means "adversary." He is the adversary of God and of every believer. We see in 1 Peter 5:8 that says, "Be sober, be vigilant; because your adversary the devil, as a roaring lion, walketh about, seeking whom he may devour." We need to remember he is our enemy; we should not dwell upon that fact. We need to keep our eye on Jesus Christ because He is our means of deliverance and our advocate in heaven. Our enemy is called "he that deceiveth the whole world," as we see in verse 9.

During the tribulation, Satan will totally deceive mankind; today, he deceives partially. Satan deceives many of people in regards to God and the Word of God. We have here the beginning of the end of the great warfare between God and His adversary, the war that began in Eden. We now move on and see rejoicing in heaven in Revelation 12:10–12. It states, "And I heard a loud voice saying in heaven, Now is come salvation, and strength, and the kingdom of our God, and the power of his Christ: for the accuser of our brethren is cast down, which accused them before our God day and night. And they overcame him by the blood of the Lamb, and by the word of their testimony; and they loved not their lives unto the death. Therefore rejoice, ye heavens, and ye that dwell in them. Woe to the inhabiters of the earth and of the sea! for the devil is come down unto you, having great wrath, because he knoweth that he hath but a short time." Now

God has shown himself to be a mighty God, Christ has shown himself to be a strong and mighty Savior his own arm has brought salvation. Now his kingdom will be greatly enlarged and established!

The salvation and strength of the church and tribulation saints are all to be ascribed to the king and head of the church, the Great King who will reign in the millennium. Though Satan hates the presence of God, he is willing to appear there to accuse the people of God. We need to take heed! We need to ensure that we give him no cause of accusation against us and that, when we have sinned, we confess that sin before the Lord. We must accuse and condemn ourselves! Then we need to commit our cause to Christ as our Advocate. John says he heard which reminds him he is still a spectator and auditor of these events. When Satan is cast out, it will cause great rejoicing among the redeemed in heaven.

Now the kingdom of God and the power of Christ are come. The angels as well as all believers who are in heaven rejoice at his defeat. We see that we are not as some claim living in the kingdom age! It is on the brink of coming at this point in Revelation! Here when Satan is cast out of heaven, understand this has not taken place, yet not today. When it does, it will be the beginning of the end for Satan. The first great demonstration of Christ's power, which is to be exerted against evil and was to occur after His death and resurrection, is the casting out of Satan.

That is setting in motion the return of the Lord Jesus to set up His earthly kingdom, the beginning of the Lord taking the reins of government upon the earth. Christ's death on the cross paved the way for Satan to be defeated for him to be cast out of heaven, ultimately to end up in the lake of fire forever! Look at Colossians 2:14. Christ made salvation possible, and by our believing on Him, we gain that precious gift—the gift of salvation. His payment was made in full for us that is for all of mankind. God cancelled our sin debt by nailing it on the cross of Christ. Colossians 2:15 says, "And having spoiled principalities and powers, he made a shew of them openly, triumphing over them in it." He conquered it all on Calvary and at His ascension. He ascended and took with Him the Old Testament saints' souls! He led captivity captive and took them into the presence of God. Christ triumph came at His ascension, and the battle we see here in Revelation 12 is yet another battle won over Satan.

Victory comes for those accused by Satan the believers of all ages in three ways seen here in this section of scripture. First, by the "blood of the Lamb" we see in verse 11. We sing of the wonder working power of the blood of the Lamb, don't we in the song, "There Is Power in the Blood!" This is one thing we should never forget: any victory you and I may win is by the power of the blood that is the blood Christ shed for us! We see the second way in which we gain victory as accused saints over Satan is by the "word of their testimony." That is why it is so important for us to live a life of faith to show the world our lives as set apart to God! We cannot deny Christ! Matthew 10:33 states, "But whosoever shall deny me before men, him will I also deny before my Father which is in heaven." We get strength when we present our testimony. If you are a believer, back it up! Tell the world about your faith, and show them your faith!

Thirdly, they "loved not their life even unto death!" This is the place we all need to get to, where we would rather die for the cause of Christ than to save our lives. That will be the tribulation saint's witness. That was the witness of the early church martyr. Where are you in your Christian walk? Would you die for the cause of Christ? These are at the place where they put Jesus first, the first love in their lives. Are you at that place? Two reactions are seen here to Satan being cast out of heaven. There is rejoicing because this horrible, untruthful, dangerous, and deadly serpent is out of heaven forever.

There is woe on earth, this is the third woe connected to the pouring out of the bowls. The only thing to hold on to for the inhabitants of the earth is that Satan's time on earth will be brief—forty-two months. The intensity of the tribulation rises in this time that is why it is referred to as the great tribulation. Satan intensifies his attack because he too knows his time is short. Great is the tribulation he brings! Our time too is short. Have we intensified our effort to win souls, or have we become procrastinators?

Revelation 12:13 says, "And when the dragon saw that he was cast unto the earth, he persecuted the woman which brought forth the man child." Satan realizes he has been cast down; he brings the attack in greater force upon Israel. Anti-Semitism will roll over the earth, as many today say God is through with Israel. But this shows just the opposite for the persecution is desperate and deadly. Satan hates Israel because of Christ, the man-child she had. His lineage was through this nation. It is from nation Israel that Christ will reign in the millennial after Satan is overthrown.

He also sees Israel as continual proof shown to mankind's eyes revealing the truth of scriptures. Proof of the truth that Jehovah God exists! This is the time of Jacob's trouble! The current land of Israel is not complete, we as believers need to understand that. Don't let someone tell you God is through with Israel as a people and nation because the Bible tells us He is not through with them. According to prophecy, there will be a remnant in the land during the tribulation. The prophecy was given in the book of the Revelation of Jesus Christ, as written by John. Understand that Israel is not back in the land at this time to fulfill prophecy for the millennium. They are in the land to fulfill prophecy concerning the tribulation. That is what we see here and in Daniels—prophecy for the tribulation. This is just as important to be fulfilled as prophecy concerning the millennial reign of Christ.

We see God's providence working in the nation Israel in Revelation 12:14 that states, "And to the woman were given two wings of a great eagle, that she might fly into the wilderness, into her place, where she is nourished for a time, and times, and half a time, from the face of the serpent." We see God bringing protection and deliverance to nation Israel. Two wings of a great eagle come so she can flee into the wilderness—the care of God for Israel, wings to carry her to safety, which He had provided for her. There she is to continue for a time, times and a half a time. We see this too fulfill prophecy again. We see Daniel 7:25 that says, "And he shall speak great words against the most High, and shall wear out the saints of the most High, and think to change times and laws: and they shall be given into his hand until a time and times and the dividing of time."

Israel is familiar with this term, for it is reminiscent of the grace of God. When He delivered them from Egypt, we see Exodus 19:4 that states, "Ye have seen what I did unto the Egyptians, and how I bare you on eagles' wings, and brought you unto myself." They had not come out of Egypt on their own effort or on their own ability. They came out because God brought them out! Eagle's wings became a symbol for them. Here again in the tribulation, the Israelites cannot deliver themselves. No one is interested in delivering them, but God will get them out. They will come out on eagle's wings by His grace.

Let's talk here about some speculations we hear today. These are, of course, speculations, and we cannot confirm or deny them. Some say the reference here to eagle's wings carrying the woman out is escape by airplane. Others speculate that the eagle, being the symbol of America today, represents the United States intervening to help Israel. That our nation is destined to be the champion of Israel's cause. We know the past administration wouldn't be the champion of Israel's cause. But now we have an administration which supports Israel. The godly influence will no longer be in the world in the tribulation understand that. Therefore, to say it is the United States of America, as things are shaping up today, might not align with the way this nation will fall during this time. What we see here is more evidence that God has a way of protecting and preserving a people, a nation when they are faithful to Him or belong to Him.

The continual onslaught of Satan, the old dragon upon Israel during this time, is real and seen here. Her obscurity could not protect her. Not from the full force of Satan who is now confined to the earth. God sends help, in the form of what we do not know just that it is described as the wings of eagles. We know it will be for a certain period of time. For it is clear God says in Revelation 12:14, "For a time, and times, and half a time." God provides nourishment and protection to Israel. For a time which is one year, for times which is two additional years, for a half a time which is six months, thus for the three and one half years of the great tribulation. The last three and one half years of the entire tribulation, we see God will protect and nourish Israel as a nation.

Remember God brought them out of Egypt. He nourished them with manna for forty years. Surely, He can do the same for them in the three and one half years of the great tribulation. He can nourish and supply our needs and protection. The woman is taken away from the face of the serpent into the wilderness just as in Exodus. Many have speculated that they go to Petra, but that is not the only place they can go. Some say it is the wilderness of the peoples of the world. Understand with this thought, that there will be another worldwide scattering of the nation Israel. Look what Christ said about this time in Matthew 24:16. It says, "Then let them which be in Judaea flee into the mountains." This seems to say it will be a literal wilderness. Possibly, the same one Israel wandered in for forty years under Moses.

The thing God wanted us to see was He would nourish and protect her for three and one half years by His grace! Just as He sustained in the wilderness by the manna and the rock as the Old Testament books tell us. He will nourish them in the same manner here, just as He does for us currently.

We see in Revelation 12:15–16 that states, "And the serpent cast out of his mouth water as a flood after the woman, that he might cause her to be carried away of the flood." Now God has shown himself to be a mighty God, now Christ has shown himself to be a strong and mighty Savior his own arm has brought salvation. "And the earth helped the woman, and the earth opened her mouth, and swallowed up the flood which the dragon cast out of his mouth." As nation Israel flees into the wilderness, the dragon sends a flood after her. This could be a literal flood of waters, or it could be armies from the nations, which are in allegiance to him.

We know God delivered the Israelites from pharaoh at the crossing of the Red Sea. We also know that He opened the Jordan River when they entered the Promised Land! Look, though, at Isaiah 8:7–8. It says, "Now therefore, behold, the Lord bringeth up upon them the waters of the river, strong and many, even the king of Assyria, and all his glory: and he shall come up over all his channels, and go over all his banks: And he shall pass through Judah; he shall overflow and go over, he shall reach even to the neck; and the stretching out of his wings shall fill the breadth of thy land, O Immanuel." Here we see the nation of Assyria called rivers of water.

We have already seen Ezekiel 38:22, which we said could be the war at the beginning of the tribulation, but it could apply here also Ezekiel 38:22. It says, "And I will plead against him with pestilence and with blood; and I will rain upon him, and upon his bands, and upon the many people that are with him, an overflowing rain, and great hailstones, fire, and brimstone." We find God rendering peculiar miraculous assistance in those terrible days to the real Israel, not those merely "of Israel" but those who keep His commandments that is—the remnant of those last days, in the "time, times, and half a time" the three and a half years of the great tribulation.

Satan is yet defeated again. His attack on Israel is thwarted by their protector, just as the Egyptian army was covered by the floodwaters of the Red Sea. God will do the same for Israel, how much more can He protect us in this present age when we remain faithful! We see the final verse of chapter 12 and Satan's reaction in Revelation 12:17 that states, "And the dragon was wroth with the woman, and went to make war with the remnant of her seed, which keep the commandments of God, and have the testimony of Jesus Christ." We see the dragon was wroth with the nation Israel. He turns his persecution to those who have trusted in Christ in all nations.

This too could be the 144,000 Jewish witnesses in the world that we saw earlier. He had destroyed many with that flood of persecution. He continues the battle with the remnant of her seed. They are called those "which keep the commandments of God and have the testimony of Jesus Christ." Paul was one of those who persecuted the remnant of Israel before his conversion. We need to see that between Revelation 12:5–6 a whole stretch of history, from the ascension of our Lord to the yet future great tribulation. The woman is protected and nourished for 1,260 days—the last part of Daniel's seventieth week. All persecution of believers in today's society is inspired by Satan. Just as he persecuted Job, just as he requested to sift Peter, this will culminate with Satan making a final attempt to destroy nation Israel and all who believe on the Lord Jesus Christ—all those "which keep the commandments of God and have the testimony of Jesus Christ." Satan has led the attack on all those who have trusted in Christ and are His children. He will continue the onslaught; it will be severe in this last three and one half years. Satan will be defeated, and he cannot destroy a work that God begins, but he can destroy those who stop serving Christ.

4
Unholy Trinity Revealed

Revelation 13:1 says, "And I stood upon the sand of the sea, and saw a beast rise up out of the sea, having seven heads and ten horns, and upon his horns ten crowns, and upon his heads the name of blasphemy." We now see the beast coming out of the sea. He is Satan's man! He will rule over nations. Satan's instrument of evil is coming, as we saw the dragon in chapter 12 falling and drawing a third of the stars or angels with him.

We now see the beast coming out of the world—a savage beast! It has seven heads, ten horns, and ten crowns. He carried the name of blasphemy! Definitely, it was the enemy of Christ, Israel, and the tribulation saints. Consider the number 13 here. As to the significance of 13, many are aware that it has come down to us as a number of ill Omens. Many superstitions have formed around it with various explanations, which we hear in our world concerning them.

The first occurrence in Scripture is seen in Genesis 14:4. It says, "Twelve years they served Chedorlaomer, and in the thirteenth year they rebelled." Accordingly, every time the number 13 appears, as well as every multiple we see of it, there is a stamp. That stamp places the connection of the number with rebellion, apostasy, defection, corruption, disintegration, revolution, or some similar idea. We see in the statement here: "A beast rise up out of the sea." In the Greek alphabet and number system, that term equals 1,664, which is the sum of 13 x 128. The description of this beast carries us back to Daniel's prophecy in Daniel 7:2–8 that states, "Daniel spake and said, I saw in my vision by night, and, behold, the four winds of the heaven strove upon the great sea. And four great beasts came up from the sea, diverse one from another. The first was like a lion, and had eagle's wings: I beheld till the wings thereof were plucked, and it was lifted up from the earth, and made stand upon the feet as a man, and a man's heart was given to it. And behold another beast, a second, like to a bear, and it raised up itself on one side, and it had three ribs in the mouth of it between the teeth of it: and they said thus unto it, Arise, devour much flesh. After this I beheld, and lo another, like a leopard, which had upon the back of it four wings of a fowl; the beast had also four heads; and dominion was given to it. After this I saw in the night visions, and behold a fourth beast, dreadful and terrible, and strong exceedingly; and it had great iron teeth: it devoured and brake in pieces, and stamped the residue with the feet of it: and it was diverse from all the beasts that were before it; and it had ten horns. I considered the horns, and, behold, there came up among them another little horn, before whom there were three of the first horns plucked up by the roots: and, behold, in this horn were eyes like the eyes of man, and a mouth speaking great things."

Numbers in scripture always have a definitive meaning. Number 1 stands for sovereignty—the number of the absolute unity of the Godhead. Two represents division and trouble. Three represents divine completion. Four is the number of the earth. Five is the number of grace. Six is the number of man; keep this in mind as we get to the number of the beast shortly. Eight is the number of new beginnings. Nine is number of judgment. Ten represents ordinal perfection and testimony. Eleven is the number of apostasy. Twelve is the number for governmental perfection and is seen in the nation Israel. Thirteen is the number of rebellion, as we enter this thirteenth chapter of Revelation, we will see rebellion on the part of mankind toward God. Now we need to realize that man placed chapter and verses into the Bible, not the original writers. While many believe God may not have inspired the division, here, isn't it striking that chapter 13 shows us the two greatest rebels who will ever be on the face of the earth? Thus God, in this spot very well, may have inspired those who broke the

Bible into chapter and verse. The political leader out of the sea and the religious leader out of the land are the two greatest rebels to ever live.

Here in Revelation 13, with the beast out of the sea, we have a symbol of the power of the world. Who will be under the control of the "prince of the world" stands in opposition to believers and Christ! During this brief time of the world's greatest sorrow, Satan will make his last great attempt to defeat the program of God! He does so by establishing his kingdom upon the earth. He does this by forming two great powers. Thus we see the revealing of the "unholy trinity."

The first is introduced here in the beginning verses of chapter 13. Two men called beast by John as they rise to power. Their reign will be vicious and cruel. They represent two movements: first, to set up a world union of nations for economic and political reason; second, to set up a world council of churches for religious reasons. Many have misidentified these two beasts. We go to the authority of God's words in the Bible to identify what is seen here. God identified them in Daniel's day. There we see God had shown that two men would rise up. They would be the heads of the opposition and hostility of Satan against the Lord Jesus Christ.

In Daniel 2, Nebuchadnezzar had a dream, which only Daniel could interpret. The king had seen a great image, the head of gold, chest and arms of silver, belly and thighs of brass, and feet of iron and clay. Daniel tells us that these are the four stages of Gentile world dominance. God had called Israel to be His chosen nation, His kingdom nation. They had rebelled against the Lord. So God scattered them throughout the world. Then He committed the government of the world to the Gentiles. We can be sure when Christ returns at the Second Advent, Israel will be converted, and the Lord will reign from Israel and more specifically Jerusalem. Gentile world power will cease. The four parts of the image in Daniel 2 are the four successive forms of Gentile power. They began with the captivity of Judah. They end at the second coming of Christ, which we see in chapter 19 of Revelation. The four forms of Gentile dominion are:

The Four Forms of Gentile Domination

1. Babylon
2. Medo-Persia
3. Greece
4. Finally, the Roman Empire

All these have oppressed God's covenant nation Israel. The two legs of the image seen in Daniel characterize the iron kingdom Rome, indicating that the Roman Empire would divide into two parts just as it later did. The two feet and the ten toes of the image illustrate a picture of the final form of the restored Roman Empire, which has taken form in the European common market nations of today.

We can see them from the old Roman Empire when they are completely formed together, when a war takes place to somehow form them into the old Roman Empire. It will be a revived Roman Empire that this beast out of the sea will rule over. That day is coming and will soon be seen! Daniel, in the vision, saw a rock—a great stone cut without hands out of a mountain, a stone that smote the image in its feet. That illustrates its final form. The rock grinds the feet to powder; the stone became a great mountain that filled the earth. Jesus is that stone—the image representing the Gentile world powers. While Israel is in dispersion, at the end of the age that is the tribulation period, the stone will come. He will destroy the oppressors of Israel and those who are tribulation saints. He will set up His kingdom!

We see this all prophesied by Daniel in Daniel 2:44–45 that says, "And in the days of these kings shall the God of heaven set up a kingdom, which shall never be destroyed: and the kingdom shall not be left to other people, but it shall break in pieces and consume all these kingdoms, and it shall stand for ever. Forasmuch as thou sawest that the stone was cut out of the mountain without hands, and that it brake in pieces the iron, the brass, the clay, the silver, and the gold; the great God hath made known to the king what shall come to pass hereafter: and the dream is certain, and the interpretation thereof sure." We then go to Daniel chapter 7, which records yet another vision to help us identify the beast described here in chapter 13 of Revelation. In this vision, Daniel saw four beasts rising in succession. The first was like a lion, the second like a bear, the third like a leopard, and the fourth was atrocious—a beast with the combination of the other three. As we see it, check to see this beast coming out of the sea as described by John.

Daniel 7:7 states, "After this I saw in the night visions, and behold a fourth beast, dreadful and terrible, and strong exceedingly; and it had great iron teeth: it devoured and brake in pieces, and stamped the residue with the feet of it: and it was diverse from all the beasts that were before it; and it had ten horns." These four beasts are the same as seen in Daniel 2 in the four parts of Nebuchadnezzar's dream. In Daniel 7, they are called the kingdoms of Babylon, Persia, Greece, and the Fourth Kingdom. Notice the beast in Daniel 7 has ten horns just as the image in Revelation 13 and just as the image in Daniel 2 had ten toes. What do we see here in this picture?

Gentile world power will run its course, under Babylon first, then the Persians, then Alexander the Great and Greece, and finally the Roman Empire, which was divided into two kingdoms. The first ended in part and ceased to be organized. The beast was thought to have died but just ceased to be dominant. The spirit of Babylon and Rome persisted, and in the great tribulation, Rome will be revived under a federation of ten nations, thus we see today the European common market nations. They will be paired down from the current number because some may have separated from one nation in the time of the writing of Revelation. The revived nation is seen in the toes of Daniel's image. As a result of battles for the territory and influence in Europe, two great powers will emerge. Here we see in Revelation 13 the leader coming to power of this federation of nations—the beast of the revived Roman Empire.

Let's look at this now in the light of Daniel's prophecy. There were to be four successive world powers, four successive stages starting with the Babylonian kingdom, the Persian, followed by Greece, and finally Rome. All this occurred just as Daniel prophesied! All came and all ceased to be at least in part! The Roman Empire was divided into two parts: Eastern and Western. Then seemingly disintegrated yet we see this in our time as Gentile world power is still ruling under republics and democracies. However, the beast that was seemingly dead will revive. In the end contest, the old Roman Empire will be the dominant force of the tribulation period.

There will be two nations that will be dominant. The other eight will have little power, represented by the eight toes. These will rebel against the Lord! Under ungodly and unholy direction from the final gentile world dictator who is seen rising here in Revelation 13:1. We will see the Antichrist, the second beast coming shortly after that. They will seek to set up an evil satanically governed union of nations. The main purpose will be to destroy the kingdom people, the nation Israel! Setting up a false messiah, the second beast who is the Antichrist, their power will be cut short by the second coming of Christ to the earth. The stone cut without hands seen in Daniel. He will crush them!

He will establish his long promised and hoped for millennial kingdom—a kingdom of peace and righteousness! This is a preview of things to come as we begin this part of Revelation. History has already proven true and has authenticated every detail to date of the prophecies in the Old Testament. Only the final formation of the ten toes must take place, and they are reasonably well in position. Then the coming of the great stone will bring an end to the chaos, horror, uncertainty, and perplexity. Revelation 13:2 says, "And the beast which I saw was like unto a leopard, and his feet were as the feet of a bear, and his mouth as the mouth of a lion: and the dragon gave him his power, and his seat, and great authority." We now see the beast coming out of the sea described by John. Understand the sea here is a symbol of the nations of the world. He will rule over nations. As we stated earlier, he will be Satan's instrument of evil. We see later in the book of Revelation what these seven heads represent a look at chapter 17 as we start with verse 9 that says, "And here is the mind which hath wisdom. The seven heads are seven mountains, on which the woman sitteth." Then we follow that with verse 12 that states, "And the ten horns which thou sawest are ten kings, which have received no kingdom as yet; but receive power as kings one hour with the beast."

Here we see in Revelation 13 the leader coming to power of this union of nations—the beast of the revived Roman Empire. The old Roman Empire's capital, the city of Rome, is known to historians as the "city of seven hills." We have a definitive identification of the place in which this beast will rule. We see Daniel in reverse here with the beast description. John saw a leopard with feet like a bear and the mouth of a lion. John reversed the order that Daniel had placed them. The reason should be evident. Daniel was at the beginning of the age of the Gentile world power. He saw Babylon, Persia, Greece, and finally Rome. John is seeing the end of Gentile world power. John is looking backward toward what has occurred. Therefore, he sees the leopard, then the bear, and the lion.

Doesn't this give a beautiful picture of perfect inspiration by the Holy Spirit—a harmony with the consistent revelation of the whole body of prophetic scripture? Remember in chapter 4, we saw the church snatched out of the world. That being seen in Section 1 the Snatching Away of the

Bride in this work. We are with Christ during this great period of the beast rising out of the nations. Satan will rise up a world dictator. This unholy trinity will succeed to a degree. Succeed for a brief time in making the nations, and the world believe that the second beast in Revelation, which we will soon see in chapter 13, is Christ. This second beast will be presented as the Jewish Messiah, the savior of the world. They will convince multitudes who have rejected Jesus Christ, that He was a fraud and imposter. The world will largely follow the advice of this first beast. They will receive the second beast (the Antichrist) as the Messiah.

We come to Revelation 13:3 that says, "And I saw one of his heads as it were wounded to death; and his deadly wound was healed: and all the world wondered after the beast." Keep in mind what these heads represent as we study. One of the heads was as it were wounded to death.

We must take this as it speaks of nations. Remember what Daniel saw earlier in the study. A stone cut without hands crushed the feet of world power, and the feet were ground to powder. Jesus is that stone. The stone cut without hands seen in Daniel. The Roman Empire lost its power and appears as dead today. But it will come back to life! Many teach that this beast physically as a man died and is brought back to life by Satan. They base this belief on Revelation 13:3 coupled with verse 8 of chapter 17 that states, "The beast that thou sawest was, and is not; and shall ascend out of the bottomless pit, and go into perdition: and they that dwell on the earth shall wonder, whose names were not written in the book of life from the foundation of the world, when they behold the beast that was, and is not, and yet is." This teaching that the beast dies and Satan raises him from the dead cannot be true.

Remember Satan is the author of death not life! God is the only one who can give life and rise from death to life. Satan doesn't have the power to give life. Satan cannot raise anyone from the dead. The Lord Jesus is the only one who can give that power. Look at John 5:21, 25, and 28–29 to see who has the power to raise the dead. We see in these verses: "For as the Father raiseth up the dead, and quickeneth them; even so the Son quickeneth whom he will. Verily, verily, I say unto you, The hour is coming, and now is, when the dead shall hear the voice of the Son of God: and they that hear shall live. Marvel not at this: for the hour is coming, in the which all that are in the graves shall hear his voice, And shall come forth; they that have done good, unto the resurrection of life; and they that have done evil, unto the resurrection of damnation." Only the Lord can rise from the dead, Satan cannot. We need to understand the beast is not just a man.

That beast represents a union of nations. Gentile world power will run its course! They will spring out of the old Roman Empire. The Roman Empire for almost nine hundred years was the greatest power on earth, and no man could reckon with it! The Roman Empire was divided into two kingdoms as was stated earlier in this chapter. The first ended in part and ceased to be organized. The beast was thought to have died but just ceased to be dominant. The spirit of Babylon and Rome persisted.

In the great tribulation, Rome will be revived under a federation of ten nations, thus we see today the European common market. Scripture declares that it would be wounded to death. But here we see Rome, the nation, coming back to life as the final world power. With a dictator who will be satanically influenced, and I believe demon possessed. Satan will bring this evil nation back to power under a central figurehead who will be this beast out of the sea. The old Roman Empire has not died. It remains in the nations of Europe today. The Roman Empire will be revitalized! It will be made a world power under the influence of the unholy trinity. The beast of the revived Roman Empire is seen here in chapter 13.

We see 2 Thessalonians 2:11, which will come into play and be fulfilled, that says, "And for this cause God shall send them strong delusion, that they should believe a lie." They have rejected the truth about Jesus and His resurrection. The majority of the people of this time will follow the beast and the Antichrist, which we see later. This beast will carry many characteristics. Great delusions and lies follow him. Daniel 11 describes him in verses 36–39, which states, "And the king shall do according to his will; and he shall exalt himself, and magnify himself above every god, and shall speak marvellous things against the God of gods, and shall prosper till the indignation be accomplished: for that that is determined shall be done. Neither shall he regard the God of his fathers, nor the desire of women, nor regard any god: for he shall magnify himself above all. But in his estate shall he honour the God of forces: and a god whom his fathers knew not shall he honour with gold, and silver, and with precious stones, and pleasant things. Thus shall he do in the most strong holds with a strange god, whom he shall acknowledge and increase with glory: and he shall cause them to rule over many, and shall divide the land for gain."

Notice he will exalt himself and do things his way. He will not regard any god but magnify himself above all gods—sounds just like Satan's fall, doesn't it! He will prosper until the indignation is accomplished. He will not regard the God of his father nor will he have a desire for women. This I take as he will have a desire for men instead of women. He will magnify himself above all gods. He honors Satan, the god of forces. This is the beast we see here in the beginning of chapter 13. The Roman Empire will spring back into existence under the cruel hand of this beast. He will be as no other dictator has been. He will show a resurrection of which is faked because that is the lie people have believed. A gullible world will respond! Those who rejected Christ will finally be taken in by this great deceiver. We first saw him in chapter 6 on the white horse, he comes preaching peace. He comes in a false platform bringing peace. Sounds a lot like our presidential candidates! That will be what the world is looking for amid the chaos of all the people who have disappeared.

We pick up now with verse 4 and more on this beast as it is called. Revelation 13:4 says, "And they worshipped the dragon which gave power unto the beast: and they worshipped the beast, saying, Who is like unto the beast? who is able to make war with him?" The people of that time will worship the dragon, Satan worship will be the religion of choice. After the believers of this age have been snatched away, he will rule over nations. Keep in mind there will be an unholy trinity formed. As we saw, the dragon is the head and is worshipped. The beast out of the sea will be the dictator of nearly all the world.

The second beast we will see in a few more verses. They have a goal, and that is destruction of all the tribulation saints. They want to dethrone Christ! The first beast carried the name of blasphemy definitely the enemy of Christ, Israel, and the tribulation saints. This is the supreme moment for Satan! His desire was to be exalted above God and heaven. Remember in Isaiah 14:12–15, we see Satan's desire, his fall. It states, "How art thou fallen from heaven, O Lucifer, son of the morning! how art thou cut down to the ground, which didst weaken the nations! For thou hast said in thine heart, I will ascend into heaven, I will exalt my throne above the stars of God: I will sit also upon the mount of the congregation, in the sides of the north: I will ascend above the heights of the clouds; I will be like the most High. Yet thou shalt be brought down to hell, to the sides of the pit."

Notice when he is cut to the earth, we saw in chapter 12 of Revelation, he weakens the nations. His sin was to have pride in his heart and say, "I will ascend into heaven. I will exalt my throne above the stars of God. I will sit also upon the mountain of the congregation in the sides of the North. I will be like the Most High!" Here in chapter 13, he is being worshipped by the world, saying who is like the beast! Who is able to make war against him? Notice they are expecting peace, but he will bring destruction. What a mockery on the worship of the true God! They say, "Look, who we are worshipping. He is someone glorious! He is much more glorious than anything the Bible offered as a God! They will soon seal their doom for eternity."

We see in Revelation 13:5 the length of his rule, which says, "And there was given unto him a mouth speaking great things and blasphemies; and power was given unto him to continue forty and two months." He is a great orator. He speaks blasphemes. Mankind will be enthralled at his masterly intelligence, accepting the concept that only with an imperial form of government in place will the world survive. This is the way to establish endless peace on earth. They will readily accept this deception. In so doing, they begin to worship the dragon that gave him his power and reverence to the beast himself. In his pride and obsession, he will speak blasphemy, speaking great blasphemies against God and Christ. He will consider himself a man of destiny of which no power on earth, or human or divine, can overthrow him. But God, whom he denies, has limited his authority because the power will be given to him for just forty-two months that is the last three and one half years of the great tribulation—the last three and one half years of Daniel's seventieth week.

He will be in authority over the prophetic earth. As we see, he speaks his blasphemous words—blasphemy against God, blasphemy in the temple in Israel! "Setting up the abomination which maketh desolate" spoken of by Daniel. Daniel 9:27 says, "And he shall confirm the covenant with many for one week: and in the midst of the week he shall cause the sacrifice and the oblation to cease, and for the overspreading of abominations he shall make it desolate, even until the consummation, and that determined shall be poured upon the desolate." For a brief time in making, the nations and the world believe that the second beast in Revelation 13 is Christ. The good news for mankind is that it is only for forty-two months! We glean from this that we need to do as John tells us in 1 John 4:1, which states, "Beloved, believe not every spirit, but try the spirits whether they are of God: because many false prophets are gone out into the world." This beast and his allies will be false prophets. This dictator will have charisma. He will be able to deceive those who have rejected Christ.

We come to Revelation 13:6–7, "And he opened his mouth in blasphemy against God, to blaspheme his name, and his tabernacle, and them that dwell in heaven. And it was given unto him to make war with the saints, and to overcome them: and power was given him over all kindreds, and tongues, and nations." We see further how much he is against Christ and His people.

The church has been snatched away (i.e. rapture). Yet we see there are saints, saved people living after the rapture. People who receive Christ after the church has been snatched away. The church is safe in heaven with Christ. The saints of the tribulation will be overcome by the beast. They will suffer great persecution! You know how we can know we aren't in the tribulation right now? Because we aren't under this great persecution many who claim to be Christians today would fall away under the great persecution that is coming in this time. Under God's will, many believers in the tribulation will become martyrs. Both Jew and Gentile will suffer together. He has power of all nations—all peoples and kindred. All tongues and all nations will be subject to him.

He is a global dictator; all the unreached peoples of the world are subject to him. Revelation 13:8 says, "And all that dwell upon the earth shall worship him, whose names are not written in the book of life of the Lamb slain from the foundation of the world. All that dwell on the earth worship him!" Notice too that has a limit. It is limited to the unsaved, those not written in the Lamb's book of life. Those who don't belong to Jesus Christ who became the propitiation for the sins of the whole world, and those who have accepted Him as their payment for sin will not worship the beast or Satan! This will be the darkest time in the history of the world. We need to be thankful that we will not be going through this time. We will not be under the rule of this beast. We are under Christ! We really need not be concerned about who the beast is. We need to be looking for

Christ's return! We need to be telling unbelievers about Christ! We need to be winning souls! Gaining rewards of intrinsic value, letting the Holy Spirit lead our lives!

The warning comes in Revelation 13:9–10 that says, "If any man have an ear, let him hear. He that leadeth into captivity shall go into captivity: he that killeth with the sword must be killed with the sword. Here is the patience and the faith of the saints." This is an awesome warning, probably one of the most awesome statements in God's Word! A gullible world will not respond to it, those who rejected Christ will finally be taken in by this great deceiver. But those who belong to Christ will see the truth. They will have ears, and they will hear the Holy Spirit! The warning is repeated several times in God's Word. Romans 10:17 states, "So then faith cometh by hearing, and hearing by the word of God."

The first chapters of Revelation say, "If any man have an ear let Him hear what the Spirit saith to the churches." Almost everyone has ears to hear, people in every age have heard the gospel presented. Many will not listen! They do not hear! As believers, we need to be studying God's Word and warning those around us of the pending time, which is coming. He that leads into captivity shall go into captivity. The doom of the beast is the lake of fire. We need to be leading folks away from captivity, leading folks so they don't end up in this period of time. Leading folks so they don't suffer the second death, but that have eternal life. John here is speaking to those who are saved during the tribulation period. Remember that the world will be deceived by this dictator. People will not be able to buy or sell without his permission! They will need a travel visa like Hitler issued in Germany. He will rule the world as no one has ever ruled the world.

God is talking to those who are His own in the world. "Don't fight him." To begin with it will not do any good. Second the "patience of the saints" of that time, the trial of their faith, with these awful trials that will come upon them. God will not have His Spirit holding back evil. Satan will be fully in control of the world at this time. At least to a point, he can't touch the 144,000 sealed at the beginning. When the Holy Spirit is removed, then evil will be permitted to have its day! Satan will have full authority on the earth. The devil and his evil minions, as well as the lost of that age, will never be able to say, "You never gave us a chance. If you had just given us a chance, we would have been able to work things out." God is going to give them a chance for a brief period of time. Matthew 24:22 states, "And except those days should be shortened, there should no flesh be saved: but for the elect's sake those days shall be shortened."

If God gave more time "there should no flesh be saved" John stated here by the inspiration of the Holy Spirit. But God does set the time, three and one half years and the destruction is great in that short period.

5

Antichrist Comes Forth

We pick up now with verse 11 and another beast as it is stated. Revelation 13:11 states, "And I beheld another beast coming up out of the earth; and he had two horns like a lamb, and he spake as a dragon." This beast comes up out of the earth. Remember the first beast came out of the sea, which represented the nations of the world.

The first beast came out of the sea or the Gentile nations. Since we see in this passage a contrast between the sea and earth then we can conclude that this means there must be something significant that the earth represents here in this verse. The earth is symbolic of the Jews as a nation. Now the unholy trinity is formed. The beast out of the sea will be the dictator of nearly all the world. This second beast will come as the Jewish Messiah, the false prophet of Israel, the Antichrist or opposite to Christ.

Jesus, the true Christ, is the incarnation of God Himself. Jesus is called the True and Faithful witness. The devil, the enemy of Christ and God, will produce a false witness. He will be the false Christ—the Antichrist, the son of perdition, the deceitful and bloody man. The false prophet, we see him in the Old Testament. As we have seen Isaac as the type of Christ so too we see this Antichrist in types throughout the Old Testament starting in Genesis 10 with Nimrod a rebellious leader after the flood. Genesis

10:8–14 says, "And Cush begat Nimrod: he began to be a mighty one in the earth. He was a mighty hunter before the Lord: wherefore it is said, Even as Nimrod the mighty hunter before the Lord. And the beginning of his kingdom was Babel, and Erech, and Accad, and Calneh, in the land of Shinar. Out of that land went forth Asshur, and builded Nineveh, and the city Rehoboth, and Calah, And Resen between Nineveh and Calah: the same is a great city. And Mizraim begat Ludim, and Anamim, and Lehabim, and Naphtuhim, And Pathrusim, and Casluhim, (out of whom came Philistim,) and Caphtorim."

Genesis 11:1–9 states, "And the whole earth was of one language, and of one speech. And it came to pass, as they journeyed from the east, that they found a plain in the land of Shinar; and they dwelt there. And they said one to another, Go to, let us make brick, and burn them thoroughly. And they had brick for stone, and slime had they for morter. And they said, Go to, let us build us a city and a tower, whose top may reach unto heaven; and let us make us a name, lest we be scattered abroad upon the face of the whole earth. And the Lord came down to see the city and the tower, which the children of men builded. And the Lord said, Behold, the people is one, and they have all one language; and this they begin to do: and now nothing will be restrained from them, which they have imagined to do. Go to, let us go down, and there confound their language, that they may not understand one another's speech. So the Lord scattered them abroad from thence upon the face of all the earth: and they left off to build the city. Therefore is the name of it called Babel; because the Lord did there confound the language of all the earth: and from thence did the Lord scatter them abroad upon the face of all the earth."

In pharaoh, the persecutor of the Jews; in Haman, the hater of the Jews—we see these types of the coming superman and religious dictator throughout scripture. We see him in Judas Iscariot. Satan's first attempt to produce this superman was at the first coming of Christ but failed. Just before the second coming of Christ, Satan will make his greatest attempt to set up this superman in opposition to the true Christ of God, Jesus. We can see that, since we have a first and second coming of Jesus the true Christ! Also we see a first (Judas) and second coming (the beast out of the earth) of the Antichrist. Was Judas a type of the Antichrist? We can look at the evidence. He speaks blasphemes. This is according to Dr. M.R. De

Haan. Let us see if we can determine this or if we will disagree with Dr. De Haan. "Judas is not the Antichrist as some want to portray him but he is a distinct type." Here are some scriptures to consider.

John 17:12 states, "While I was with them in the world, I kept them in thy name: those that thou gavest me I have kept, and none of them is lost, but the son of perdition; that the scripture might be fulfilled." Notice what Judas is called: the "son of perdition." Then we see Paul in 2 Thessalonians 2:3, which says, "Let no man deceive you by any means: for that day shall not come, except there come a falling away first, and that man of sin be revealed, the son of perdition." Notice both these verses have the term the "son of perdition" used in them.

The first instance is applied to Judas, the second to the Antichrist. Dr. De Haan says, "Surely, here, is a close association. They are the same. They are called the same." Notice another verse concerning Judas. We see in Luke 22:3, which says, "Then entered Satan into Judas surnamed Iscariot, being of the number of the twelve." This is the only place we see that states that Satan entered into a man. We can find many, which state a demon entered a human. But this speaks of Satan personally as the prince of demons, taking up his temporary abode in Judas. Dr. De Haan states, "The argument is still more conclusive by the statement in the gospel according to John."

We see John 6:70, which says, "Jesus answered them, Have not I chosen you twelve, and one of you is a devil?" Judas is called "devil" not a "demon." Dr. De Haan says the original verse is translated "one of you is devil." The Greek diabolis refers to the devil and Satan. Jesus does not say that Judas is a demon but devil. Judas then was a type of Antichrist. The Antichrist coming out of the Jews that is the earth he will be the imitation of the true Christ. He will come in fulfillment of prophecy. He will claim to be Messiah. Israel will not accept him if he didn't come from the Jewish race out of Israel. This beast will be false prophets. He will come out from the Jews. He will be able to deceive those who have rejected Christ.

We see too that "he had two horns like a lamb." We see an imitation of Christ in this symbol. The first beast is opposed to Christ and therefore Antichrist. The second beast imitates Christ, he too is Antichrist. Consider anti as being instead of therefore he poses as Christ. Both oppose Christ! He has two horns as a lamb, but he is a wolf in sheep's clothing! He imitates the Lamb of God, "which taketh away the sins of the world," as John 1:29 states. This beast is a fake lamb, which cannot take away sin! He adds and multiplies sin in the world. He does not come to do his own will but to do the will of the first beast. He is a counterfeit Christ! As the first beast comes speaking of peace, this one will come speaking of loving everyone! Underneath he is a dangerous beast, just like the first one, deceiving the world! Jesus warned of false prophets in Matthew 7:15, which says, "Beware of false prophets, which come to you in sheep's clothing, but inwardly they are ravening wolves."

This second beast is the example of all false prophets. He is Antichrist! It takes two men to fulfill the position Christ fills. Yet they cannot fill them, but Satan needs two men in an attempt even an imitation of Jesus. We see more on what the Lord Jesus Christ taught concerning these false ones in Matthew 24:24, which states, "For there shall arise false Christs, and false prophets, and shall shew great signs and wonders; insomuch that, if it were possible, they shall deceive the very elect."

The false prophet does like John the Baptist, he steers people to the first beast. He speaks as a dragon, he carries Satan's message. Under the name of religion, he will deceive the souls of mankind. He gives forth those false doctrines and cruel decrees, which show him to belong to the dragon and not to the Lamb. We see next verse 12 of Revelation 13, which says, "And he exerciseth all the power of the first beast before him, and causeth the earth and them which dwell therein to worship the first beast, whose deadly wound was healed." He has delegated authority from the first beast. Thus he is a servant to the first. He promotes the same interest, pursues the same design in substance, which is to influence men to change from worshipping the true God to worshipping those who are not gods. He influences a gullible world which he works to influence to subject their souls and conscience to the will and authority of men bringing them into opposition to the will of God. But those who belong to Christ will see the truth. They will have ears, and they will hear the Holy Spirit. This false prophet will offer the world something new to worship.

The first beast, the evil dictator, the man of sin, the second beast is presented to us! He will exalt the first beast to a place of worship. He will exalt Satan to a place of worship. The deadly wound healed, thus the revived Roman Empire comes to power, with the same power and authority of the former empire. This time having the support of the one who in Israel claims to be their Messiah and yet he will be influencing them to worship the beast, influencing Satan's worship. Do you remember when Jesus was in the wilderness? Satan came and tempted Him. We see Matthew 4:8–9 that says, "Again, the devil taketh him up into an exceeding high mountain, and sheweth him all the kingdoms of the world, and the glory of them; And saith unto him, All these things will I give thee, if thou wilt fall down and worship me."

Christ told Satan in Matthew 4:10, "Then saith Jesus unto him, Get thee hence, Satan: for it is written, Thou shalt worship the Lord thy God, and him only shalt thou serve." Here we see this false one and the first beast receive what Satan promised to Jesus. They have all the kingdoms of the world in their power. They are falling down and worshipping Satan, and he is giving them the world. Notice from this, Satan had the authority to give the kingdoms of the world to Jesus. Jesus rejected the offer these men will not!

We pick up now with verse 13 and another beast which it is called. Revelation 13:13 says, "And he doeth great wonders, so that he maketh fire come down from heaven on the earth in the sight of men." This beast comes up out of the earth; he performs great wonders, to give acceptable proof to mankind of the beast title before them. Compare 2 Thessalonians 2:1–17. He deceives the dwellers on earth by his miracles, causing them set up an image to him. This image he gives breath to, that it speaks and causes those to be killed who do not worship it. Thus possibly a demon takes up residence in this image.

The Antichrist or opposition to Christ will continue his reign of terror for three and one half years. Notice the resemblance to Judas in this, Judas a type of the Antichrist. Notice how Judas typifies the Antichrist. The antichrist will preside over the worship of the false kingdom. Judas was one of Christ's disciples and treasurer of the company. Satan entered him and he became the devil's son. The Antichrist also will come with a message of peace, but he will betray his friends. Judas served with Christ for three and one half years, the reign of Antichrist will be three and one half years. Judas was an apostle, and from indications in scripture, he performed wonders and miracles, just as we see Antichrist perform wonders and miracles here in verse 13.

Judas worshipped idols, he was an idolater. The Antichrist too is an idolater. Scripture tells us every covetous man is an idolater. Ephesians 5:5 says, "For this ye know, that no whoremonger, nor unclean person, nor covetous man, who is an idolater, hath any inheritance in the kingdom of Christ and of God." The Antichrist will be a great idolater. Jesus gave signs to those who followed him to the garden in Matthew 26:48. The Antichrist, as we see shortly, will institute the mark of the beast, making all on earth take the sign or be put to death. Isn't this too a striking type many other resemblances could be found. After three and one half years when the nations of the earth, deceived by Satan, will gather together for the great battle of Armageddon, the heavens will suddenly open as we see in Revelation 19:11. The true King, the King of kings and Lord of lords, will descend. He will destroy those armies, the beast and false prophet will be cast into the lake of fire.

Satan, who indwelt the man of sin, will be cast into the bottomless pit, loosed after the millennial kingdom has been complete. Satan will muster an army of nations, one last opportunity to deceive the nations. This is what we see here in chapter 13—a perfect harmony with all the deception and lying wonders. We see Revelation 13:14 that states, "And deceiveth them that dwell on the earth by the means of those miracles which he had power to do in the sight of the beast; saying to them that dwell on the earth, that they should make an image to the beast, which had the wound by a sword, and did live." This false prophet is a miracle worker.

Matthew 24:24 states, "For there shall arise false Christs, and false prophets, and shall shew great signs and wonders; insomuch that, if it were possible, they shall deceive the very elect." Jesus warned against this false prophet. He mimics Elijah in bringing fire down from heaven. He is like Jannes and Jambres in Exodus 7:11–12. They were clever magicians. They had satanic power, so too will the Antichrist. The world is taken in by his deception with the exception of the elect. Those who are Christ cannot be deceived.

The false prophet shows his hand when he causes them to make an image to the beast. The big production is a likeness of the first beast. It emphasizes the deadly wound that was healed. Isn't it interesting that Jesus did not allow anything connected with his physical appearance to survive? That way, no one could worship His image! They must worship

Him in spirit and in truth. Yet the likeness of Antichrist will be placed in the temple in Jerusalem. "That will be the abomination that maketh desolate," spoken of by Daniel.

Jesus referred to this in Matthew 24:15. This image is the abomination that makes desolate set up in the temple in Jerusalem. The image of the first beast out of the sea, the function to which this beast out of the earth devotes himself is religious, not secular. We see Revelation 13:15–17 that says, "And he had power to give life unto the image of the beast, that the image of the beast should both speak, and cause that as many as would not worship the image of the beast should be killed. And he causeth all, both small and great, rich and poor, free and bond, to receive a mark in their right hand, or in their foreheads: And that no man might buy or sell, save he that had the mark, or the name of the beast, or the number of his name."

We see life given to the image by this second beast. I wonder if this is a sort of computerized robotic image, not your usual statue or idol but a modern version with computer and operating system. Isaiah and all the prophets made it clear idols cannot speak. Paul mentioned it too! But here the idol can speak. That gives us two choices: it is an idol made of metal and or stone, or it is a robot with a computer controlling it. This image is something that will influence the whole world to turn and worship the beast. He is in partnership with business and religion. Notice the cleverness of this plot!

This second beast comes out of the land where the prophets announced Christ would be born. Many believe this Antichrist is from the tribe of Dan. The Danites were given to idolatry. We must compare scripture and let it show us what it says. Matthew 24:15–20 says, "When ye therefore shall see the abomination of desolation, spoken of by Daniel the prophet, stand in the holy place, (whoso readeth, let him understand:) 16 Then let them which be in Judaea flee into the mountains: Let him which is on the housetop not come down to take any thing out of his house: Neither let him which is in the field return back to take his clothes. And woe unto them that are with child, and to them that give suck in those days! But pray ye that your flight be not in the winter, neither on the Sabbath day." What does the Word say to us here?

Notice the deception of this beast. Underneath he is a dangerous beast, just like the first one, deceiving the world. Don't we see in our world today people are seeking an authoritative religious leader who makes them feel good and not bad about sin? They want an authoritative religious leader. When we are in an age of doubt and uncertainty, people are longing for someone who can speak a final word on all the ethical, religious, and political questions that trouble folks today. The world will turn away from Christ and God. Look around, it is happening today, isn't it? They will stretch out open arms to accept the false. He steers people to the first beast, welcoming this man of sin. He will be on time. God's Word says he will arrive on earth just when God says he will!

Just as it says, Christ will return first in the air for His church and then later to set up His kingdom. In the meantime, the great false church of evil does away with every truth of scripture. Have you noticed today, the throngs turning from churches that teach the true Word of God, Churches where the pastor won't step on toes? Churches that call sin what it is sin. They are turning to liars as 1 John 2:22 that states, "Who is a liar but he that denieth that Jesus is the Christ? He is antichrist that denieth the Father and the Son." People are seeking pastors to tickle their ears. One of the signs that we are close to this period today is the unhealthy craving for marvels and wonders. It is a most dangerous condition of the mind. Christians might very well beware of anything of the kind! We are too near the end of this age to expect divine miracles in great numbers.

Satanic signs and wonders will increase and are on the rise currently. When Antichrist himself will appear, he will give to mankind all the wonders and signs that they seek, only deceiving them, leading them to accept his ungodly affection. His coming will be the culmination of apostasy. The signal for all believer's Gentile and Jews of the tribulation, who are under great persecution, to hold on fast to the Lord Jesus Christ! To flee from Jerusalem, hiding themselves as best they can in distant areas of their countries until the appearing of the Lord Jesus!

We finish Revelation 13:18, which says, "Here is wisdom. Let him that hath understanding count the number of the beast: for it is the number of a man; and his number is Six hundred threescore and six." We have here the number for the beast. We are to count the number of the beast here in Revelation 13:18, which contain the number of man. Man's number is 6 for on the sixth day man was created. E.W. Bullinger is considered by many to be an authority on numbers, so we look to his book. "When the name of Antichrist is known, its gematria will doubtless be found to be the number 666.

Gematria is an Assyro-Babylonian system of numerology later adopted by Jews and Greeks that assigns numerical value to a word or phrase in the belief that words or phrases with identical numerical values bear some relation to each other or bear some relation to the number itself as it may apply to a person's age, the calendar year, or the like. The number 666 has, we believe, a far deeper reference to and connection with the secret mysteries of the ancient religions, which will be again manifested in connection with the last great apostasy. Many names may be found, the numerical value of whose letters amounts to 666. Gematria is not a means by which the name is to be discovered; but it will be a test and a proof by which the name may be identified after the person is revealed.

If six is the number of secular or human perfection, then 66 is a more emphatic expression of the same fact, and 666 is the concentrated expression of it. The number 666 is therefore the trinity of human perfection; the perfection of imperfection; the culmination of human pride in independence of God and opposition to His Christ. The number 666 was the secret symbol of the ancient pagan mysteries connected with the worship of the devil. It is today the secret connecting link between those ancient mysteries and their modern revival in spiritualism. Apostasy is before us. The religion of Christ has, in the past, been opposed and corrupted. But when it once comes, as it has come in our day to be mocked, there is nothing left but judgment. Roman numerals have been used in many things such as movies released. These are significant here too! Look at the Roman numerals and what they equal.

Roman Numerals

1. D=500
2. C=100
3. L=50
4. X=10
5. V=5
6. I=1

If you add those, what is the number you get? 500 + 100 = 600 + 50 = 650 + 10 = 660 + 5 + 1 = 666. So even in this, we have the Roman Empire and its use of their alphabet and numbers. The M appears to have been merely two D's." (End of E.W. Bullinger's excerpt.)

What this mark is we may not know, but with technology as it is today, we can see many things it could be. The beast will be a man who claims to be God. Three 6's imply that he is a false God and a deceiver. He is what the Jews called Christ! He is a mere man either possessed by a demon or at times possessed by Satan himself. He will reach the highest peak of power and wisdom. But He will still be merely a man, yet mighty wonders and so great his wisdom this superman shows to the world! That mankind will believe that he is god and that many Jews will believe him to be their Messiah! But remember his number shows him to be a mere man! Six is the number of mankind. With this warning, we must conclude many will not be deceived. Many will faithfully refuse and remain or become faithful to God.

We see in chapter 14 the 144,000 Jewish witnesses appearing after this incident. They refuse to worship the beast because they understand that his number is the number of mankind. We need to be busy in this age witnessing to others about the Lord Jesus because we see this time coming and don't want to see others go through this great tribulation.

6

A Third Pause in Judgment

We come now to Revelation chapter 14. This chapter changes scenes and contains several events, which we will see. It is as if Christ said, "You see the evil now, let me give you an interlude from the destruction and evil." We see the Lamb on Mount Zion in this chapter. We hear a proclamation of the everlasting gospel—the pronouncement of judgment upon Babylon and those who receive the mark of the beast. We see those who have died for the cause of Christ in the tribulation receiving praise. We see a preview of Armageddon. We see certain participants in this chapter. We have just seen the darkest days of mankind in chapter 13—the most horrible time in the history of the world.

The question might have come to mind: how did God's people fare during this period? Did they remain faithful to the Lord through this period of overwhelming odds against them? We see in chapter 14 the answer to that and other questions. The shepherd who began with the 144,000 sheep is identified with them, something to notice which answers the question. He doesn't have 143,999. He still has the 144,000! Not one was lost! He redeemed them all! They had been sealed and remained sealed!

Thus we see once saved, always saved in this chapter because He is the Great Shepherd! He brought them through the great tribulation. That is how chapter 14 opens. This should encourage us as to our eternal security.

We see too that the Lamb, the Lord Jesus Christ, has the last Word, not the two beasts and Satan. He is not a lamb, which speaks like a dragon; He is the Lord Jesus Christ! With Him having the last Word, Babylon will fall—the great political capital, the great commercial center of that time! The great religious capital of the world during the great tribulation will fall! As will the followers of the beasts, they all will be judged!

Many believers in the tribulation will become martyrs but won't lose. They will win in the end! We pick up now with verse 1 of chapter 14. Revelation 14:1 says, "And I looked, and, lo, a Lamb stood on the mount Sion, and with him an hundred forty and four thousand, having his Father's name written in their foreheads." We come back to the Lamb, the Lord Jesus, and see Him standing on Mount Zion. This means He is not in heaven but is on earth in Jerusalem. The vision John sees confirms a fact to us. An event that takes place after Israel had been desolated. Yet the desolation will end!

The glory of the dawning in the land where Jesus had been rejected in His first Advent where he had died and rose from the grave is coming. He is going to return, that is the gospel. We see a peaceful scene here beginning in chapter 14. The evil was so intense we get a break from it. We see a peaceful scene in this. We see a glimpse of the millennial kingdom here. The Lord Jesus is going to reign from Jerusalem in the land of Israel! He is going to reign in Jerusalem! Upon David's throne just as prophecy tells us, this is a glimpse of the fulfillment of Psalm 2:6, which states, "Yet have I set my king upon my holy hill of Zion." The Father has every intention to fulfill that scripture, to place Jesus on the throne of David in Jerusalem and specifically at Mount Zion.

We see the 144,000 who were sealed in chapter 7. Remember there were twelve thousand from twelve tribes? We were told they were sealed in Revelation 7:3, which says, "Saying, Hurt not the earth, neither the sea, nor the trees, till we have sealed the servants of our God in their foreheads." We weren't told then how they were sealed, but we see now. Here in Revelation 14:1, we see the final statement that states, "Having his Father's name written in their foreheads." This shows us these are, in fact, that very same 144,000. Notice they have a mark on their foreheads but not the number of the beast, which we saw last chapter as 666! They have the name of God the Father on theirs, they are both sealed and in the presence of the Lamb. These 144,000 are the ones who were to preach the gospel. The result of which we have seen a great multitude of Gentile believers from every tribe, tongue, and nation were saved. They will be very effective evangelist in that day.

We see next Revelation 14:2, that says, "And I heard a voice from heaven, as the voice of many waters, and as the voice of a great thunder: and I heard the voice of harpers harping with their harps." John hears a voice from heaven as He sees the Lord Jesus on Mount Zion. Notice how loud they are singing, the sweetness of the sound, melodious music as the sound of well-skilled harpers, playing their harps. It is the music that is ever in God's presence, not the music of angels only or glorified saints or a redeemed creation. Most probably, it is that of all them together. You and I will be a part of the singing more than likely. We see what they are singing in Revelation 14:3 that says, "And they sung as it were a new song before the throne, and before the four beasts, and the elders: and no man could learn that song but the hundred and forty and four thousand, which were redeemed from the earth."

It's a new song. I have spoken with many from several sects who tell me that only the 144,000 will sing the new song and that the 144,000 already know that song. Notice it says here in verse 3 that only the 144,000 could learn it, one sect will tell you that only those who know the new song will be in heaven. Yet here we see these are on earth, and the voice from heaven was heard as harps. The 144,000 learn the new song and join in chorus with the voices from heaven. God has His harpers in heaven while the 144,000 are on the earth. They are on Mount Zion. The 144,000 were redeemed from the earth we are told. They have been purchased to enter the millennium upon the earth. Notice they are not taken into heaven. This is a picture of the millennial kingdom upon the earth. These will live with Christ on the earth.

The unsaved of the tribulation will not be living on earth, they will face judgment! We learn more about the 144,000 in Revelation 14:4–5 as we see, which says, "These are they which were not defiled with women; for they are virgins. These are they which follow the Lamb whithersoever he goeth. These were redeemed from among men, being the first fruits unto God and to the Lamb. And in their mouth was found no guile: for they are without fault before the throne of God."

Notice the life they live and how we are told about their character. They are described by their chastity and purity. They are virgins! They had not defiled themselves either with corporal or spiritual adultery. They had kept themselves clean from the abominations of the anti-Christian generation. That is the spiritual interpretation. Can this have a literal meaning as well? Remember the great tribulation is a period of great suffering. These 144,000 men have been through that period. This is an abnormal time, and so the abnormal occurs. Remember the beast is said to have no natural affection for women. These 144,000 have affection but are said not to be defiled by women.

By their loyalty and steadfast adherence to Christ, they follow the Lamb wherever He leads them. Where He goes, they follow the conduct of his Word, Spirit, and direction! Leaving it to Him to lead them into whatever duties and difficulties He leads! During the tribulation and the great tribulation, as we have seen, things are going to be evil and corrupt. It will be wise for them not to marry. In Jeremiah's time, there was great tribulation. We can look at what he was told in Jeremiah 16:1–4, which states, "The word of the Lord came also unto me, saying, Thou shalt not take thee a wife, neither shalt thou have sons or daughters in this place. For thus saith the Lord concerning the sons and concerning the daughters that are born in this place, and concerning their mothers that bare them, and concerning their fathers that begat them in this land; They shall die of grievous deaths; they shall not be lamented; neither shall they be buried; but they shall be as dung upon the face of the earth: and they shall be consumed by the sword, and by famine; and their carcases shall be meat for the fowls of heaven, and for the beasts of the earth." Jeremiah was told not to marry!

The time of the Babylonian captivity was upon Israel and Judea. Because of the wretched days of that period, God forbade Jeremiah to marry. Also we see the 144,000 are virgins; they will not marry! That would let a few of those sects who believe only the 144,000 out of this mix also, for many are married. We see too what Jesus warned in Matthew 24:19, which says, "And woe unto them that are with child, and to them that give suck in those days!" It used to be that marriage was honorable and encouraged. Today we see quite the opposite. In Noah's day, it is said they were marrying and giving in marriage. Christ said when He returns, it will be as it was in the days of Noah. We see again this time in Matthew 24:37–38, which states, "But as the days of Noah were, so shall also the coming of the Son of man be. For as in the days that were before the flood they were eating and drinking, marrying and giving in marriage, until the day that Noe entered into the ark."

To see Noah's time, we see Genesis 6:5 that says, "And God saw that the wickedness of man was great in the earth, and that every imagination of the thoughts of his heart was only evil continually." We can see that there is spiritual and literal meaning to their being not defiled! As we see right now, so too will the great tribulation be a great emphasis upon sex. Immorality will prevail! As we saw of the beast, he will not desire women, but as we said, we believe he will have a desire for men. The 144,000 will have kept themselves from the immorality of the great tribulation.

Let's look a little further at this and consider spiritual immorality. Spiritual fornication, as it is called, Ezekiel 6 shows the gross spiritual state of Israel. They had gone into idolatry. The 144,000 will not have bowed themselves to the beast. They had not worshipped him or his image. They remained true to the God who had sealed them! They are found chaste both spiritually and literally so that they are able to do the work of the Lord and are under His protection. We see in verse 5 in them was found no guile. Their words are sincere! No deceit or hypocrisy! They are just the opposite of the two beasts of the tribulation. God's people should always be polar opposites of the world. These 144,000 did not participate in the lie of the beast, when he used his lying wonders. Remember Jesus said the beast words and wonders would be so great an influence that if it were possible even the elect would be deceived.

Here we see these weren't deceived but remained faithful through it all. What an example for us to follow, what a great testimony they will have. Shouldn't we also have that type of testimony! With this interlude, we must conclude many will not be deceived by the beast and false prophet. Many will faithfully refuse and be unfaithful to God. We see in chapter 14 the 144,000 Jewish witnesses appearing. They have refused to worship the beast because they understand that his number is the number of mankind.

We come now to Revelation 14:6 that states, "And I saw another angel fly in the midst of heaven, having the everlasting gospel to preach unto them that dwell on the earth, and to every nation, and kindred, and tongue, and people, we see now a scene from Heaven an Angel flying in the midst of Heaven." This vision represents the spread of the gospel. In other words, the everlasting gospel is the same gospel that has always been proclaimed from the very beginning. It is the good news of all ages, showing us that God is sovereign, and man's happiness consists in recognizing His authority, not that of the beasts and Satan—the gospel of the grace of God as we see in our age most especially. The gospel of the kingdom is just another aspect of the everlasting gospel—the emphasis from heaven, showing the lordship of Jesus Christ!

There can be only one gospel! The apostle Paul emphasizes that in Galatians 1:8, which says, "But though we, or an angel from heaven, preach any other gospel unto you than that which we have preached unto you, let him be accursed." That one gospel has different phases. In

Galatians, for instance, Paul talks about it being a "gospel of the circumcision" and a "gospel of the uncircumcision." John the Baptist and Jesus preached of the gospel of the kingdom. It was rejected by the Jewish people as a whole. The kingdom was set aside for a time. Thus we have the day of the church and the preaching of salvation by grace through faith, and that is the gospel, the everlasting gospel.

The Son of Man is like a man who went into a far country to receive a kingdom for himself. He will return to earth one day, someday. When the Word is given by the Father, the Son will descend to take His kingdom. To be proclaimed the King of kings and Lord of lords! In our age, the church age or the age of grace, He is by the Holy Spirit calling out from among Jew and Gentile, all who believe on the name of Jesus Christ—making them all one in unity as the body of Christ, the church, the bride of Christ. Not one will be left behind who has trusted in Christ in this church age. When we have been snatched away, then God will begin to work among the Jews. He will send the 144,000 and the two witnesses out to preach the gospel of the kingdom once again to all the earth.

Now we see the last big proclamation of the gospel, preceding His coming the second time to earth. It is the final call for the guilty nations to receive Christ as Savior and Lord! God's mercy on those who, in that time of judgment, come to Christ, before the final blow, the call will still go out to mankind everywhere to acknowledge that Jesus is Lord and Savior! We will not see any responses recorded here in chapter 14. But in other scripture, we do see that many, who had never heard, will open their hearts to the message of the angel and receive Christ as their Savior!

We pick up now with verse 7 of chapter 14. Revelation 14:7 says, "Saying with a loud voice, Fear God, and give glory to him; for the hour of his judgment is come: and worship him that made heaven, and earth, and the sea, and the fountains of waters." Look at the message in verse 7: "Fear God" and "give Him glory!" That is the message of the eternal gospel. The psalmist says in Psalm 111:10, "The fear of the Lord is the beginning of wisdom: a good understanding have all they that do his commandments: his praise endureth for ever."

Solomon tells us in Proverbs 9:10, "The fear of the Lord is the beginning of wisdom: and the knowledge of the holy is understanding." Both tell us the beginning of wisdom is the fear of the Lord. The angel is virtually saying, "Wise up, you need to fear God!" Salvation comes by the grace of God. The gospel is the means in which mankind is brought to fear or reverence God. Not only are they to fear or reverence God, we see they are to give Him glory. What the beast and false prophet are offering will not bring salvation, only destruction.

The preaching of the everlasting gospel shakes the foundations of the Antichrist in the world. The downfall of the unholy trinity is at hand here in this proclamation! "If any persist in being subject to the beast, and in promoting his cause, they must expect to be forever miserable in soul and body," Matthew Henry states at this point. More of the everlasting gospel is seen at the end of verse 7. Worship Him who made heaven, worship Him who made the earth. Worship Him who made the sea, worship Him who made the fountains of the waters. Everything that was attacked in the tribulation belongs to God. He created it all, and He can withhold it from mankind. Understand that this message goes further—worship God, not the beast.

We see next in Revelation 14:8 that states, "And there followed another angel, saying, Babylon is fallen, is fallen, that great city, because she made all nations drink of the wine of the wrath of her fornication." Another messenger appears this with a pronouncement of the fall of Babylon. The great period of the worship of the beast and his image has fallen. The end is here, this messenger proclaims. The great time of idolatry is gone, that time of great spiritual fornication has ceased. That is the message he brings, while we haven't seen the fall, the angel proclaims it.

God has said it, and therefore, the angel declares it as truth, as if it has already occurred. The city in which the first beast will be ruling from will fall. The idolatry of Babylon has been intoxicating the world; this time of Satan worship will cease to occur. The cults we see so rampant today will be destroyed.

Look at Isaiah 13:11 that says, "And I will punish the world for their evil, and the wicked for their iniquity; and I will cause the arrogancy of the proud to cease, and will lay low the haughtiness of the terrible." This is God's wrath coming upon the world. We see too in Isaiah 13:19 that states, "And Babylon, the glory of kingdoms, the beauty of the Chaldees' excellency, shall be as when God overthrew Sodom and Gomorrah." We see more when we get to chapter 17 and the culmination in chapter 18. The reason for this fall, I know, is quite obvious because of the opposition to God, Jesus, and the Holy Spirit but look at it like this too. The wine of the wrath of her fornication, the idolatry, which the unholy trinity brought into being during this period, is like the wine of wrath, so intoxicating that it drew them in. They saw the riches and honors. The pleasures of the world and it all looked good! The unholy trinity promised all these to those who would worship them. Just as wine intoxicates and inclines and excites to lust, and by the "wrath" of it is meant either the heat of lust unto it or the wrath of God against them, which is stirred up by it. Now the provocation of her sin is that she not only drinks of this wine herself or commits idolatry, being drawn to it by its allure, even though she enjoys its pleasure, now the wrath of God is coming. She had drawn all nations into the same idolatrous practices.

We see yet a third angel or messenger comes in Revelation 14:9–10, which says, "And the third angel followed them, saying with a loud voice, If any man worship the beast and his image, and receive his mark in his forehead, or in his hand, The same shall drink of the wine of the wrath of God, which is poured out without mixture into the cup of his indignation; and he shall be tormented with fire and brimstone in the presence of the holy angels, and in the presence of the Lamb." The message those who turn away from God, those who reject His Word, those who turn to worship the beast and his image will have to drink of God's wrath. It will take great courage for anyone to stand against the beast and his worship, those who turned to the beast will suffer the wrath of God.

Look at Psalm 75:8 that states, "For in the hand of the Lord there is a cup, and the wine is red; it is full of mixture; and he poureth out of the same: but the dregs thereof, all the wicked of the earth shall wring them out, and drink them." Again we see fulfillment of Old Testament prophecy. The Old Testament prophet picked up this theme too. They saw the cup of wrath filling up to the brim. When that cup is filled, God will bring His full wrath upon those who have not turned to Him. Rebellious men kept this up! Judgment will break it to pieces! They will be "tormented with fire and brimstone!" Great will be their eternal punishment. They enjoyed the things on earth, now they will suffer God's wrath in the presence of holy angels, in the presence of the Lamb. Clearly, we should be busy at telling others about Christ and His salvation.

Brimstone is a term used for sulfur. What will hot sulfur do to the body? Thus will be the torment of all who worship the beast and take his mark! We see more in Revelation 14:11 that states, "And the smoke of their torment ascendeth up for ever and ever: and they have no rest day nor night, who worship the beast and his image, and whosoever receiveth the mark of his name." The smoke of their torment will ascend up forever. They have no rest day or night. Eternal will be their punishment. They will forever be miserable in soul and body. The Lord will inflict punishment upon them. The holy angels will see it and approve of it. Their idolatry will prove fatal to those who follow after the beast and worship his image and take his mark.

Let's look at what Jesus said about the punishment of the unrighteous. Luke 16:19–23, in the story of Lazarus and the rich man, says, "There was a certain rich man, which was clothed in purple and fine linen, and fared sumptuously every day: And there was a certain beggar named Lazarus, which was laid at his gate, full of sores, And desiring to be fed with the crumbs which fell from the rich man's table: moreover the dogs came and licked his sores. And it came to pass, that the beggar died, and was carried by the angels into Abraham's bosom: the rich man also died, and was buried; And in hell he lift up his eyes, being in torments, and seeth Abraham afar off, and Lazarus in his bosom." He was in torments, and look at what he told father Abraham.

We see in Luke 16:24 that states, "And he cried and said, Father Abraham, have mercy on me, and send Lazarus, that he may dip the tip of his finger in water, and cool my tongue; for I am tormented in this flame." He was tormented in the flame! So too will the beast and false prophet suffer. So too will all who follow and take the mark in the forehead on their hand, tormented in the lake that burns with fire and brimstone.

We come to Revelation 14:12 that says, "Here is the patience of the saints: here are they that keep the commandments of God, and the faith of Jesus." Now we transition to the saints and their patience. We see in Matthew 24:13 that states, "But he that shall endure unto the end, the same shall be saved." Why will the saints endure till the end? Because they are sealed by God! Also they keep the commandments of God. They have faith in Christ! They are clothed with Christ's righteousness! They overcome by the blood of the Lamb! Look too at Luke 21:19 that says, "In your patience possess ye your souls." Waiting upon God, depending upon Him, we possess our souls! The patience of the saints will be tried, that is the tribulation saints. There will be far less who are church members and not saved in that time. The true worshippers of Christ will be discovered, comforting them with an assurance of that rest—a rest that remains after death for the faithful followers of Christ.

We see in Revelation 6:10 that states, "And they cried with a loud voice, saying, How long, O Lord, holy and true, dost thou not judge and avenge our blood on them that dwell on the earth?" Those martyred tribulation saints see their blood avenged. This is the patience of the saints. This is the answer to their prayer. We come now to Revelation 14:13 that says, "And I heard a voice from heaven saying unto me, Write, Blessed are the dead which die in the Lord from henceforth: Yea, saith the Spirit, that they may rest from their labours; and their works do follow them."

We see now a very striking statement here in verse 13. Notice the word henceforth. How often do we hear this word at a funeral? Its full meaning refers to a coming day. The point being that while the declaration of the doom of the beast and false prophet is announced the fact that God will avenge those who are His saints is stated clearly. The darkest days of the great tribulation are yet to occur. The greatest part of God's judgment is coming. Those who trust Him during this great period of tribulation will enter into the kingdom on earth. Those who die in the tribulation period will also have a part in the kingdom. Therefore, a special blessing will be theirs. What is it saying here, from this point on, it will really be better to die as a believer than to live. They will rest in their labors. They will be spared further tribulation on earth. They will have their place with their Lord in heaven, which will be far better than the highest place in the kingdom on earth as glorious as it will be. Their works will follow them just as ours do for us.

We receive our reward at the bema seat judgment, which occurs at The Snatching Away of the Bride. Those saints of the tribulation will also receive their rewards. First, we see they are blessed in their rest from all sin, temptation, sorrow, and persecution. They are blessed in their reward, their works don't go before them instead they will follow them. It will be the evidence of their having lived and died in the Lord. The reward will be glorious, far above the measure of all their service. Death is a happy thing in that time because they will have lived to see the cause of God reviving. It doesn't matter where they die or what type of humiliation they die from—whether labeled as a heretic, religious freak, Bible thumper, intolerant bigot as we are now being called—no matter what label is put on them when they die, or if they are cast out as the cleaning off all things. They will be blessed. Their works follow them to heaven to bear witness of their faith.

Can we say that about our works for God or the lack thereof, spiritually they continue to live on this earth? Their death as a witness, the gracious seed that they laid down their lives to plant during this evil time, never before has this been spoken or could it of works following the believers. In our age, Paul said in Philippians 1:21, "For to me to live is Christ, and to die is gain." Our lives on this earth are to be lived for Christ. The most important thing in our lives should be living for Christ—having the reality of Christ showing forth to the world, people today, church members, like to talk about being dedicated, wanting to serve Him, doing this for Christ or that for Christ. The most important thing for us as believers is to have fellowship with Him. That way our joy is full! We have a powerful witness when people around us see us full of joy and praise for God. If living for us is Christ, we aren't fazed by criticism that is leveled at us by people in the world. You see a person in fellowship with God, with Jesus, and with the Holy Spirit can't be hurt! But for the tribulation saint, it is better to die.

Notice the second half of Philippians 1:21: "to die is gain!" For the tribulation saint, it is better to die and gain being in the presence of Jesus in heaven. Their works follow them. Rest from their labor is found in death. We find rest in Christ as we walk with Him. For those tribulation saints, it will not be so. Daniel 7:25 says, "And he shall speak great words against the most High, and shall wear out the saints of the most High, and think to change times and laws: and they shall be given into his hand until a time and times and the dividing of time."

We see Revelation 13:7 that states, "And it was given unto him to make war with the saints, and to overcome them: and power was given him over all kindreds, and tongues, and nations." They can't live a life of disciplined service as we do. Death will be better for the faithful of those days. Those "in the Lord" find rest only in death. You see we find comfort in knowing that the Lord will return for us before the tribulation comes. The book of 1 Thessalonians 4:13–18 says, "But I would not have you to be ignorant, brethren, concerning them which are asleep, that ye sorrow not, even as others which have no hope. For if we believe that Jesus died and rose again, even so them also which sleep in Jesus will God bring with him. For this we say unto you by the word of the Lord, that we which are alive and remain unto the coming of the Lord shall not prevent them which are asleep. For the Lord himself shall descend from heaven with a shout, with the voice of the archangel, and with the trump of God: and the dead in Christ shall rise first: Then we which are alive and remain shall be caught up together with them in the clouds, to meet the Lord in the air: and so shall we ever be with the Lord. Wherefore comfort one another with these words."

For them, this prophecy will have been completed. Now in chapter 14, we see they have forty- two months left. Paul doesn't want us ignorant of prophecy; he doesn't want them ignorant either. The believers in Thessalonica were ignorant until Paul wrote this. We shouldn't be ignorant because we have this teaching. We see for our age the dead in Christ will rise first, those whose bodies are sleeping in death, their Spirit and soul are in heaven. Because the soul and Spirit of the believer can't die they live on forever. The unbeliever is spiritually separated from God and therefore is spiritually dead in trespasses and sin to begin with. Paul tells us what happens to believers who die in 2 Corinthians 5:8–10, which says, "We are confident, I say, and willing rather to be absent from the body, and to be present with the Lord. Wherefore we labour, that, whether present or absent, we may be accepted of him. For we must all appear before the judgment seat of Christ; that every one may receive the things done in his body, according to that he hath done, whether it be good or bad."

Do you see when we die separation occurs, that is what death is. Absent from the body which is asleep, but we—our being, our soul, and our spirit—are present with the Lord. So too will the tribulation believer be with the Lord. But notice verse 10, we will face the bema seat and receive our rewards. That happens when the Lord descends from heaven with a shout. Notice verse 16 of 1 Thessalonians 4, the dead, those who sleep will rise first, when we meet Him in the air, we face the bema seat judgment in heaven. Verse 17 of 1 Thessalonians 4 says we who are alive will be caught up, that is snatched out or the rapture. We will meet Him in the air and be with Him forever. In verse 18, we are to find comfort in these words. The tribulation saints can't find comfort in them because it has been fulfilled three and one half years prior to the things occurring in Revelation 13 and following.

The last three and one half years of the tribulation are at hand here in chapter 14. The tribulation saint who dies will be blessed when death occurs. Their works accompany them. We see four times in chapter 14 the Greek word translated follow used in verse 4, verse 8, verse 9, and of course, here in verse 13. It is the word used of the disciples in Matthew 4:25 and 8:1 along with other scripture. Matthew 4:25 says, "And there followed him great multitudes of people from Galilee, and from Decapolis, and from Jerusalem, and from Judaea, and from beyond Jordan." Matthew 8:1 states, "When he was come down from the mountain, great multitudes followed him."

These are the last martyrs. They are seen as the third company of those who reign with Christ in Revelation 20:6, which says, "Blessed and holy is he that hath part in the first resurrection: on such the second death hath no power, but they shall be priests of God and of Christ, and shall reign with him a thousand years." You see this is their reward for their works. So who is the first company? We see them in 1 Corinthians 6:2 that states, "Do ye not know that the saints shall judge the world? and if the world shall be judged by you, are ye unworthy to judge the smallest matters?" It is you and I as believers in this age, as the church or bride of Christ who will be sitting in judgment as the first company who reign with Christ. We see the second company as those in Revelation 6:1–17, those martyrs seen in the fifth seal who are waiting for their blood to be avenged, those who were martyred up to the reign of the beast and false prophet.

Then these are the last, when their company is made. They will reign with Christ. John was commanded to write, which further substantiates that it is true and will happen. The Holy Spirit's inspiration is seen in this. This is of special importance. It is to be taken to heart, especially for those believers of the great tribulation. It should be taken to heart at the death of any believer. But it is written especially for these last martyrs. It is addressed to them directly, connected to them by the words from henceforth. It is definitely a marked time. It shows us a change in circumstances and conditions that means "from now."

We come now to Revelation 14:14 that says, "And I looked, and behold a white cloud, and upon the cloud one sat like unto the Son of man, having on his head a golden crown, and in his hand a sharp sickle." The time is getting close for the Lord to return. We see Him sitting on a cloud. What is the significance of the cloud? To find the answer, we look to Matthew 24:30 that states, "And then shall appear the sign of the Son of man in heaven: and then shall all the tribes of the earth mourn, and they shall see the Son of man coming in the clouds of heaven with power and great glory." He is coming as the King of kings with great power. Notice the crown upon His head. This time, it isn't a crown of thorns but a golden crown showing His authority to do all that He has done, whatever He will do! Gold, of course, represents deity; and this, of course, goes along with the great glory spoken of in Matthew.

Thus we have Christ coming as King and God ready to judge the world. Notice what He has in His hand. He is coming to reap. In several passages, the Lord speaks of the reaping of His people. He declared it as the end of the age. Look at John 5:22, which says, "For the Father judgeth no man, but hath committed all judgment unto the Son."

Then verse 27 that states, "And hath given him authority to execute judgment also, because he is the Son of man." Christ is ready with a reaping instrument. It is a sickle, which is for reaping. The word sickle is mentioned twelve times in the Bible, twelve the number of governmental perfection or completion. But it is of further note that it is mentioned seven times here in chapter 14. Seven is the number of spiritual completion or perfection as we have mentioned. Numbers in scripture are important for believers to understand. They reveal to us God's plan, almost as much as the Bible does. Another thing that I felt quite significant is the number 14. While man divided the books into chapters and verses, I believe this is one more incident where we can see the Holy Spirit's hand in the division of the Bible.

The number 14 of which is the chapter in which this appears, and the number 14 the verse in which we have this vision, the number 14 is a double measure of spiritual completion or perfection! Of course, 7 times 2 is seen in the number 14, and 2 represents division and 2 natures, thus 14 is double spiritual perfection and the incarnation—the two natures of Christ. Not only is sickle of importance but notice it is sharp. The word sharp (oxus) occurs seven times in the book of Revelation. There are four times here describing the sickle, while three times as the sharp two edged sword which proceeds out of the Lord's mouth in judgment. Who is the sharp sickle as we see here in Revelation 14? Understand the number 4 represents creation, the creation of all material things. The number 3 is divine completion or perfection and thus the culmination of all things God has planned. Since the end of the tribulation is soon to follow, then Christ is coming not to reap a harvest of the good, He is coming to reap the bad.

He is coming to reap that which He has authority over. The church was removed as we saw in Revelation 4. The 144,000 are preserved and can't be killed. The martyrs under the beast have been seen in verse 13 as the blessed who shall die, Are there any left for this sharp sickle? Yes, the wicked on earth are left. We see then the command to reap in Revelation 14:15 that says, "And another angel came out of the temple, crying with a loud voice to him that sat on the cloud, Thrust in thy sickle, and reap: for the time is come for thee to reap; for the harvest of the earth is ripe."

Another messenger appears. He comes from the temple in heaven, from the presence of the Father. The Father who has set the time and seasons, Acts 1:7 states, "And he said unto them,

It is not for you to know the times or the seasons, which the Father hath put in his own power." As well Matthew 24:36 that says, "But of that day and hour knoweth no man, no, not the angels of heaven, but my Father only." The command is sent by the Lord with this angelic voice. The command given thrust in thy sickle and reap. God's judgment is going to be thrust upon those on the earth. They will reap what they have sown. The Father's message to Christ is clear: the time of reaping has come! The harvest work is beginning for the Lord. God's justice is seen in this sharp sickle. God's justice is reaping the world. Cutting it asunder, remember Hebrews 4:12. This reaping will cut the inhabitants of the earth. In the end, they will be carried off. The harvest time has come, what does that mean? When as it was in the days of Noah, they did evil continually in Luke 17:26–27 that says, "And as it was in the days of Noe, so shall it be also in the days of the Son of man. They did eat, they drank, they married wives, they were given in marriage, until the day that Noah entered into the ark, and the flood came, and destroyed them all."

As well as in Genesis 6:5–7, it states, "And God saw that the wickedness of man was great in the earth, and that every imagination of the thoughts of his heart was only evil continually. And it repented the Lord that he had made man on the earth, and it grieved him at his heart. And the Lord said, I will destroy man whom I have created from the face of the earth; both man, and beast, and the creeping thing, and the fowls of the air; for it repenteth me that I have made them." At this point in the tribulation, they are ripe for ruin. God will spare them no longer. The sharp sickle will be thrust in, and the earth will be reaped.

We see Revelation 14:16 that says, "And he that sat on the cloud thrust in his sickle on the earth; and the earth was reaped." Christ thrust in His sickle, the reaping begins, the enemies of God and the believers of the tribulation are not going to be destroyed until the time is right. Until by their sin, they are ripe for ruin. Then He will spare them no more, He will thrust in His sickle. The earth shall be reaped. We see Revelation 14:17 that states, "And another angel came out of the temple which is in heaven, he also having a sharp sickle." Another angel comes to help with the reaping. An angel comes from the temple in heaven. He too has a sharp sickle. He too helps with the reaping.

We see Matthew 13 and the parable of the sower in verses 37–42. We see this scene that says, "He answered and said unto them, He that soweth the good seed is the Son of man; The field is the world; the good seed are the children of the kingdom; but the tares are the children of the wicked one; The enemy that sowed them is the devil; the harvest is the end of the world; and the reapers are the angels. As therefore the tares are gathered and burned in the fire; so shall it be in the end of this world. The Son of man shall send forth his angels, and they shall gather out of his kingdom all things that offend, and them which do iniquity; And shall cast them into a furnace of fire: there shall be wailing and gnashing of teeth." The tares are gathered first before the kingdom. They are burned in judgment.

We see here this reaping and the tares, the evil ones of the earth being gathered for judgment. The gathering of those who offend and do iniquity is occurring here in this vision. We finish Revelation chapter 14 with verses 18–20, which states, "And another angel came out from the altar, which had power over fire; and cried with a loud cry to him that had the sharp sickle, saying, Thrust in thy sharp sickle, and gather the clusters of the vine of the earth; for her grapes are fully ripe. And the angel thrust in his sickle into the earth, and gathered the vine of the earth, and cast it into the great winepress of the wrath of God. And the winepress was trodden without the city, and blood came out of the winepress, even unto the horse bridles, by the space of a thousand and six hundred furlongs." Notice the next angel has power over fire, crying out thrust in thy sharp sickle. Gather the clusters of the vine.

Verse 18 tells about the vine of the earth and for her grapes are fully ripe, man's evil is fully ripe. J. Vernon Magee says the term conveys the thought that they are being dry like Raisins. Isaiah 63:1–6 can be seen here, and it says, "Who is this that cometh from Edom, with dyed garments from Bozrah? this that is glorious in his apparel, travelling in the greatness of his strength? I that speak in righteousness, mighty to save. Wherefore art thou red in thine apparel, and thy garments like him that treadeth in the winefat? I have trodden the winepress alone; and of the people there was none with me: for I will tread them in mine anger, and trample them in my fury; and their blood shall be sprinkled upon my garments, and I will stain all my raiment. For the day of vengeance is in mine heart, and the year of my redeemed is come. And I looked, and there was none to help; and I wondered that there was none to uphold: therefore mine own arm brought salvation unto me; and my fury, it upheld me. And I will tread down the people in mine anger, and make them drunk in my fury, and I will bring down their strength to the earth."

In verses 19–20, we have a glimpse of Armageddon—the battle, which destroys the beast, the false prophet, and their armies. The blood up to the bridle of the horses that means it is about four feet deep. It stretches "a thousand and six hundred furlongs." That is about 185 miles, which is the distance from Dan to Beersheba. All of the land of Palestine is the scene of this war. Some see a war beginning here in the middle of the tribulation. If you remember, we talked about they are in Ezekiel 38 and 39 in an earlier book. I taught that, that war would begin after the peace was dissolved. This could be that war, or it could be yet another. We know that it is not Armageddon, it is a war not fought to gain land or a spoil but to fight against the Lord who is returning. This is seen in the reaping. Which is God's judgment upon mankind, so I believe this is God's beginning judgment and will conclude it at the second coming of Christ. We see now the beginning of the end for the beast and false prophet. As well as those who follow them. God is bringing judgment, and it will be a furious judgment—the separation of the sheep and goats. Man's evil has reached its point of ripening, and the time for them to reap what they have sown is upon them. Fulfillment of scripture of prophecy is upon mankind. It will culminate in chapter 19 with the second coming of Christ.

7 The Sickle Thrust In

John now tells us of the next sign he sees, a great and marvelous sign in heaven. Revelation 15 is a continuation of chapter 14. As the reaping of judgment begins, the sickle, being thrust in, brings us to the seven plagues that will come. This chapter presents a picture of the redeemed that has not worshipped the beast and false prophet and has escaped the judgment of God. We see in chapters 15 and 16 the final scenes of the tribulation period, the period of great judgment that will come upon mankind. My congregation asked me the question before we started as to why most pastors will not teach this book. Well, I believe we see the answer in the books I have written to date. It is a book of judgment! Some see it as a pessimistic book occupied with many fearful scenes. The end is bright for those who believe, though, because at the end, we see our eternal home. We see Christ gain the victory. We see Satan defeated. We see our eternal dwelling place with all the beauty of eternity—an eternity spent with God and our Lord Jesus Christ.

There should be no reason for apologies for continually bringing you picture after picture of God's dealing with those of the tribulation with great judgment—the prophecies of what is yet to occur for mankind. These prophetic verses and these revelations are given to us out of God's kindness, in order that we are warned to avoid what lies ahead. So we can warn others of what is prophesied and what lies ahead for those who reject Christ. That we need to make sure we have sound solid doctrinal teaching and are not falling prey to any form of apostasy that God will soon judge. Remember back to Revelation 12:1. Let's look at it. It states, "And there appeared a great wonder in heaven; a woman clothed with the sun, and the moon under her feet, and upon her head a crown of twelve stars."

The beginning of the judgment is seen here in 12:1. The first sign to appear was showing Israel. The seven angels of wrath are seen in the judgments that follow. They will not end until chapter 19, when we see the return of Christ. So from chapter 12 until the return of Christ, we see a continuous chain of events. But understand they are not chronologically in order. They are in logical order based on Christ logic. They are in order of reviewing events and adding more detail. That is how the Holy Spirit reveals things. He did the same in the book of Genesis chapters 1 and 2 and told us of creation in chapter 3, reviewed it, and gave more details. We saw Satan cast to the earth, and with that casting down, he brought with him wrath. That wrath is directed first at the believers then he brings it upon Israel with a fury. He makes a final attempt at world domination through the two beasts.

God is now ready here to display His wrath and brings the conclusion of the world's tragedy of sin. We see the fulfillment of Psalm 110:1 that says, "The Lord said unto my Lord, Sit thou at my right hand, until I make thine enemies thy footstool." God's wrath is seen in the final judgment of the great tribulation. God has been slow to anger, but here is where His patience is seen finally coming to an end. The final stages of the day of wrath are now beginning, not from Satan or wild beast but coming directly from the throne of God. God will Judge.

In verse 1 of Chapter 15 of Revelation, the seven angels hold the last seven plagues. Do you see the final judgment is coming? This is leading up to the pouring out of the seven vials. John said too that this was a marvelous event. How can judgment be marvelous many might ask? The more we study this book and see the coming judgment, the greater the realization of the judgment that is coming. God's last big judgment in which He is attempting to reach those who have not taken the mark and still haven't trusted Christ. This is all prior to the return of Christ at His second coming. Remember the culmination of the Jewish age of the tribulation requires one great event that we see in Isaiah 63:3–5, which states, "I have trodden the winepress alone; and of the people there was none with me: for I will tread them in mine anger, and trample them in my fury; and their blood shall be sprinkled upon my garments, and I will stain all my raiment. For the day of vengeance is in mine heart, and the year of my redeemed is come. And I looked, and there was none to help; and I wondered that there was none to uphold: therefore mine own arm brought salvation unto me; and my fury, it upheld me." Christ must come to tread down the winepress.

God's wrath here is not just upon Israel, not just upon the two beasts and their followers—it will come because of man's sin and idolatry. Yes, Christ's wrath is coming against the beast and false prophet, against kings and armies who will be gathered to fight against Him. Psalm 83:4 says, "They have said, Come, and let us cut them off from being a nation; that the name of Israel may be no more in remembrance." And they are attempting to prevent His bringing Israel back into their land.

Look at Zechariah 12:10, which states, "And I will pour upon the house of David, and upon the inhabitants of Jerusalem, the spirit of grace and of supplications: and they shall look upon me whom they have pierced, and they shall mourn for him, as one mourneth for his only son, and shall be in bitterness for him, as one that is in bitterness for his firstborn." We see in Zechariah 12:11, where this will occur, which says, "In that day shall there be a great mourning in Jerusalem, as the mourning of Hadadrimmon in the valley of Megiddon." Judgment is on the way, and yet we see something marvelous in verses 2 and 3.

We see Revelation 15:2–3, which states, "And I saw as it were a sea of glass mingled with fire: and them that had gotten the victory over the beast, and over his image, and over his mark, and over the number of his name, stand on the sea of glass, having the harps of God. And they sing the song of Moses the servant of God, and the song of the Lamb, saying, Great and marvelous are thy works, Lord God Almighty; just and true are thy ways, thou King of saints." We see before the vials of judgment are poured out to God giving a vision of those who gained the victory during the tribulation.

They gained victory over the beast and the false prophet. They gained victory over Satan. They gained victory during these violent last days these last days in which the two beasts are in charge of the earth with satan to lead them. In verses 2 and 3, we see the saints who have won the victory, notice what over. First, it says over the beast then over his image. They didn't take the mark. They didn't receive the number of his name. They stand on the glass; they have harps. Understand this is not the church. They sing the song of Moses, the servant of God. Then they sing the song of the Lamb. Yet the glass they stand on is mixed with something else—the glass is mixed with fire!

This is believed to have a twofold significance—first, the glassy sea as we have seen before is like the brazen sea in Solomon's temple. It is like the Word of God, needed for cleansing here in heaven crystallized. It is a glassy sea upon which the victorious saints take their stand to praise Him who has redeemed them to Himself. He has made them like us forever clean. Second, the fire is the representation of the fiery trial they have gone through for the sake of Christ. Fire is normally spoken of as judgment in scripture. Fire can also be for trials, which the saints of the tribulation endured and by which God purifies His people. These are standing upon the sea of glass mingled with fire, having been delivered from their adversaries. The troubles they have overcome. They sing this double song in celebration of their victory, the second song in praise to Christ the redeemer.

Then verse 3 finishes with the words King of saints. This can also be translated as King of the nations, Ruler of the ages. They are praising and adoring Him for his justice and truth, recognizing the righteousness of His character, the holiness of His person. Thereby, all nations will come and worship Him when His judgment has been made known. We see the term King of nations in Jeremiah 10:7 that says, "Who would not fear thee, O King of nations? for to thee doth it appertain: forasmuch as among all the wise men of the nations, and in all their kingdoms, there is none like unto thee." Then in Jeremiah 10:10, it states, "But the Lord is the true God, he is the living God, and an everlasting king: at his wrath the earth shall tremble, and the nations shall not be able to abide his indignation." He is here an everlasting King. When His wrath comes, the world shall tremble. They shall not abide or be able to stand up to His indignation. For His anger will be great against them.

Remember Genesis 6:5–7, which says, "And God saw that the

wickedness of man was great in the earth, and that every imagination of the thoughts of his heart was only evil continually. And it repented the Lord that he had made man on the earth, and it grieved him at his heart. And the Lord said, I will destroy man whom I have created from the face of the earth; both man, and beast, and the creeping thing, and the fowls of the air; for it repenteth me that I have made them."

The same was said by Christ concerning His second coming. Luke 17:26 states, "And as it was in the days of Noe, so shall it be also in the days of the Son of man. 27 They did eat, they drank, they married wives, they were given in marriage, until the day that Noah entered into the ark, and the flood came, and destroyed them all." The world at the return of Christ is doing evil continually. Do I need to give examples, or do you see it in the news every single day? God will bring judgment just as He judged the Noah age. Just as He did in Noah's age, he does for every believer. In every age, He has a saved remnant. This is true here in Revelation as it is today in our age.

We see now in verse 4 of Revelation 15 the continuing of praise. It says, "Who shall not fear thee, O Lord, and glorify thy name? for thou only art holy: for all nations shall come and worship before thee; for thy judgments are made manifest." Everyone is soon to worship Christ. This will be reverential fear of the Lord. Something we find very little of in our day, even among believers. Many are caught up in the love attitude, while we should not lose sight of God's love. We need to remember that God is light—that is He is Holy. Our God is to be feared because He is Holy. The day will soon come, and here in Revelation 15, it is close, in that all nations shall come and worship Christ.

We don't see that today! We will see it one day, some day! The world will bow at His feet. They will acknowledge Him because of His judgment. Look at Psalm 86:8–9, which states, "Among the gods there is none like unto thee, O Lord; neither are there any works like unto thy works. All nations whom thou hast made shall come and worship before thee, O Lord; and shall glorify thy name." This is fulfillment of this prophecy and the prophecies of what is yet to occur for mankind. These prophetic verses and these revelations are given to us out of God's kindness.

We can see Christ is going to reign someday. Here, at this point in Revelation, that someday will be a short time away. Christ is going to execute judgment. He will bring justice to the earth. For all must be done to redeem the earth for Him. Can we say thank God for that? We see Philippians 2:9–11 that says, "Wherefore God also hath highly exalted him, and given him a name which is above every name: That at the name of Jesus every knee should bow, of things in heaven, and things in earth, and things under the earth; And that every tongue should confess that Jesus Christ is Lord, to the glory of God the Father." Do you see those who are in Hell will not acknowledge Him as their redeemer? But they are going to recognize Him as the ruler. Acknowledge that He runs the universe, that it belongs to Him. They will acknowledge the glory of God, they have to do that.

Why, because His judgments were made manifest. This is the testimony of those on the glassy sea, those who are living in that period. He will be known for His works that are made public for all to see. The testimony opened not a covenant, which was secured in the hour of evil, a testimony of His power and authority. Judgment is coming to bring the restoration of Israel, judgment of the Gentiles and all who corrupted the earth. Psalm 7:9 states, "Oh let the wickedness of the wicked come to an end; but establish the just: for the righteous God trieth the hearts and reins." Psalm 11:7 says, "For the righteous Lord loveth righteousness; his countenance doth behold the upright." Psalm 107:1 states, "O give thanks unto the Lord, for he is good: for his mercy endureth for ever." And Psalm 107:40 tells, "He poureth contempt upon princes, and causeth them to wander in the wilderness, where there is no way." This will happen when God is in charge.

We see Revelation 15:5–6 that says, "And after that I looked, and, behold, the temple of the tabernacle of the testimony in heaven was opened: And the seven angels came out of the temple, having the seven plagues, clothed in pure and white linen, and having their breasts girded with golden girdles." John sees the temple of the tabernacle in heaven. It has opened. We again see God bring Israel to the forefront. These judgments are for the carrying out of God's covenant with His ancient people Israel. Let's note here all the attacks and all that people are doing to destroy Israel in this present time we are living are for naught. All those who want to say God is through with Israel are just as wrong.

God is going to punish all those who have oppressed them. Zechariah 12:3 states, "And in that day will I make Jerusalem a burdensome stone for all people: all that burden themselves with it shall be cut in pieces, though all the people of the earth be gathered together against it." The nations that have vented their hatred upon Israel, upon the Jewish people, cannot escape the wrath of God. Notice again there is a literal temple in heaven. Understanding this keeps things from becoming obscure.

The angels come out of the temple. This is the main object of chapter 15: the seven angels with the seven plagues. They are coming to complete the wrath of God. They introduce judgment in the plagues. They close His final visitation in judgment upon the Gentiles. This will fulfill many prophecies concerning the judgment, which abounds in scripture. The book 2 Thessalonians 1:6 says, "Seeing it is a righteous thing with God to recompense tribulation to them that trouble you." If this was promised to the church age believer, how much more for this time in which Israel is oppressed? The plagues are coming with these seven angels.

We see then in Revelation 15:7 that states, "And one of the four beasts gave unto the seven Angels seven golden vials full of the wrath of God, who liveth for ever and ever." Seven angels, seven golden vials—here again is the emphasis on the number 7, the number of completeness. Everything in Revelation guides us to completeness. Sometimes, completeness is perfection. God's plan is nearing completeness here in Revelation. Before the Lord comes in chapter 19, we have these angels coming with the seven plagues. God, in His grace and mercy, is making one last call to the people on earth.

God will not destroy man until He gives one last and loud call of warning. The last the vials full of wrath are being handed to these angels. This seems to be a scene of finality—a finality that brings the utmost awe into our hearts, the temple, which these angels come out of, their holy glittering aspect. The bowls or vials of wrath handed off ready to be poured out. The presentation of the bowl is a solemn occasion. The material of these bowls is gold which shows both the deity of God in sending them out, the setting forth of God's glory. The fullness of these bowls shows us the fullness of the wrath to come; they are not full of grace or are they mixed with mercy and wrath. They are "full of the wrath of God!"

Let us speak this slowly and allow it to sink in. This last and final judgment is the greatest of all. Let us reverence God. Observe the wickedness that is on the earth and it will be punished. But let us observe it with awe and deep humility. We come to the close of Revelation 15:8 that states, "And the temple was filled with smoke from the glory of God, and from his power; and no man was able to enter into the temple, till the seven plagues of the seven angels were fulfilled."

Smoke filled the sanctuary. The smoke was from the glory of God. This brings to mind Exodus 40:34, which says, "Then a cloud covered the tent of the congregation, and the glory of the Lord filled the tabernacle." The Shekinah glory of God that filled the temple is seen here in the temple in heaven.

We see that with these seven angels on the brink of delivering judgment in the plagues, there is great concern in heaven—the smoke of God's glory, this from His power. The redeemed in heaven standing outside the temple is found in awe, awaiting the developments. Then we will see in Revelation 16:1 a voice sound. Judgment is upon the earth. A world that has rejected the blood of Christ will now bear the last and final judgment. Why must they bear it, because of their sin—the sin of rejecting Christ! This judgment is not the result of man's or Satan's hatred. It is the direct action of the Lord Jesus! The gentle Jesus, we saw in His earthly ministry, is now seen as the wrath of the Lamb.

We can't separate God's attributes. His judgment and wrath cannot be separate; they go together. His love and holiness go right along with His power. Because of that, these angels stand ready to pour out these seven plagues upon the earth. Wrath and mercy are linked together. Consider John 3:16, the verse is filled with the love of God. It tells us how much God loved mankind. That He gave His only Son to die for our sins. It speaks of a willing Christ, at that point covered with His love, bringing salvation. That is solemn, yet it is also terrifying in the perish portion. Those who believe will not perish. Think about it, though, those who believe not will perish. They will face the wrath of God. Know anyone who has not believed?

They will perish if they aren't reached for Christ. If they don't believe in Him, God's wrath remains upon their lives, and it could be for eternity. We see now the coming of the vials of judgment. The time is now getting short for His coming even His coming for us the bride, His church. The vials or bowls of plague are ready to be poured out upon the earth. Judgment is close, and the redemption of the tribulation saints is near.

What do we learn here? We need to be busy at His work this side of the tribulation, sowing and watering reaching souls for Christ. God will give the increase we are promised that. This book, with all its warnings, should be the thing to spur us on to labor for God and Christ. That is why Revelation should be studied, taught, and understood properly. Each day, we get one day closer to His return for us and then the tribulation will begin. Seven long years of tribulation, seven long years of evil desperately wicked evil upon the earth. Yet even in that, God will have a saved remnant that will survive and go into the millennial kingdom to reign with Him one thousand years. Praise God for that.

Wrath of God

We see now in verse 1 of Revelation 16 the command to the angels, and it states, "And I heard a great voice out of the temple saying to the seven angels, Go your ways, and pour out the vials of the wrath of God upon the earth." The last plagues are now to be poured out upon the earth. As we saw, the angels had in their hands the plagues, as well as the vials of God's wrath. But they did not move until their orders came.

They are now commanded to go their way to pour out the vials of the wrath of God. They will leave the temple and heaven. They will go to all the parts of this now antichristian empire. They will pour out all the wrath, vengeance, and judgment of God upon His enemies, leaving nothing behind in their wake, pouring out the contents of every vial of God's fury. The whole earth is to be taken here.

These vials and plagues will be poured out upon the land, the sea, the fountains, the rivers, the firmament—which is the atmospheric air—and also the sun in the firmament. The pouring out of these vials upon them shows that all will be encompassed in judgment, any remnant of the apostate church—all things of earthly sinful men, all the inhabitants of the earth. Those who worship the beast will receive the full brunt of the contents of the vials. Let's be clear here about the church and the age we now live, just to refresh our memories.

The age in which you and I currently live is referred to in scripture as the "dispensation of the grace of God." Look at Ephesians 3:2 and what it has to say, "If ye have heard of the dispensation of the grace of God which is given me to you-ward." Our age, also referred to as the church age by many, began at Pentecost with the birth of the church, also known as the body of Christ or the bride of Christ. This age will end at the snatching away of the bride so that when the things we are viewing, the vials and plagues occur, the church will not be on earth. Christ will have taken us out of this world prior to the tribulation beginning. The dead in Christ will rise first. Then we, who are alive and remain, will be taken up to meet Him in the air. Once we are snatched away, then the brief seven-year period of the tribulation will begin.

A period which will be split into two, three and one half year periods making seven years. During the tribulation period, the world will experience travail, sorrow, and war. It will see the worst destruction and death in its entire history. As you may recall, Christ said if it wasn't shortened, no flesh would survive. At the end of this period, Christ will return. He will subdue His enemies and destroy the wicked. Then set His kingdom up on the earth. For one thousand years, there will be prosperity and peace among the nations. Nature and earth will be back as pre-flood. At the end of the one thousand years, the wicked dead will be raised, judged, and cast into the lake of fire—there with Satan, their leader. We have studied the history of the church here in Revelation in the section, The Snatching Away of the Bride. In chapters 2–3, we saw the stages of church history. Chapter 4 shows the snatching away of the true believers, while the professing church on earth will be left behind. It is, as you may remember, called "Mystery Babylon."

We are now in the stretch of chapters 15 to 18 of Revelation, a portion that describes for us the final phase of the false church, the false Christ, and the beast. The last three and one half years of the tribulation, the worst part of that short seven-year period. These seven vials and plagues of the wrath of God are coming here in chapter 16. The command to pour them out is issued here in verse 1. John now continues the account of what will occur when the bowls of wrath are poured out. God will not bring judgments upon the earth until He had made safe those who belong to Him.

Just as He promised the church that she would not go through that great time of temptation or trial as the Greek word means. Remember Revelation 3:10 states, "Because thou hast kept the word of my patience, I also will keep thee from the hour of temptation, which shall come upon all the world, to try them that dwell upon the earth." The church is snatched away prior to the tribulation starting. He will not have these vials poured out until His ancient people, the Jews, are made safe. Once He has done that. The judgments will fall—they will fall quickly and terribly. Remember the Lord Jesus Christ is still in charge.

Remember back in Revelation 5:5, "And one of the elders saith unto me, Weep not: behold, the Lion of the tribe of Juda, the Root of David, hath prevailed to open the book, and to loose the seven seals thereof." The Lord Jesus is the only one worthy to open the seven-sealed book. His opening of the seals brought about this entire series of sevens. He is still in command here in chapter 16. He is in command to the end of the book of Revelation of Jesus Christ. He is the One who is marching toward victory. The power and glory of His majesty belong to Him. He is finalizing His judgment upon a Christ rejecting world.

The Father has committed to Him all judgment. Christ gives the command, which sends these seven angels moving with the final judgments. There is now no longer a delay. The interval of intermission seen in chapter 15 has ended. The hour of judgment is now here! The order to move is given the seven angels follow the command. We now see Revelation 16:2 that says, "And the first went, and poured out his vial upon the earth; and there fell a noisome and grievous sore upon the men which had the mark of the beast and upon them which worshipped his image." The first angel begins to pour out his vial or bowl. It lands upon the earth, the first thing God created.

Notice too, the plagues, these resemble some seen before. This appears like the boils of Exodus 9:8–9, which states, "And the Lord said unto Moses and unto Aaron, Take to you handfuls of ashes of the furnace, and let Moses sprinkle it toward the heaven in the sight of Pharaoh. And it shall become small dust in all the land of Egypt, and shall be a boil breaking forth with blains upon man, and upon beast, throughout all the land of Egypt." When pharaoh persecuted the children of Israel and refused to let them go, God sent plagues. He did it until pharaoh and his house had been destroyed. That judgment of plagues was a type of Revelation 16. The difference is the scope of the intensity.

The Exodus plagues were limited to Egypt. These will be worldwide. Moses predicted a similar plague like this, it has not been fulfilled. We find it in Deuteronomy 28:15 that says, "But it shall come to pass, if thou wilt not hearken unto the voice of the Lord thy God, to observe to do all his commandments and his statutes which I command thee this day; that all these curses shall come upon thee, and overtake thee." Then we see the list in Deuteronomy 28:27 that states, "The Lord will smite thee with the botch of Egypt, and with the emerods, and with the scab, and with the itch, whereof thou canst not be healed." These diseases are incurable according to Deuteronomy 28:35, which states, "The Lord shall smite thee in the knees, and in the legs, with a sore botch that cannot be healed, from the sole of thy foot unto the top of thy head." These are Moses predictions or prophecies. They are fulfilled for the Jews here as well as all who follow the Antichrist and the beast.

Now we see here in verse 2 these sores are "noisome and grievous." They are for all who have taken the mark of the beast. Remember those who had not taken the mark were protected. But under severe persecution even of being put to death, the ones who don't have the mark can't buy or sell anything. These are desperate times in these last three and one half years of the great tribulation. Now the end is here, and those who had been enjoying the privileges of having the mark are now going to be judged. God's judgment during the tribulation will be a terrible one.

AIDS is our big epidemic today. Recently there was the Ebola virus in Africa. Yet these will be even worse. That is hard to comprehend. These people will mark themselves with a mark, and by their sin now, God marks them out by His judgments. This sore will be similar to ulcers. Think about this and the AIDS/HIV of today. Don't lesions come up on the bodies of those with AIDS—virus lesions that cause cold sores, similar to shingles, accompanied by fluid-filled blisters?

What is the tribulation period known for? Remember Daniel 11:37 states, "Neither shall he regard the God of his fathers, nor the desire of women, nor regard any god: for he shall magnify himself above all." The beast will have no desire for women. Romans 1:26–27 says, "For this cause God gave them up unto vile affections: for even their women did change the natural use into that which is against nature: And likewise also the men, leaving the natural use of the woman, burned in their lust one toward another; men with men working that which is unseemly, and receiving in themselves that recompence of their error which was meet." The tribulation will be a time of great homosexuality. The noisome and grievous sores sound a lot like those of people with AIDS. The beast worshippers are the final rebels, they are shortly condemned. Now they taste just a portion of what their eternity will resemble. The torments—they will suffer for all eternity. This is not a time for mercy on their part. They hate God more and more and are still stricken.

We now come to verse 3 of Revelation 16, which states, "And the second angel poured out his vial upon the sea; and it became as the blood of a dead man: and every living soul died in the sea." Now the sea is affected, with greater intensity than we had seen in the beginning of the judgment. Remember the second trumpet affected one-third of the sea life? Now we see every sea creature is affected. The sea is the great reservoir of life. It is teaming with life. The salt water is cleansing for the filth of the earth. However, in this plague, blood is the symbol of death. The sea becomes a grave of death instead of a womb of life. The cool sea breezes become a stench from the carcasses floating on the water. Commerce will be paralyzed.

In the Egyptian plague, humans died in Exodus 7:20–25, which says, "And Moses and Aaron did so, as the Lord commanded; and he lifted up the rod, and smote the waters that were in the river, in the sight of Pharaoh, and in the sight of his servants; and all the waters that were in the river were turned to blood. And the fish that was in the river died; and the river stank, and the Egyptians could not drink of the water of the river; and there was blood throughout all the land of Egypt. And the magicians of Egypt did so with their enchantments: and Pharaoh's heart was hardened, neither did he hearken unto them; as the Lord had said. And Pharaoh turned and went into his house, neither did he set his heart to this also. And all the Egyptians digged round about the river for water to drink; for they could not drink of the water of the river. And seven days were fulfilled, after that the Lord had smitten the river." Remember the sea covers the greatest portion of the earth.

The God who made it now turns it to blood "as of a corpse lying in its own blood." So the billions, trillions of sea creatures die. They come floating to the surface in horrible, rotting witness of the wickedness of men. There is no escaping these words of God: "every living soul died." What a frightful stench! What fearful possibilities of disease! Yet remember that this is exactly what God is doing. Behold, Jehovah maketh the earth empty, and maketh it waste and scattereth abroad the inhabitants thereof. Therefore few men left. When thus it shall be in the midst of the land among the people, there shall be as the shaking of an olive tree, and as the gleaning grapes when the vintage is done. (Isa. 24:1–13) I will make a man more rare than fine gold, even a man than the golden wedge of Ophir. As the shaking of an olive tree, two or three berries in the top of the uppermost bough, four or five in the outmost branches of a fruitful tree, saith Jehovah, the God of Israel." (Isa. 13:12; Isa. 17:6)

When God cleared off this race in the days of Noah, He left eight persons. It will be "as it was in the days of Noah" again, shortly, and although God will yet suffer the human race to have another thousand years on earth (Rev. 20:4–6). Nevertheless, He will so reduce earth's population, that "few men will be left" to start that thousand years. This will be so whether you believe it or not because God cannot lie.

We see next Revelation 16:4–7, "And the third angel poured out his vial upon the rivers and fountains of waters; and they became blood, And I heard the angel of the waters say, Thou art righteous, O Lord, which art, and wast, and shalt be, because thou hast judged thus. For they have shed the blood of saints and prophets, and thou hast given them blood to drink; for they are worthy. And I heard another out of the altar say, Even so, Lord God Almighty, true and righteous are thy judgments." Now not just the sea is affected but the rivers and fountains. They too turn to

Blood fresh water is affected. The very source of life is destroyed, just as the plague that fell upon Egypt, when the river became blood. All freshwater is affected that would be the wells like many country folks have. The water supply is cutoff. That would mean that the animal life would begin to die off. Man's life destroyed in unparalleled fashion.

Notice the fountains, we see from the first judgment that fell upon men were used in the judgment and salvation. Genesis 7:11 says, "In the six hundredth year of Noah's life, in the second month, the seventeenth day of the month, the same day were all the fountains of the great deep broken up, and the windows of heaven were opened." In that judgment, the fountains of the deep were broken up. They spewed forth water to help in the deluge that came from God's judgment. Here they are turned to blood. God uses the life sustaining things He supplied to bring judgment. What God gave for a blessing for mankind, He is now using for His wrath and judgment.

Just as Christ said, "As it was in the days of Noah." God works His judgment upon man. He uses the creation to accomplish His mission. Again, we see the plague similar to the third trumpet, and again, it is more severe. We see God's righteousness dealing with those who had slaughtered His servants. We see this in verses 5 through 7. God is righteous in all His ways, whether in grace or in judgment. "The angel of the waters" is the superintendent of God's water department. Can you see yet another function of God's holy angels here? They have different parts of the earth to care for, different departments shall we say.

We see another mystery here revealed that the angels affect creation. This is not the angel to whom it was given to smite the waters but the waters themselves speaking through their angel. Here we see that angelic being in charge of the waters that supply the earth, a benevolent being certainly. You think maybe our nation's angel is being told to withhold rain in some parts of this nation? Draught is prominent in many parts of this nation, especially where folks have turned away from God. We saw in the beginning of our study four angels are holding the four corners and winds of the earth. The angel who knows the whole story of the waters, he now declares that God is right and holy in this act of judgment.

Whatever God does is right! God is righteous! All His ways are righteous! We see the reason God is doing this. Verse 6 says they had poured out the blood of saints and prophets. So God gave them blood to drink. God's poetic justice in His vengeance. Those who live by the sword shall die by the sword. The shedding of blood leads to God shedding their blood. These are those who are being judged for making martyrs of God's people. God is forcing them to drink blood. For the righteous blood, they had spilled.

We hear a voice out of the altar as we see in Revelation 16:7 that says, "And I heard another out of the altar say." The brazen altar as seen in Revelation 6:9 states, "And when he had opened the fifth seal, I saw under the altar the souls of them that were slain for the word of God, and for the testimony which they held." The voice responds to the judgment being executed. They recognize the true and righteous character of Almighty God. They welcome His manifest judgment upon those wicked and evil humans in charge on earth at this point.

Here we see the prayers of those seen in chapter 6 being answered. God took some time to get to it but now is the time for the answering of their prayers. All sympathy of heaven is with God. This should be a wake-up call to those who are not saved in our age. This should make them tremble, coming to Christ for safety. This should spur us on to serve God and bear witness of the truth. The altar's message is loud and clear. True and righteous are thy judgments. All God does is true and righteous, especially in His judgments.

In their praise, they recognize the true and righteous character of the Lord God Almighty. We are now fully seeing God's judgment coming swiftly upon all those who have taken the mark and/or worshipped the beast. All that the Beast claimed and told them is now falling apart. The water needed to sustain life has now turned to blood. Even the ecosystem that man is desperately trying to keep in balance has now been destroyed. The souls in heaven are worshipping and praising God. The souls who have cried out for vengeance are now seeing it come to pass. God is pouring His wrath out on the enemies of the believers on earth and those who are against Israel. Great is the burden of God's wrath upon them. Great are these plagues! The evil ones are reaping what they have sown. God will not hold back His wrath any longer.

We now come to verse 8 and 9 of Revelation 16 that says, "And the fourth angel poured out his vial upon the sun; and power was given unto him to scorch men with fire. And men were scorched with great heat, and blasphemed the name of God, which hath power over these plagues: and they repented not to give him glory." Now the sun is affected. Global warming comes about but not because of man's environmental practices. Or maybe as the global warming folks say, the ozone layer is removed or altered. The sun, which they cherished, will grow hot as judgment comes to the idolaters. God is demonstrating His power over His creation.

God, we are told, would bring signs in the sun, moon, and stars, and here are those signs. Look at Luke 21:25 that states, "And there shall be signs in the sun, and in the moon, and in the stars; and upon the earth distress of nations, with perplexity; the sea and the waves roaring." Here is that prophecy fulfilled as God is pouring out judgment upon mankind. The supreme source of light, which had affected a third of the sun earlier in the study when the trumpets sounded now, becomes a curse and brings intense heat. Bittersweet suffering comes.

Though their suffering is great, they still fail to be brought to repentance by this punishment. God's name is still blasphemed! His creatures refuse to give Him glory! Old Testament prophecy is not left out in all this. The great tribulation and the judgment it would bring is seen in Old Testament scripture. Such as Deuteronomy 32:24, which says, "They shall be burnt with hunger, and devoured with burning heat, and with bitter destruction: I will also send the teeth of beasts upon them, with the poison of serpents of the dust." Not just Moses in the Pentateuch but also Isaiah. Where we see in Isaiah 24:6 which states, "Therefore hath the curse devoured the earth, and they that dwell therein are desolate: therefore the inhabitants of the earth are burned, and few men left." We see also Isaiah 42:25 that says, "Therefore he hath poured upon him the fury of his anger, and the strength of battle: and it hath set him on fire round about, yet he knew not; and it burned him, yet he laid it not to heart."

Now we have seen Jesus, Moses, and Isaiah prophecy of this time. Let's look to yet another Old Testament prophet Malachi in chapter 4 verse 1 that states, "For, behold, the day cometh, that shall burn as an oven; and all the proud, yea, and all that do wickedly, shall be stubble: and the day that cometh shall burn them up, saith the Lord of hosts, that it shall leave them neither root nor branch." To accomplish this, all that the Lord has to do is to remove one of the two blankets of the atmosphere. Just maybe it is a depleted ozone layer. He could also grab the sun or earth and pull them closer together. Neither would have to move too much. Just that little bit and man would have a hard time surviving.

Isaiah, as we saw, said the world would be decimated. We go back to Christ's words in Matthew 24:22 that says, "And except those days should be shortened, there should no flesh be saved: but for the elect's sake those days shall be shortened." One thing we can be sure of, He will protect His own. We see Psalm 121:6 that states, "The sun shall not smite thee by day, nor the moon by night." This verse is not as much of a comfort for us today. For the saints of the tribulation, it will be a great comfort. Yet Revelation

16:9 says, "And men were scorched with great heat, and blasphemed the name of God." In spite of all these judgments and plagues, instead of turning to God for mercy, they blaspheme His name! Doesn't this show man's heart is wicked!

Turning back to Genesis 6 and the flood—Noah's day we see Genesis 6:5 that says, "And God saw that the wickedness of man was great in the earth, and that every imagination of the thoughts of his heart was only evil continually." Look at what Christ said in Luke 17:26, which states, "And as it was in the days of Noe, so shall it be also in the days of the Son of man." No amount of punishment will turn them from the great wickedness. The great tribulation is not a purification of the church, understand that, please! It is a judgment upon the earth, it is part of the redemption of the inheritance. God "hath power over these plagues: and they repented not to give him glory." If they turned, God could end the plagues. But they repented not! They refused to give Him glory. The intense heat continues.

We see next Revelation 16:10–11 that says, "And the fifth angel poured out his vial upon the seat of the beast; and his kingdom was full of darkness; and they gnawed their tongues for pain, And blasphemed the God of heaven because of their pains and their sores, and repented not of their deeds." Reeling from the first four, now the fifth plague is poured out. Now the capital city of the beast is directly hit! His kingdom becomes dark, from intense heat to darkness! Men gnaw their tongues in pain!

Have you ever hurt that much hurt enough to gnaw your tongue? We see yet another of the plagues of Egypt here. Exodus 10:21–22 states, "And the Lord said unto Moses, Stretch out thine hand toward heaven, that there may be darkness over the land of Egypt, even darkness which may be felt. And Moses stretched forth his hand toward heaven; and there was a thick darkness in all the land of Egypt three days." Do you see it says, "Even the darkness which may be felt?"

These judgments, like those in Egypt, are placed upon all those who oppress God's people, mainly the redeemed of the Jews but all tribulation saints in this case. The end of Gentile world domination is near with the pouring out of these vials. The seventh vial will bring an end to Gentile rule as the world has known it for one thousands of years. The battle of Armageddon is a few chapters away with that Gentile world power comes to an end. My first thought on reading that darkness came was that with the heat comes fires and with fires come smoke. Look back at Revelation 9:2 that says, "And he opened the bottomless pit; and there arose a smoke out of the pit, as the smoke of a great furnace; and the sun and the air were darkened by reason of the smoke of the pit."

Several of the prophets mention this event. The whole kingdom of the beast is darkened. Again, we need to go to Old Testament prophecy and Isaiah's prophecy. We see Isaiah 60:2 that states, "For, behold, the darkness shall cover the earth, and gross darkness the people: but the Lord shall arise upon thee, and his glory shall be seen upon thee." We have now a minor prophet too in Joel. We see chapter 2 of Joel verses 1–2 and 31 that says, "Blow ye the trumpet in Zion, and sound an alarm in my holy mountain: let all the inhabitants of the land tremble: for the day of the Lord cometh, for it is nigh at hand; A day of darkness and of gloominess, a day of clouds and of thick darkness, as the morning spread upon the mountains: a great people and a strong; there hath not been ever the like, neither shall be any more after it, even to the years of many generations. The sun shall be turned into darkness, and the moon into blood, before the great and terrible day of the Lord come."

The darkness arrives here in Revelation 16. John seems to be saying as it is given to him by Christ, "This great tribulation period is where these prophecies fit into the program of God." The Lord Jesus confirmed it. We see His words in Mark 13:24 that states, "But in those days, after that tribulation, the sun shall be darkened, and the moon shall not give her light." Because of this darkness, they gnawed on their tongues because of the pain. Just think about the intensity of the suffering. While they will be thinking this is hell on earth and it is, they still have a future and eternity to spend in the lake of fire.

This is a preview for them of what is to be their eternal destiny. But they don't turn from their wickedness they just keep on doing it continually. There are two self-evident things we see here. First, God is righteous in pouring out the bowls of wrath. Remember after all, Jesus is the judge. He is in charge here, as well as He is in our world today. He is in charge here in Revelation of handing out judgment.

Second, we see mankind is not led to repentance through suffering. We see Paul and his prophetic words in Romans 2:4–5 that says, "Or despisest thou the riches of his goodness and forbearance and longsuffering; not knowing that the goodness of God leadeth thee to repentance? But after thy hardness and impenitent heart treasurest up unto thyself wrath against the day of wrath and revelation of the righteous judgment of God." Here we are seeing the righteous judgment of God being poured out. Man continues to harden his heart to God and refuses to repent.

They continued to blaspheme God. They gnawed their tongues and blasphemed God. What a reaction to the immense judgment God is placing on them! Darkness, extreme heat, and still they harden their hearts. They blasphemed because of their pains, sores. They repented not of their deeds. All this judgment placed upon them, and yet they refuse to repent. In other words, they did not repent of their wicked deeds, idolatries, murders, sorceries, fornications, and thefts.

In order to own and confess them, which is the meaning of giving glory to God in repentance these people are shut in with their sores and pains. There is no relief now. They are in darkness, and the pain is much more intense. We need to be busy telling others about the Lord, warning of the judgment to come. Yet people today harden their hearts toward God too.

We need to warn the unbelievers, don't we? We need to seek out souls. We now come to Revelation 16:12–13 that states, "And the sixth angel poured out his vial upon the great river Euphrates; and the water thereof was dried up, that the way of the kings of the east might be prepared. And I saw three unclean spirits like frogs come out of the mouth of the dragon, and out of the mouth of the beast, and out of the mouth of the false prophet." Now the great Euphrates River is affected. That great river dries up. We are told it dries up to prepare the way for the kings of the East. That would be China, Korea, Vietnam, and many others now coming in the picture. They can pursue an uninterrupted march to the place of destruction. God is demonstrating His power over His creation.

We go again to Old Testament prophecy and Isaiah 11:15–16, which says, "And the Lord shall utterly destroy the tongue of the Egyptian sea; and with his mighty wind shall he shake his hand over the river, and shall smite it in the seven streams, and make men go over dryshod. And there shall be an highway for the remnant of his people, which shall be left, from Assyria; like as it was to Israel in the day that he came up out of the land of Egypt."

Now we see here that these nations are gathering to the mountain of destruction, Armageddon. The gathering of all nations is seen in the sixth vial. They are coming to make warfare against Almighty God. Think about this: the Euphrates river runs some 1,500 to 1,800 miles long. In some places, it is a mile wide. It is ten to thirty feet deep. Yet we are told it will dry up when the sixth vial is poured out. God's wrath is great upon the earth at the end of the tribulation. The dry riverbed will become a highway. This highway will play an important role in the bringing together the armies of the world for the next to last great battle. The border that once was a formidable boundary between East and West will be removed.

The king of the rising sun, as the original calls it, can now come and join in allegiance to the king of the West in a valley called Megiddo. For centuries, the Euphrates River has been a formidable natural barrier between the East and West. But here now, at the end of the tribulation, the armies of the world will prepare themselves for a great battle. The beast and false prophet set to take a final stand in battling against God and His people. Daniel states at least four armies will be gathered: the king of the North, the king of the South, the king of the East, and the ten-horned beast mentioned by Daniel and Revelation. The king of the North, Gog and Magog, Russia and its subsidiary nations will join in.

The king of the West the revived Roman Empire, the European common market nations, and probably the USA will come. The king of the South coming up out of Africa he too will be joining the forces. The kings of the East are the Asian countries. These are all going to meet in the valley of Megiddo to make way for the king of the East to reach the battlefield the river Euphrates is dried up. It makes a natural roadway by which they can come. God can dry up waters. For Israel, He dried up two bodies of water—the Red Sea for deliverance, the Jordan River at flood stage for them to enter the land of promise. If he was able to do that, He can surely dry up the great river Euphrates.

We see next Revelation 16:13 that states, "And I saw three unclean spirits like frogs come out of the mouth of the dragon, and out of the mouth of the beast, and out of the mouth of the false prophet." We see an interlude, a break from the pouring out of the vials here in verse 13. We see unclean spirits like frogs. Remember in Exodus one of the plagues was that of frogs? Here we see frogs yet again. Yet these are unclean spirits.

Leashed upon the earth by the dragon aka Satan—the beast of the revived Roman Empire, the Antichrist or false prophet, which is the unholy trinity.

They act in unison in forcing the nations of the world to march against Israel first, but we are shown the real reason they gather in chapter 19. Keep in mind, Satan knows scripture; he knows that the end of the tribulation is upon them. He knows what the book of Revelation states. So he sends these unclean spirits to gather them to battle. We see Revelation 16:14 that says, "For they are the spirits of devils, working miracles, which go forth unto the kings of the earth and of the whole world, to gather them to the battle of that great day of God Almighty." They are gathering because they know Jesus is to return soon. You see they know about Jesus but will not submit to Jesus. Remember the Bible is a literal book with pictures or types.

We are told that the tribulation is a seven-year period. Satan knows that and knows that his final battle will soon be here. Satan is moving to destroy God Almighty to destroy God's covenant with Israel. He brings all the armies of the world together, that would include the USA, would it not? These frog-like symbols are unleashed and somehow gathered the armies of the whole world.

There are three of them. Remember the beast has control of the Western nations. Three are for the kings of the North, South, and East. The greatest world conflict will be a direct result of these unclean spirits because as we are told, they come from the mouth of the dragon. Understand the beast, the false prophet, and demons working together as the unholy trinity. They are working miracles that are signs, visiting kingdoms upon the earth. The purpose is to gather them to battle of the Great and mighty day of God Almighty. This will be a showdown at Armageddon. The place they will meet one another, in an attempt to settle the final issue. This is a war, which they are gathered for, the battle is never joined.

The Lamb only needs to come forth. When He does, the beast is taken—the false prophet too. They will be cast into the lake of fire. The devil cast into the Tartarus abode of Hades. The gathering unto war becomes the business of the whole world. For how long they fight among themselves, we aren't sure. The source of the conflict is the unclean spirits of the frogs—three special evil spirits, doubtless leading millions of others, who will help them from hell's trinity. The dragon, the beast, and the false Christ will all be sending them forth. They accomplish their mission by one method. One many look for today. Miracle working, sign gifts you see Satan can deceive by having miracles performed. They do it before the rulers of the earth.

Remember Jannes and Jambre, Egypt's magicians! They blinded pharaoh from the truth. They also brought up frogs in Exodus 8:7 that states, "And the magicians did so with their enchantments, and brought up frogs upon the land of Egypt." Scriptures constant testimony is that of "signs and wonders," but these will be performed in that time by Satan's agency.

Let's now look at Revelation 16:15–16 that says, "Behold, I come as a thief. Blessed is he that watcheth, and keepeth his garments, lest he walk naked, and they see his shame. And he gathered them together into a place called in the Hebrew tongue Armageddon." John hears Christ say He comes as a thief, but blessed are those who watch for His coming! The time of His coming is close for us more than even these. We are to keep ourselves looking and prepared, ready for His return at any time. We are not to get distracted by signs and miracles today. But we are to keep our garments undefiled, not following after Satan's inspired movements, walking with God in holy separation from the abounding apostasy. We are to be following the truth of scripture rather than the lies of Satan. Remember Satan knows how long he has and he has marked the day from the time of the rapture of the church. He knows he had seven years. He knows the beast had three and one half years the last three and one half. That is why he is gathering the armies. He gathered them to a place in the Hebrew tongue Armageddon.

Now comes Revelation 16:17 that states, "And the seventh angel poured out his vial into the air; and there came a great voice out of the temple of heaven, from the throne, saying, It is done!" The seventh angel pours out his vial. It is poured into the air. The consequences of which are the voice out of the temple of heaven—a voice declaring it is done. It is believed the point here is that the vial fell upon the prince and power of the air, which is Satan. His powers are now restrained. His policies confounded.

The earth's reclamation is done. The price of its redemption fulfilled. It is now time for Christ to return. We will see that return in Revelation 19:11 that says, "And I saw heaven opened, and behold a white horse; and he that sat upon him was called Faithful and True, and in righteousness he doth judge and make war." Prior to seeing His return, we have chapters 17–18, which will come and are descriptive chapters. Explanatory chapters which deal with Babylon the great as it is called and her doom. Here we are in chapter 16 verse 17, and we have come to the end of the final series of sevens. The judgments coming before the second coming of Christ to set up His Kingdom are seen. The seventh and last vial and plague are broken and poured out by the Angel. This culminating with the end of the great tribulation the battle of Armageddon with Christ return to the earth.

We hear the voice of the only one who can deliver these people, the only one who can set up a righteous kingdom upon the earth. The only one who can bring peace to the World! None other than the Lord Jesus Christ! He says it is done! Do you remember His final words on the cross? It is finished. He finished paying the redemption price for mankind. Now we see the price to redeem the earth is finished. Christ is the judge, and His judgment in the great tribulation is completed—the redemption price for the world has been paid.

As Revelation 16:18 thus states, "And there were voices, and thunders, and lightning's; and there was a great earthquake, such as was not since men were upon the earth, so mighty an earthquake, and so great." Voices, thunders, lightning's, and great earthquake so great that they have not come upon the earth while man has been walking on it, not since the curse was placed on it we might say. So mighty, so great, we just think we have had bad earthquakes in our time. Yet we are told this is by far the worst. The voice said it is done. Then the earth begins a terrible shaking. Just think what this will cause, and we see what happens.

Revelation 16:19 tells us, "And the great city was divided into three parts, and the cities of the nation's fell: and great Babylon came in remembrance before God, to give unto her the cup of the wine of the fierceness of his wrath." So great is the earthquake that it divides the city into three parts. Great Babylon comes into God's remembrance, giving her the cup of wine—the wine of the fierceness of His wrath. First, it is called the great city. We see in Zechariah 14:4 that states, "And his feet shall stand in that day upon the Mount of Olives, which is before Jerusalem on the east, and the mount of Olives shall cleave in the midst thereof toward the east and toward the west, and there shall be a very great valley; and half of the mountain shall remove toward the north, and half of it toward the south." Many theories on what the mention of Babylon is here. Some believe it is Jerusalem, others say it is Rome, some say the real city of Babylon since the Euphrates runs through it.

We see what Zechariah says in chapter 14, that a great earthquake will occur when Christ sets foot on the Mount of Olives at His second coming. Some see it as the vial poured out upon the entire kingdom of the beast. Take a look at verse 19 again. This is called the city of nations. Could this be the city where the United Nations sits? Do you see how we can speculate? It is the city, which at this point in the great tribulation has the rule over the nations. God's places His full wrath upon her upon the nations of the world at this period of time.

As Revelation 16:20 comes into view, "And every island fled away, and the mountains were not found." Every island fled away. Mountains were not found. Remember Hawaii is a group of islands. Japan is an island nation. The mountains were not found. The fierceness of this earthquake moves islands and mountains. Islands are shifted. Remember that great earthquake a few years back that caused a tsunami? Japan was covered for a while. Mountains didn't disappear, but it was a bad earthquake. If that isn't bad enough, we see the final blow in

Revelation 16:21 that states, "And there fell upon men a great hail out of heaven, every stone about the weight of a talent: and men blasphemed God because of the plague of the hail; for the plague thereof was exceeding great." Now we see here the hailstones fall. These fall upon men. Do you see how the atmosphere is affected that is the air? The great hailstones weigh a talent. So what does a talent weigh, I know you're thinking. The Greek talent weighed about fifty-six pounds. The Hebrew talent was 114 pounds. It is said that when Titus leveled Jerusalem in ad 70, the Roman catapults, according to Josephus, threw stones the weight of a talent upon Jerusalem.

Great are these hailstones, big balls of ice. Instead of turning to God, look what the effect is— they blaspheme God. They do it because of the plague of hail. For we are told the plague was exceeding great.

Here we see again the plagues of Egypt here. Exodus 9:23–25 says, "And Moses stretched forth his rod toward heaven: and the Lord sent thunder and hail, and the fire ran along upon the ground; and the Lord rained hail upon the land of Egypt. So there was hail, and fire mingled with the hail, very grievous, such as there was none like it in all the land of Egypt since it became a nation. And the hail smote throughout all the land of Egypt all that was in the field, both man and beast; and the hail smote every herb of the field, and brake every tree of the field."

The same result followed in Exodus 9:34–35 that states, "And when Pharaoh saw that the rain and the hail and the thunders were ceased, he sinned yet more, and hardened his heart, he and his servants. And the heart of Pharaoh was hardened, neither would he let the children of Israel go; as the Lord had spoken by Moses." The miraculous hailstorm ends the great tribulation plagues and judgments. The intolerable judgment of God hits the earth in the final vial being opened.

Chapter 16 shows all these vials of God's judgment falling upon mankind. Christ is redeeming the earth from the curse. In these final two judgments, what do we see? The two worst awful things, the gathering of the earth's armies in Palestine, coming to battle the Almighty God in the sixth vial. The seventh brought even greater tragedy. First, the fearful, shaking of the earth, dividing the great city into three parts. So great is the swell from all the tsunamis that islands disappear. Mountains disappear. If that isn't bad enough, great hailstones fall upon the earth.

These will crush cars and destroy airplanes. All this happens after Christ says it is done. The redemption price of the purging of the earth is complete. It is finished. Yet these people still will not praise God. They continue to blaspheme God.

9

Antichrist Religious System Destroyed

We now come to Revelation 17:1 that says, "And there came one of the seven angels which had the seven vials, and talked with me, saying unto me, Come hither; I will shew unto thee the judgment of the great whore that sitteth upon many waters." An angel, which poured out one of the seven vials, comes and sits with John. At the end of chapter 16, we saw the end of the judgments. The series of seals, the trumpets, and the bowls are now done. We now see other visions and judgments here in chapters 17 and 18. We reached an end at Revelation 6:17. We saw another at Revelation 11:18. Both carried the same general theme. The same truths presented. They were in different aspects. Now we have the same type thing.

We will see again this city called great Babylon, and she will fall. The city is called in verse 1 "the great whore that sitteth upon many waters." Now John describes a new vision for us, not in matter but as Revelation of what we have seen before. An invitation is issued. "Come hither and I will show you the judgment of the great whore." The description carries with it the thought of a married woman who has been untrue to her husband. Having forsaken the guidance of her youth and broken the covenant of God by means of rebellion. She became a prostitute with the kings of the earth. This great harlot is of course the remnant of the worldly church in the tribulation, composed of those in the churches who never trusted Christ as their personal savior. She "sitteth upon many waters." The waters will be explained in verse 15. She will be pretty much in control of the world at this point.

Now we see in Revelation 17:2 that states, "With whom the kings of the earth have committed fornication, and the inhabitants of the earth have been made drunk with the wine of her fornication." See here she has committed fornication, spiritually with the kings of the earth. She is drunk with the wine of her fornication. These are the ten kings of the revived Roman Empire. Enticed to commit spiritual fornication, that is idolatry, the church and state in an unholy alliance to worship idols of gold, silver, brass, and wood. Keep in mind, in our day; we have the World Council of Churches trying to unite all Christian denominations. God will bring judgment upon this unholy alliance.

As we see Revelation 17:3 that says, "So he carried me away in the spirit into the wilderness: and I saw a woman sit upon a scarlet coloured beast, full of names of blasphemy, having seven heads and ten horns." John is carried away into the wilderness, where he sees a woman sit upon a scarlet-colored beast. This is, of course, the rule of the beast over the revived Roman Empire. The woman will be identified in verse 18. The woman is said to be a city. Many believe that city to be Rome, which at the time of the writing Rome was the religious capital of the world. She is religious Rome, we might say.

All true believers had been ruptured at the beginning of the tribulation. Folks will be saved during the tribulation as we have seen. But religion will be the course of the day, and the true believer will be subject to torture and death. As stated in the previous chapter, many theories on what the mention of Babylon is here. Some believe it is Jerusalem, others say it is Rome, some say the real city of Babylon since the Euphrates runs through it. We saw what Zechariah said in chapter 14, that a great earthquake will occur when Christ sets foot on the Mount of Olives at His second coming. Some see it as the vial poured out upon the entire kingdom of the beast. But notice back in chapter 16 verse 19, again this is called the city of nations. Could this be the city where the United Nations sits? Again, you see how there can be much speculation? We know it is said to be full of blasphemies.

We see Revelation 17:4 that states, "And the woman was arrayed in purple and scarlet colour, and decked with gold and precious stones and pearls, having a golden cup in her hand full of abominations and filthiness of her fornication." We get closer and closer to identifying what Babylon is referring too with each verse here in chapter 17. The beast is the one we saw in chapter 13. Therefore, we know it to be the revived Roman Empire and its dictator, the beast, and his protégé Antichrist, the religious leader.

The woman, as we go through, can be seen as a religious system who dominates world power, at least for a little season. The name she carries on her forehead helps to identify her as we see Revelation 17:5 that says, "And upon her forehead was a name written, Mystery, Babylon The Great, The Mother Of Harlots And Abominations Of The Earth." The church was a mystery because it was not revealed in the Old Testament. Here we have Mystery Babylon in the fact that it was not revealed until chapter 17. The true church left at the rapture.

The phonies those who are only church members were revealed at that moment. They entered the tribulation. I believe some will be saved after the rapture. But most will go right on not realizing they were left behind. The church system continues but is a harlot. The antichurch is the opposite of the true church—it is Mystery Babylon because it is given this designation just as Jerusalem is called Sodom. Babylon is the fountainhead for all false religions scriptures most abominable sin. Sex and false religion are related here. Mystery Babylon is called the mother of harlots—not singular but plural. In our day, we are seeing the church attacked, at least those who stand up for the truth.

Each group of these churches water down biblical truth in order not to offend people. For instance, those who believe in immersion will immerse folks during baptism. Those who believe in sprinkling will sprinkle for baptism. Those who want an elaborate ritual type ceremony will have that type of ceremony. You see, there will be more than just mother of harlots. There will be many in that day. They are forming today. They will be stronger in the tribulation. They will focus on the beast and false prophet and enter into that unholy alliance.

Now Revelation 17:6 states, "And I saw the woman drunken with the blood of the saints, and with the blood of the martyrs of Jesus: and when I saw her, I wondered with great admiration." Drunk on the blood of saints!

Those would be people who trusted Christ after the rapture. So here we see people will be saved after the church; the bride is in heaven with Christ. Many of those saints, those who trust Christ after the rapture, will become martyrs for Jesus. John says when he saw her, he wondered with great admiration. She is drunk with persecuting the saints of the tribulation. She has cruelly and inhumanly persecuted the saints of the tribulation. She is a composite of religious systems, which includes Protestantism, Romanism, and the occults.

John wondered with great wonder at her. The emphasis is on the revived Roman Empire more than the beast who is its leader. The emphasis on the unholy deeds of the religious system of the Antichrist is the focus. The emphasis on the martyrdom of the tribulation saints. We have before us the great harlot—the world's religious system and Mystery Babylon.

All deal with one thing that is cruelty toward anyone who worships the true God. The people who have turned from the true God and turned to the beast and false prophet thus turned to Satan are not repenting; instead they are blaspheming and rejecting God, killing those who receive God and His way. This great harlot is, of course, the remnant of the unholy church in the tribulation. Thus composed of those in the churches whose members never trusted Christ as their personal Savior.

We now come to Revelation 17:7 that says, "And the angel said unto me, Wherefore didst thou marvel? I will tell thee the mystery of the woman, and of the beast that carrieth her, which hath the seven heads and ten horns." The angel asks John why he marveled at her that is in amazement, which was joined by John's indignation toward her. The angel is going to reveal something to John we are told. He is going to reveal what is mysteriously or mystically designed by her. Until it is revealed to him, this will be a mystery to him, just as we are still looking at what is being seen in all this. When it is revealed, the interpretation is given in a vague manner.

It can only be understood with spiritual wisdom. It still remains a mystery to carnal mankind, just as the gospel itself, seems vague and unclear to the unbeliever. The hidden meaning of the woman or the mystery of her is told to John by the angel in verse 8.

We go now to Revelation 17:8 that states, "The beast that thou sawest was, and is not; and shall ascend out of the bottomless pit, and go into perdition: and they that dwell on the earth shall wonder, whose names were not written in the book of life from the foundation of the world, when they behold the beast that was, and is not, and yet is." The beast is to be understood as not Satan himself. It is in fact the revived Roman Empire. It was a very powerful and thriving empire.

Understand Satan's final attempt to fulfill his desires will occur during this period we have called the tribulation. The true church having been snatched away, ruptured, and in heaven. Satan brings to power the Antichrist, as well as the beast. His goal, as with the ancient time, is to set up a super federation of nations to guarantee safety for the world in union with the last great political empire the revived Roman Empire. We see in verse 8 that the beast was, is not, and yet is. Thus the reference "was" speaks of the history of the Roman Empire in the past. It now describes its present condition today fragmented yet not dead. It has fallen apart into the European nations of today. It is about to rise again from the abyss or the bottomless pit. We came next to the fourth message to the church at Thyatira.

We saw in the name Thyatira a continual sacrifice. It can also mean an incense offering. This was the church from ad 500 to the dark ages. In this church, we saw the union of the church with the state. They had a religion of works not grace. They suffered the woman Jezebel to seduce the church. They made use of the name of God to oppose the truth of his doctrine and worship. They abused the patience of God to harden themselves in their wickedness. The seductress will be cast into a bed. Thyatira is the first that will continue even in her wicked state until the coming of the Lord.

The wicked worshippers shall pass through the tribulation. But religion will be the course of the day, and the true believer will be subject to torture and death during the tribulation. We can see the beast in the revived Roman Empire here. We see in the harlot a form of the church. The church at Sardis was seen. This was the church of the reformation. The reformation fell short of accomplishing all that it could have achieved, while it was a protest and reaction against the rigid ecclesiastical hierarchy of Thyatira. It went to another extreme becoming free of restraints of absolute priest and sovereign of the church. It was split by the abuse of liberty and freedom and split into various sects and denominations.

Christ says of this confusion, "Thou hast a name that thou livest, and art dead." God's estimate of the church as a whole was they had a name and lived but were dead. There is a remnant of true believers as with each church and each era. The church at Sardis had a great reputation; it had a name, a very honorable name. It was a flourishing church—a name for a vital lively religion, for purity of doctrine, unity among themselves. Everything appeared well outwardly! But it was not really what it appeared to be the message of the reformation churches the great truths of God's Word. In the end, some fell away, and this is the part we see here as the woman.

We had the Laodicean church, the lukewarm church, the church of today—the church of the rights of the people, the church which exists when Christ will return for His bride. It is the last and worst church of all. Christ as the Amen, the one steady and unchangeable God. He never changes in his purpose or promise. This church completes the series of the seven churches. It is about the rights of people to do as they please here in our time—the time of democratization in the world and in churches. The authority of God's Word is being denied. This church receives a severe punishment. As lukewarm water turns the stomach, so this church turns Christ's stomach.

Understand the word spew here in the Greek means to vomit. To vomit in Webster, we see one meaning and that is to "eject violently." The masses have rejected Christ and aren't chosen because of that rejection of Christ. Many are seen here in the Laodicean church. Those who have a form of godliness and claim to be Christians but really aren't. They will go into the tribulation, and many will be absorbed into the woman.

Look to Revelation 17:9 that states, "And here is the mind which hath wisdom. The seven heads are seven mountains, on which the woman sitteth." We see now that the woman sits upon seven mountains. Rome is said to be the city of seven hills. Understand though this can't definitely say this is Rome. Babylon is also said to sit upon seven hills. So too is Jerusalem. Rome, throughout history, is called the city of seven hills—infamous for idolatry, tyranny, and blasphemy. The seven hills on which Rome stands; and seven kings, seven sorts of government. Five were gone when this prophecy was written.

One was then in being. The other was yet to come. Can you see the progression of the churches we saw in Pergamon and Thyatira? The marriage of the church with the emperor Constantine declaring the Roman Empire Christianized came in ad 312. The church after that period made a continual sacrifice, and the church came into a union with the state Rome and will continue in its false teaching throughout the tribulation.

Revelation 17:10 states, "And there are seven kings: five are fallen, and one is, and the other is not yet come; and when he cometh, he must continue a short space." Seven kings seen, five are fallen, one is the other is not yet come. When he comes, he must continue a short space. Five kingdoms have ruled the earth. At the point of this writing, there had been five world powers that had existed but were no longer—all oppressed the children of God: Egypt, Assyria, Babylonia, Persia, and Greece. One was in power at the time, Rome. The final one would come for a short space. That would be the revived Roman Empire. The European confederation of nations that is the European common market nations have formed. They will make up this revived Roman Empire.

They cannot come into power until the church has been snatched away. Then they will come and oppress the remnant of that day and align with the Antichrist who will spread false doctrine. The short space of their rule will be the seven years of the tribulation. The apostate church will have as its head the Antichrist, spreading the false doctrines and deceitful lies, the churches as seen in Thyatira, Sardis, and Laodicea. After the true church has been snatched away their doom is coming shortly as we press on through the chapters of Revelation. The doom of the woman and the beast is immanent. We need to be busy in this age because soon and very soon, the Lord will be returning for His bride, the true church and the tribulation will commence.

Revelation 17:11 states, "And the beast that was, and is not, even he is the eighth, and is of the seven, and goeth into perdition." The beast was and is not even, he is the eight and of the seven. This is the last great world dictator. He will dominate the League of Nations that is beginning with the European common market nations. His capital will be the eternal city. Again, Rome is called the eternal city. He will be destroyed. He will be cast into the lake of fire.

We go now to Revelation 17:12 that says, "And the ten horns which thou sawest are ten kings, which have received no kingdom as yet; but receive power as kings one hour with the beast." The beast is to be understood as not Satan himself. It is in fact the revived Roman Empire and its leader. It was a very powerful and thriving empire. These ten kings align with the beast. These ten have one mind. They are subservient to the beast. They become puppet leaders. They receive their authority from the beast. They rule with the beast for one hour. One hour or they rise up at one and the same hour.

In Revelation 17:13 it states, "These have one mind, and shall give their power and strength unto the beast." These are sovereign nations with one mind. But they give their power and authority in alignment with the beast. As we talked about, we are to be of one mind, the mind of Christ in our age. Yet our power and authority come from Him as the Lord and Savior of our lives.

Here we see these ten kings and all their subjects are to have one central religion. Being zealous for that religion and worshipping the beast, following his principles and practices, allowing him to exercise all authority both political and ecclesiastical. We come next to Revelation 17:14 that says, "These shall make war with the Lamb, and the Lamb shall overcome them: for he is Lord of lords, and King of kings: and they that are with him are called, and chosen, and faithful." They will make war with the Lamb.

This we will see in chapter 19. He will overcome them because He is Lord of lords and He is King of kings! Notice the army with Him, they are called and chosen and faithful. Sounds like us as the church, the bride. Are we not called, chosen, and to remain faithful? Romans 8:30 states, "Moreover whom he did predestinate, them he also called: and whom he called, them he also justified: and whom he justified, them he also glorified." Ephesians 1:4 says, "According as he hath chosen us in him before the foundation of the world, that we should be holy and without blame before him in love."

In the book 1 Corinthians we see chapter 4 verse 2 states, "Moreover it is required in stewards, that a man be found faithful." All three of these things can be said of us, as we will see in chapter 19 we will be with the Lord when He returns at His second coming. We see now Revelation 17:15 that says, "And he saith unto me, The waters which thou sawest, where the whore sitteth, are peoples, and multitudes, and nations, and tongues." The angel continues to reveal things to John.

The waters are peoples. The nations of these kings! She has dominion over the whole earth. So she will have rule over all the earth. Is that why Babylon is here? The whole earth in which she reigns, or was it she reigns in one specific city over the whole world? These multitudes of nations are seen as the waters. They are subject to the beast, with the approval of the great harlot. She reigns over the kings, they are her subordinates. We see Revelation 17:16 that states, "And the ten horns which thou sawest upon the beast, these shall hate the whore, and shall make her desolate and naked, and shall eat her flesh, and burn her with fire."

The ten nations under the harlot hate her. They turn on her. They hate her principles, sentiments, doctrines of devils, wicked practices, idolatries, adulteries, murders, and thefts. They will change their mind about her. Their love will turn to hate. Then they will make her desolate and naked. Then they will attack her and burn her with fire. Remember Christ's words to the church of Laodicea? Christ said He would spew her out of His mouth. He would vomit her up. He will eject her violently. Now the masses have turned against her, she is being violently rejected and ejected by those who followed her.

Now comes Revelation 17:17 that says, "For God hath put in their hearts to fulfil his will, and to agree, and give their kingdom unto the beast, until the words of God shall be fulfilled." God will work in them to overthrow her. He will fill them with hatred toward her. He will incline their hearts to overthrow her, while he turns their hearts against the whore; they will turn against her as predicted.

The same God who has turned them to a reprobate mind now puts in their heart to move away from the apostate church and move now toward the beast. They now turn their kingdoms over to the beast. This until the Word of God is fulfilled. The destruction of the armies by Christ in chapter 19 is the culmination. By overthrowing the apostate church, the way is paved for the Antichrist and beast to gain full power. That is God's purpose.

As we see Revelation 17:18 stating, "And the woman which thou sawest is that great city, which reigneth over the kings of the earth." Now we see she was that great city. The city of "which reigneth over the kings of the earth." At the time of this writing, the great city, which ruled over the kings of the earth, was Rome. So is this city Rome? The great whore is the apostate church. First followed by the kings then hated by them. Left desolate and naked and burned, the kings and people turn to the beast and Antichrist for direction—this to fulfill God's Words.

10

Babylon's Reward, Double Judgment

Revelation 18:1 says, "And after these things I saw another angel come down from heaven, having great power; and the earth was lightened with his glory." We have another angel or messenger who comes with great power and lightened the earth with his glory. A messenger sent with God's Word. We see Ezekiel 43:2. The gospel of Christ is the light that lightened with God's glory. He has power with him to accomplish God's plan.

Further we see Revelation 18:2 "And he cried mightily with a strong voice, saying, Babylon the great is fallen, is fallen, and is become the habitation of devils, and the hold of every foul spirit, and a cage of every unclean and hateful bird." The angel pronounces to all the earth that Babylon is fallen, is fallen. She is become the habitation of devils. Compare Isaiah 21:9 that states, "And, behold, here cometh a chariot of men, with a couple of horsemen. And he answered and said, Babylon is fallen, is fallen; and all the graven images of her gods he hath broken unto the ground." The emphasis on her destruction, the habitation of devils and every foul spirit is seen.

A cage or home for every unclean bird is spoken of. A buzzard came to my mind, those that eat flesh in order to cleanse the area of death. The end of apostasy of the church was seen in chapter 17. Now what is the reference here? The state of Babylon is that of ruin. We see in Revelation 18:3 that says, "For all nations have drunk of the wine of the wrath of her fornication, and the kings of the earth have committed fornication with her, and the merchants of the earth are waxed rich through the abundance of her delicacies." The reason for her destruction is given to us here. All nations had drunk the wine of the wrath of her fornication. They followed her idolatries. The kings of earth had committed fornication with her. Notice here too that all nations of the earth are guilty during the tribulation that would include the good ole United States of America. The multi-corporations become rich in alignment with her. Making the almighty dollar is more important than serving God, too busy for God and too busy in making money.

Next to Revelation 18:4 that states, "And I heard another voice from heaven, saying, Come out of her, my people, that ye be not partakers of her sins, and that ye receive not of her plagues."

Another voice speaks, saying, "Come out of her, my people." God's remnant now separated out. Remember this is not the church. The church was snatched out back in chapter 4 and at this point in Revelation. That means seven years had taken place. Yet more proof that people will be saved during the tribulation period. Remember that God called out 144,000 Jewish believers at the beginning of the judgments of man. There are 144,000 Jews to evangelize the world. We see their fruits being called out of the apostate church. Jesus is calling for them to come out and separate themselves from Babylon, which has fallen.

In this we see God warned Israel to separate from the sins of Babylon in Jeremiah 51:5–6, 45, as well as Isaiah 48:20. These are two part warnings. Do not have fellowship with the sins found in Babylon. Flee before the judgment comes. This should be a warning to us separate from sinful doctrines of devils today. Separate from the worldliness, many churches have given into, but this is also inward for we are to separate ourselves from the temptation the old sin nature brings upon us and follow the mind of Christ. We see as Lot was ordered out of Sodom and Gomorrah, so too the remnant here is told to separate. Before judgment fell on those cities Lot and his daughters were forced out. His wife looked back and was turned to a pillar of salt. As the church was removed from the time of trial in Revelation 4 now the Tribulations Saints are called out of hiding.

As we come now Revelation 18:5 that says, "For her sins have reached unto heaven, and God hath remembered her iniquities." God sees the sins of people. One after another, her sins were seen by God. They were piled one upon another in a heap. They all reached heaven, and God remembered her iniquities. Judgment will come because of the failure to repent and turn to God.

Then in Revelation 18:6 we see, "Reward her even as she rewarded you, and double unto her double according to her works: in the cup which she hath filled fill to her double." She will be rewarded with judgment. Not just judgment but double judgment is coming to her. It is spoken to the people of God to reward her double what she had rewarded them. Take vengeance upon her! God says to retaliate on her. Do it for what she had done, not for what she had done to them but to their predecessors in the faith of Christ. Those in former ages, those persecuted in the beginnings of the church, she had hated them. Made war with them, now they are to make war with her.

Next we see Revelation 18:7 that says, "How much she hath glorified herself, and lived deliciously, so much torment and sorrow give her: for she saith in her heart, I sit a queen, and am no widow, and shall see no sorrow." We see the same thinking in Revelation 3:17 with the Laodicean church. We see here in verse 7 "she hath glorified herself!" We see the Laodicean church "Because thou sayest, I am rich, and increased with goods, and have need of nothing." Do you see Babylon the great harlot lived deliciously? The Laodicean church said "I am rich, and increased with goods" is not that living deliciously. The apostate church gave torment and sorrow to all those who opposed her. She sat as a queen in her glory. She was no widow, yet Christ had taken the bride out. She thought she would see no sorrow, but God's judgment will come upon her. God said He would spew the Laodicean church out. This is that spewing out that ejecting violently double what she gave.

Revelation 18:8 that states, "Therefore shall her plagues come in one day, death, and mourning, and famine; and she shall be utterly burned with fire: for strong is the Lord God who judgeth her." The seven last plagues that came fall upon her in a very short time. Very speedily and very quickly! One right after another! If not, all together. The suddenness of the destruction will be by fire. Death and mourning occur. Actually death, mourning, and famine come that is what we saw with the four horsemen. They come upon Babylon with a vengeance. The destruction is God's final judgment upon her, and she is totally destroyed. The destruction is with fire as the city of Sodom and Gomorrah was destroyed with fire and brimstone. The emphasis is upon the method of destruction here. Which is by fire, this had been prophesied and referred to throughout scripture. We just saw last chapter the ten kings would burn her with fire. A voice had said, "She shall be utterly burned with fire." Thus is her fate.

As we see in Revelation 18:9–10 that says, "And the kings of the earth, who have committed fornication and lived deliciously with her, shall bewail her, and lament for her, when they shall see the smoke of her burning, Standing afar off for the fear of her torment, saying, Alas, alas that great city Babylon, that mighty city! for in one hour is thy judgment come." The kings who committed fornication with her, who lived deliciously with her, now mourn over her. They weep over her destruction. When they see the smoke billowing up, similar to what we saw with the twin towers only this is the whole city and the entire world.

In chapter 17, religious Babylon was taken down. Here we see the commercial center of the world is now destroyed. That is why we see the kings of the earth weeping over her destruction. The revenue she produced is now up in flames and smoke. Her destruction came speedily and very quickly. They ran to the outskirts of her in fear of her torment. They are seen saying alas, alas or woe, woe that great city Babylon, that mighty city. For in one hour is thy judgment come that is speedily and very quickly. The great city Babylon is destroyed but not before God calls out His remnant. Destruction was speedily and swiftly accomplished. Double was her punishment for her sins had reached unto heaven. God had remembered her iniquities. She had glorified herself, lived deliciously, arrogant, self-centered, and prideful. But judgment came, and they didn't expect it. God brings judgment upon the whole earth in the tribulation, but the center of their commerce and government is brought down.

We pick up now with Revelation 18:11 that says, "And the merchants of the earth shall weep and mourn over her; for no man buyeth their merchandise anymore." The merchants who bought her delicacies, they weep and mourn over her. Their livelihood has been destroyed. No one is buying their merchandise anymore. We see what that merchandise is in the next two verses.

Looking to Revelation 18:12–13 that states, "The merchandise of gold, and silver, and precious stones, and of pearls, and fine linen, and purple, and silk, and scarlet, and all thyine wood, and all manner vessels of ivory, and all manner vessels of most precious wood, and of brass, and iron, and marble, And cinnamon, and odours, and ointments, and frankincense, and wine, and oil, and fine flour, and wheat, and beasts, and sheep, and horses, and chariots, and slaves, and souls of men." The merchandise of gold and silver, the first thing mentioned is precious metals. Things for treasure and show, which we were told the great whore was to be decorated with. Not only gold and silver but precious stones, sound familiar. Those three are the items Paul said the believers would receive at the bema seat judgment. Here they are the merchandise of the world.

They had pearls, fine linen another thing we are to have, fine linen clean and white, do see how the things they have are the earthly treasures, yet ours are eternal. Purple and silk, scarlet and all thyine wood were all for those who were rich. All manner of vessels of ivory and of precious wood and brass, iron and marble were theirs. Riches upon riches being lost, as well these vessels would be no more for them. All the things mankind holds dear and of value on earth. Things that delight and bring pleasure, that gratify the senses: cinnamon and odors, ointments and frankincense, wine and oil, fine flour, and wheat, beasts and sheep and horses and chariots, and slaves and souls of men.

Whether slavery is the case here or just slaves to the merchandise cannot be determined. But with the current slavery of women and young girls in many countries, this in a corrupt world could be very possible. The souls of men, hooked on the lust of the false prophet and the beast taking the mark took their souls. Making the almighty dollar is gone, and they weep and mourn over their losses. Do you see that!

Look next to Revelation 18:14–15 that says, "And the fruits that thy soul lusted after are departed from thee, and all things which were dainty and goodly are departed from thee, and thou shalt find them no more at all. The merchants of these things, which were made rich by her, shall stand afar off for the fear of her torment, weeping and wailing." The fruits they lusted after the riches too, they lost all they are gone. The dainty and goodly things are gone. The worst thing is they will see them no more. The things of this earth pass away, but the things of God in heaven will never pass away.

The book 1 Corinthians 7:31 states, "And they that use this world, as not abusing it: for the fashion of this world passeth away." Merchants who became rich from her will stand afar off from her, they will keep Revelation 18:16–17 that says, "And saying, Alas, alas that great city, that was clothed in fine linen, and purple, and scarlet, and decked with gold, and precious stones, and pearls! For in one hour so great riches is come to nought. And every shipmaster, and all the company in ships, and sailors, and as many as trade by sea, stood afar off." They say alas, alas the great city that was clothed in fine linen. Using the same words as the kings, but adding how beautiful the city was. The things they had traded with her, the fine things in man's eyes, all those linens and jewelry and precious stones, all the things they lost when she fell. Again, for one hour or a short period of time, everything was destroyed. The verse tells that the shipmasters and all the ships all the sailors and as many as trade by the sea stood afar off.

As Revelation 18:18–19 opens, "And cried when they saw the smoke of her burning, saying, What city is like unto this great city! And they cast dust on their heads, and cried, weeping and wailing, saying, Alas, alas that great city, wherein were made rich all that had ships in the sea by reason of her costliness! For in one hour is she made desolate." They cried at her destruction. They saw the smoke billowing up in the sky from her. They said, "What city is like unto this great city!" Then they cast dust on their heads and cried, weeping and wailing over this city.

We see the reason for all this had made rich all ships in the sea because of her extravagances. Their ships had lost revenue. Remember by this time only if you had the mark of the beast in your hand or forehead could you buy and sell. Could be here that the beast had all the merchandise locked up in this city and everything that could be bought and sold was in her. In one hour, she was made desolate. The Lord brought her destruction quickly.

As the judgment continues to unfold in Revelation 18:20–21 that says, "Rejoice over her, thou heaven, and ye holy apostles and prophets; for God hath avenged you on her. And a mighty angel took up a stone like a great millstone, and cast it into the sea, saying, Thus with violence shall that great city Babylon be thrown down, and shall be found no more at all." Heavens are to rejoice over her destruction. The apostles and prophets are to rejoice. Then an angel appears and took a stone, we are told it was like a giant millstone. He cast it into the sea. He says, "Thus with violence shall that great city Babylon be thrown down. And found no more at all." They are gone forever never to be rebuilt again.

The final three verses in Revelation 18:22–24 that states, "And the voice of harpers, and musicians, and of pipers, and trumpeters, shall be heard no more at all in thee; and no craftsman, of whatsoever craft he be, shall be found any more in thee; and the sound of a millstone shall be heard no more at all in thee; And the light of a candle shall shine no more at all in thee; and the voice of the bridegroom and of the bride shall be heard no more at all in thee: for thy merchants were the great men of the earth; for by thy sorceries were all nations deceived. And in her was found the blood of prophets, and of saints, and of all that were slain upon the earth."

No more music will be heard from her. It tells us that not one builder and craftsmen, whatever his craft is, will no longer be found in her for she is destroyed never to be rebuilt. The sound of a millstone will no longer be heard grinding. No light will shine from her. No marriage will be performed. The merchants of the sea had been seduced by her sorceries. All nations were deceived by her. The blood of prophets and of saints and all that were slain upon the earth were found in her. She was judged by God, as Sodom and Gomorrah were judged and she was destroyed by fire just as those cities were. The great city Babylon is destroyed all her riches up in smoke.

Kings and merchants weep and wail over her because of lost revenue. You see, this is the great city of trade and commerce was in her. They are losing everything. In heaven, we see a scene of rejoicing, for she has received her just reward. The blood of prophets and saints, she was destroyed.

CONCLUSION

The beginning of the great tribulation and the reaping of the wicked ones was seen here. The unholy trinity was introduced to us and is going to come into being. Each day we live is one day closer to that occurring. Everything we see in the book of Revelation was prophesied to take place and is showing fulfillment of Old Testament prophecy. Yet this prophecy is not given by John but by Jesus Himself and John was the scribe who transcribed it all. Everything will happen just as seen on the pages of the book of Revelation and as laid out in these books. In the end, the unholy trinity will find its doom. That is for the final work on the Revelation study.

Right here we have seen the religious and economic system of the unholy trinity destroyed here at the end of chapter 18. We saw too that there will be a remnant of believers, people born again in this the tribulation period. We see a great multitude through the pages of chapters 6 through 18 on earth and the souls of martyr's in heaven, proof that folks will be saved in this seven-year period of time. For those who want to avoid going through these judgments, one must only receive Christ as their personal savior in the age in which we are currently living. The way to accomplish that was covered in the introduction and will be in the following portion of this conclusion. It is that important that you know how you stand and how to receive so great a salvation.

How do you stand today? Have you believed on Jesus as your Lord and Savior? If not, you need to do so right now. Don't miss being snatched away in the rapture! Don't be one of those who will end up in the tribulation facing the judgment of God! John 3:16 says, "For God So Loved the Word that He gave His only begotten son, that whosoever believeth on Him will not perish but have eternal life." Do you see God by grace gave His Son, Jesus Christ, and you must believe on Him! Romans 10:13 states,

"For whosoever shall call upon the name of the Lord shall be saved." Believe then call is God's order. Look at what Jesus said in John 3:17–21: "For God sent not his Son into the world to condemn the world; but that the world through him might be saved. He that believeth on him is not condemned: but he that believeth not is condemned already, because he hath not believed in the name of the only begotten Son of God. And this is the condemnation, that light is come into the world, and men loved darkness rather than light, because their deeds were evil. For every one that doeth evil hateth the light, neither cometh to the light, lest his deeds should be reproved. But he that doeth truth cometh to the light, that his deeds maybe made manifest, that they are wrought in God."

Do you see believe and call upon Him, admit you are condemned already because you haven't believed on Jesus Christ? Believe you are sinner in need of salvation, and believe that Jesus died for your sins. Call on the Lord and admit all to Him even that you believe Jesus died for your sins. You see, it isn't a matter of your sin that has condemned you; it is a matter of your unbelief. Believe and call upon Christ for salvation and you too can be snatched away at the rapture.

SECTION 4

History's Finale, God's Plan Finished

CONTENTS

INTRODUCTION

A great time of praise and adulation is seen in heaven as "History's Finale God's Plan Finished" opens. As we open Chapter 19 of Revelation with verse 1. The scene has now changes to Praise. God changes scenes and the prelude to war opens this book. We see Praise and honor being given to the Lord. The defeat of Babylon the great whore has been completed. Now the scene leading up to Armageddon and completion of Earth's redemption will finally be accomplished. Worshipping God in Heaven opens this book. Then we see the marriage feast and the marriage of the Lamb is now here the marriage supper taking place. Then Heaven will open up and Christ will return to Earth as conqueror and King. Let's cover a few things that must happen before you can receive the message which the Holy Spirit's purpose is in you reading this book. Before you can receive the message and serve God as He commands, before you can walk for Him you must have a personal, intimate relationship with Him. Romans 10:13 states "Whosoever shall call upon the name of the Lord shall be saved." Acts 16:31 says "And they said, Believe on the Lord Jesus Christ, and thou shalt be saved, and thy house." Of course John 3:16 is known by almost everyone but verse 17 & 18 state, "[17] For God sent not his Son into the world to condemn the world; but that the world through him might be saved. [18] He that believeth on him is not condemned: but he that believeth not is condemned already, because he hath not believed in the name of the only begotten Son of God."

You must admit you are a condemned sinner because of not having believed, you also must believe and then call upon Christ for salvation. Next if you are a believer you must practice 1st John 1: [9]"If we confess our sins, he is faithful and just to forgive us our sins, and to cleanse us from all unrighteousness." Before you can receive God's message you need to confess all known sin and God will forgive that sin and all the things which you don't realize are sins, as I like to say unknown sins.

1

Praise and the Marriage of the Lamb

We are at the brink of the marriage of the Lamb. First we see the celebration of the fall of mystery Babylon and the great whore. As we begin with Chapter 19 and verse [1]"And after these things I heard a great voice of much people in heaven, saying, Alleluia; Salvation, and glory, and honour, and power, unto the Lord our God:" After the Angel declared the fall of Babylon, a voice from heaven called the people of God. They are given specific orders take vengeance on her! After the weeping and mourning from the kings, merchants and the captains of the sea. Another voice had called the people of God to rejoice at the overthrow of this great city! Then right on cue those in Heaven rejoice just as commanded in Chapter 18. They say "Alleluia, salvation and glory and honor and power, unto the Lord our God!" God is given praise! Those souls we saw earlier in Revelation. Those under the throne who asked how long oh Lord! They are rejoicing over her destruction. The Bride the church that had been Snatched Away is rejoicing in Heaven with them. For in them there had been Martyr's too. The Prophets of old were rejoicing for they too had been avenged. Verse 2 the praise continues, [2]"For true and righteous are his judgments: for he hath judged the great whore, which did corrupt the earth with her fornication, and hath avenged the blood of his servants at her hand." They praise God saying

He as a true and righteous God, He hath judged the great whore! She was guilty of corrupting the Earth with her fornication. God has avenged the blood of His servants. We come next to verse [3]"And again they said, Alleluia And her smoke rose up for ever and ever." Again they rejoice and say Alleluia! The smoke from her is said to rise for ever and ever. As we saw in chapter 18 she will never be seen again. God in His vengeance for her great sin has avenged His people. We see the representatives of the Church offer up praise in verse [4]"And the four and twenty elders and the four beasts fell down and worshipped God that sat on the throne, saying, Amen; Alleluia." The twenty four elders as we saw earlier in Chapter 4 those who represent the church in Heaven and the four beasts who were flying round about the throne of God give praise and adoration. They fall down and worship God! He that sat upon the Throne in Heaven God the Father! They say Amen; they are in full agreement with God. They say Alleluia in worship of Him! We see verse [5]"And a voice came out of the throne, saying, Praise our God, all ye his servants, and ye that fear him, both small and great." A voice out of the Throne pipes in, the voice of Christ saying, Praise our God, all ye His servants! All ye that fear that is reverence Him, both small and great, the common believer who was in the Background as well as the Prophets and Apostles are all to praise God! We now come to verse [6]"And I heard as it were the voice of a great multitude, and as the voice of many waters, and as the voice of mighty thunderings, saying, Alleluia: for the Lord God omnipotent reigneth." Now the voice of the multitude in Heaven, the Old Testament Saints as Well as the Bride all chime in, all in one accord. The voice of many waters, Jew and Gentile who are saved worship Him. The voice of Thundering's they sound like thunder clapping. Again they cry out! Alleluia for the Lord God Omnipotent reigneth! God has conquered this great satanic ruled city. He has avenged the Martyrs of all ages. Soon we will see the full redemption process for both mankind and the earth completed. The fall of Babylon is to be praised and rejoicing comes by those who are saved both in Heaven and on Earth. For those who aren't, there is weeping and mourning over her destruction. We now see verse [7]"Let us be glad and rejoice, and give honour to him: for the marriage of the Lamb is come, and his wife hath made herself ready." All in Heavenly Saints and all Earthly ones too are to be glad and rejoice. They are to give God honor. Now the great event is ready, the marriage of the Lamb is come! Having now completed the full redemption process of man at the first advent and now the earth's redemption has been completed, the marriage can take place. The 7 year Tribulation is now at its end. We have seen the awful judgments that had to come to cleanse the earth and prepare it for the rule of Christ. Which occur in that period having appeared after the Snatching away of the Bride, she had been snatched away in Chapter 4 and has been in Heaven since the beginning of that Great and Terrible day, the Tribulation period. Just as she was promised in Revelation 3: [10] "Because thou hast kept the word of my patience, I also will keep thee from the hour of temptation, which shall come upon all the world, to try them that dwell upon the earth." But understand that the Wedding had not taken place. She had received her rewards and was preparing herself for the marriage. While the Bride, the Church resided in Heaven with Christ, God was judging the people on earth. Israel and the nations on earth were under great judgment. Great tribulation or Trial the Prophesied time of great temptation is coming to an end. The Final Chapter in man's history that is History's Finale and God's Plan for mankind will be Complete. Christ was still concerned with the Church now in Heaven. We see that the marriage will take place just as the Tribulation ends and right before the 2nd coming of Christ. The Bride has been in heaven preparing herself for the marriage. If you will recall in the marriage at Cana as we see in John 2 that the third day of the wedding they ran out of wine. Here is the process of a marriage in Jesus' time. The betrothal process, this would be the age in which we currently live. A suitable spouse for the Bridegroom was sought out. The church in our day is the Bride which will be suitable for the Bridegroom Christ. The second part of the betrothal was a "prenuptial agreement". The two parties would enter that agreement and sign it before witnesses. Remember Mary was "betrothed" to Joseph, they had entered this stage. Once this had been entered then there would be no sexual relations between them. If either was found in adultery as it would be considered, a bill of divorcement would have to be issued. If either party died before the actual ceremony then the other would be considered a widow or widower. The next step was the Wedding itself. The length of the betrothal was generally a year. The wedding was a special ceremony. We see that ceremony begin in Chapter 4 and continue to where we are now in Revelation 19. The wedding started with the procession of the groom and his companion's to the bride's home that occurred in chapter 4. The company would then escort the Bride and her companions back to the groom's home. Where there would be a special meal prepared. A celebration ensued until a written marriage contract was issued. The couple would then be escorted to a special "bridal chamber". Where they consummated the marriage, marriage festivities continued for up to a week. Remember what we see in 1st Peter 3:7-9, 7 "But the heavens and the earth, which are now, by the same word are kept in store, reserved unto fire against the Day of Judgment and perdition of ungodly men. 8 But, beloved, be not ignorant of this one thing, that one day is with the Lord as a thousand years, and a thousand years as one day. 9 The Lord is not slack concerning his promise, as some men count slackness; but is longsuffering to us-ward, not willing that any should perish, but that all should come to repentance." Then Daniel 9:24-25, 24" Seventy weeks are determined upon thy people and upon thy holy city, to finish the transgression, and to make an end of sins, and to make reconciliation for iniquity, and to bring in everlasting righteousness, and to seal up the vision and prophecy, and to anoint the most Holy. 25 Know therefore and understand, that from the going forth of the commandment to restore and to build Jerusalem unto the Messiah the Prince shall be seven weeks, and threescore and two weeks: the street shall be built again, and the wall, even in troublous times." God's timetable for the marriage celebration has been ensuing for 1 week or the last 7 years of Daniel's prophecy. The time to issue the marriage contract has come. The Bride is now adorned and ready for the marriage. We see verses 8 & 9 now, 8 "And to her was granted that she should be arrayed in fine linen, clean and white: for the fine linen is the righteousness of saints. 9 And he saith unto me, Write, Blessed are they which are called unto the marriage supper of the Lamb. And he saith unto me, These are the true sayings of God." She is now arrayed and prepared. Fine linen clean and white, fine linen the righteousness of saints. Now others are called to the marriage feast of the Lamb. Do you see the marriage process? The Bride was brought and the festivities have been taking place. Now is the time for the Marriage contract to be issued and the marriage feast to continue.

The great city Babylon is destroyed all her riches went up in smoke. Kings and merchants wept and wailed over her. In heaven rejoicing was occurring. God has avenged those martyred for His cause. Now the wedding and the wedding feast are at hand, ready for "History's Finale God's Plan Completed." The bride arrayed in fine linen clean and white, the fine linen of the righteousness of the saints. Those called to the marriage supper are the Old Testament Saints and the Saints who have died in the Tribulation. The finality of the Marriage process has come and a great marriage will occur.

2

Christ Return, the 2nd Advent

I want to ensure that it is understood about the marriage and ceremony. Therefore, let's ensure the point became clear on the Marriage of the Lamb and the Marriage supper as seen in verses 7-9 of Revelation 19. The Bride has been preparing herself for a week, every spot and every blemish was being removed. The wood, hay, and straw, which many believers received, had to finish burning. Each of the rewards not of intrinsic value had to be consumed. You see those were the rewards of the things done in the flesh by the believer. The Bride had been preparing herself. She had been 7 years or as we see in Daniels 70 weeks the last week of Daniel's weeks was in full swing on the Earth! The Bride had been in Heaven during this time preparing for the wedding, all her works done in the flesh had to be fully consumed. Her dress made spotless for the wedding and verse 7 said the time for that marriage had come. We pick up now with Chapter 19 verse [10] "And I fell at his feet to worship him. And he said unto me, See thou do it not: I am thy fellowservant, and of thy brethren that have the testimony of Jesus: worship God: for the testimony of Jesus is the spirit of prophecy." John falls down at the angel's feet to worship him. He is quickly told not to worship him for he was a fellow servant just as John was a servant of God. He was one who revealed God's plan! The point, worship God not angels or objects! We are to Worship the Lord our

God! John was rebuked by this messenger. Now the Lord is set to return to the Earth this is the Second Coming of The Lord Jesus seen here in verse [11] "And I saw heaven opened, and behold a white horse; and he that sat upon him was called Faithful and True, and in righteousness he doth judge and make war." Heaven is opened and a white Horse was beheld by John. The marriage now complete the Lord will come forth to complete the redemption of the earth. The marriage now fully completed. The Bride and Bridegroom having completed the marriage process, it is time for Him to reign in His Kingdom. Heaven is opened! The Bridegroom comes forth on a white horse! Remember this is a different White Horse and rider than what was seen in Chapter 6. He is coming forth here to return as King of Kings and Lord of Lords! What a thrilling scene! Does it give you chills just to think He is returning just as He said? Remember where we have been from chapter 4-18. The Bride was removed in Chapter 4 verse 1. The Tribulation began and billions of people died. The Beast and False Prophet came to reign. The Great Tribulation began. The time of Jacob's trouble, the time of Trial, of temptation had occurred. Now it is coming to an end after 7 years and for those on earth it has been a long seven years especially for those who believed on Christ during that time. We are told this rider is called Faithful and true, in righteousness He is coming! He has a purpose in coming. He is coming to judge those who did not receive Him! He is coming to make war and defeat the Beast, the False Prophet and satan which make up the unholy trinity. Remember God has always had a plan! God laid the plan out even to Adam and Eve. A Son would be born who would redeem mankind's soul first, and He would then redeem the lost inheritance the earth second. That plan of redemption was going to culminate with the 2nd coming of the Savior that is the 2nd Advent, here we see it beginning! We see now verse [12] "His eyes were as a flame of fire, and on his head were many crowns; and he had a name written, that no man knew, but he himself." We are given His description, His eyes as a flame of fire, which speaks of him coming in judgment. He is coming to judge those on the Earth. He is coming to put down its unrighteousness. On His head are many crowns. He is coming as Isaiah said, in Isaiah 9:5-7, He is coming to a battle. Garments will be rolled with blood. He will come with burning and fuel of fire. The government will be upon His Shoulders! His name will be Wonderful, Counsellor, the Mighty God, The Everlasting

Father, The Prince of Peace. Of the increase of His government and Peace there shall be no end! He will sit Upon the Throne of David and upon His Kingdom. It will be established with judgment and justice from henceforth and forever. The Zeal of the Lord of Host will perform this! He will be the Supreme ruler of the Earth. He is King of Kings and Lord of Lords. Can you see this as a figurative or symbolic reign? Some teach it that way and believe it that way. I can't, I see it that way and I believe it to be a physical Earthly Kingdom just as Isaiah prophesied and as it will be fulfilled by God, just as He promised it would be. Jesus sitting on the throne of David in Jerusalem as King not just of Israel but as the King of Kings and Lord of Lord's! We are told He has a name that no man knew but He himself. We saw Isaiah said He would be, Wonderful Counsellor, The Mighty God, the Everlasting Father the Prince of Peace. We see in the Gospels He is called, King of kings, Faithful and True, Word of God, Lord of Lords. Here we are told He has a name no man knows. We aren't told because God doesn't want us to know. His divine Nature is seen here in this Name that no man knows. He is coming as the one who will overcome. He is the Son of God. Isaiah said He would be called Immanuel! But this name cannot be comprehended by man. We now come to His clothing in verse [13] "And he was clothed with a vesture dipped in blood: and his name is called The Word of God". Remember what Isiah said his garment was rolled in blood! Here that prophecy is seen and fulfilled, a vesture dipped in blood. This also fulfills Isaiah 63:1-6. He comes in Battle. He died for our sins in Bloody agony there on the cross. The whipping and beating He took soaked his garments with Blood. In the Garden He sweat drops of Blood. He is coming to battle already having fought once for man's redemption. He comes now to complete the battle for the Redemption of all creation! He will stain His clothing more with the blood of His enemies in this coming war! His name is called "THE WORD OF GOD"! Note here John 1 verses 1 & 2, "In the beginning was the Word, and the Word was with God, and the Word was God. [2] The same was in the beginning with God." John 1: [14] "And the Word was made flesh, and dwelt among us, (and we beheld his glory, the glory as of the only begotten of the Father,) full of grace and truth." In His first advent John says the Word was made flesh. Now He comes in His resurrection Body still as "THE WORD OF GOD"! He comes in his eternal Character. As He was before creation so is He here at His second coming. Eternal Lord, Savior God. "THE WORD OF GOD!" The marriage we saw takes place in verse 7, verse 8 we are told how the bride was arrayed. Here is what verse 8 is stated "…arrayed in fine linen, clean and white…" Now we are told "THE WORD OF GOD" has an Army with Him. Notice how this army is arrayed, verse [14] "And the armies which were in heaven followed him upon white horses, clothed in fine linen, white and clean." Do you see who this army is? It is the Bride coming with her Husband the Bridegroom. Let's go all the way back to Revelation 4: [4] "And round about the throne were four and twenty seats: and upon the seats I saw four and twenty elders sitting, clothed in white raiment; and they had on their heads crowns of gold." Do you see it again? The 24 elders were clothed in Fine linen Clean and White. All this shows the Church, the Bride is the Army that comes with Christ. She has been with Him for one week of celebration. Leading up to the marriage ceremony and coming with Him in His finest moment. The church has been with Him in Heaven during the Tribulation all 7 years. Scripture to me is clear on that, although many would debate it, I believe it to be so! We see just exactly where we will be at Christ second coming. We will be with Him! Can you see that here? You will have your own white horse it says. You will be clothed extravagantly. You follow Him into Battle! How about the battle rights now, are you in the Battle or are you leaving it to others? You know the battle to win souls! Are you working to reach others! Working for an eternal reward! If you're not you should be! Jesus fought the battle for our souls, and if you have placed your faith and trust in Him, you should be in the battle today, as a Christian Soldier! Because you can be sure you are going to be in the battle at His second coming! We see the Weaponry in Verse [15] "And out of his mouth goeth a sharp sword, that with it he should smite the nations: and he shall rule them with a rod of iron: and he treadeth the winepress of the fierceness and wrath of Almighty God." A sharp sword proceeds out His mouth. Do you know you have that same weapon today? We see Hebrews 4:11-13, the Word of God we are told "…is quick, and powerful, and sharper than any twoedged sword, piercing even to the dividing asunder of soul and spirit…" The same weapon that proceeds out of the Lords mouth is the same weapon we use today, the Bible which is the Word of God, we use it to witness to people at least some of us do! How well are you utilizing that sword? The Bible, the Word, is designed as Hebrews states to pierce even to the dividing asunder the soul and Spirit of mankind! The sword the word that proceeds out of Jesus' mouth here in verse fifteen is used to smite the nations! He speaks and people fall down dead. Remember the night of His arrest when Judas brought the soldiers and servants to arrest Jesus? John 18:5 & 6 tells us, [5] "They answered him, Jesus of Nazareth. Jesus saith unto them, I am he. And Judas also, which betrayed him, stood with them. [6] As soon then as he had said unto them, I am he, they went backward, and fell to the ground." They fell backwards to the ground! He could have said "I am He" as He speaks here in Revelation and they would have fallen backwards dead. He treads the winepresses of the fierceness of His anger; He comes in judgment and justice! God's wrath against sinners is compared to a winepress. Those followers and armies of the unholy trinity are like clusters of grapes ripe for destruction! It is like He cast them in and presses and squeezes them and they are crushed under, just by His Speaking. The return of Christ at the Second Advent will be a time of Judgment first. He comes with His bride to defeat the wicked on the earth. The Lord is on His way to defeat the unholy trinity. The Battle of Armageddon is at hand here in Chapter 19. We will see next chapter the rest of the battle!

3

Armageddon, the End of the Unholy Trinity

As we saw heaven opened last chapter the Lord ready to return we now see the name written on his vesture and thigh as we come to verse 16 of chapter 19, [16]"And he hath on his vesture and on his thigh a name written, King Of Kings, And Lord Of Lords." He is coming to reign for we are told on His vesture and thigh a name written "King Of Kings, And Lord Of Lords!" This leaves no doubt who the One is riding upon this white Horse. He is the Champion of Salvation! The champion of Redemption! He is Jesus Christ! The Bridegroom, the "King Of Kings, And Lord Of Lords!" He is coming to conquer the unholy trinity. Retaking possession of the now restored Earth. He is coming with God's vengeance upon them for their shedding the blood of God's people. He is coming to deliver His people, Israel first and Foremost. Also He is coming for those gentiles who had trusted Him during this the Tribulation Period. Coming to execute Righteous Judgment! Coming to establish His divine authority over all the Earth as The Eternal Son of God! The promised seed of woman! We pick up now with Chapter 19 verse [17]"And I saw an angel standing in the sun; and he cried with a loud voice, saying to all the fowls that fly in the midst of heaven, Come and gather yourselves together unto the supper of the great God;" We see now another angel this one standing in the sun, crying with a loud voice. Not to mankind this time or to those of the army with Christ. But we are told he cries out to all the fowls of the air! Gather yourselves together unto the supper of the Great God. There is going to death to those standing in the Valley of Megiddo. The great armies of the world will fall! Great will be the death toll! Great will be the feast for the fowls in heaven. The supper provided by God, the Lord Jesus Christ! We are given the menu for the fowls of the heaven called to the supper of the Great God in verse [18] "That ye may eat the flesh of kings, and the flesh of captains, and the flesh of mighty men, and the flesh of horses, and of them that sit on them, and the flesh of all men, both free and bond, both small and great." They will eat flesh they have a smorgasbord of delicacy at least for them, the flesh of Kings that is rulers over nations, the flesh of captains, military leaders. As well as the flesh of mighty men that would be the rank and file soldiers. The flesh of horses, yes these armies will be on literal horses according to this. The flesh of them that sit upon them, the cavalry troops will be their meal. The flesh of all men, both bond and free, both small and great! That is all who rejected Christ that is those who received the mark of the beast, all will be food for these fowls of the air. This Great battle is a decisive victory! It will leave the enemies of Israel and the Tribulation Saints as a feast for the birds. God's divine vengeance will be completed! The birds of prey will swoop down and feast, the Eagle, the Vulture, the Buzzards all of those that eat flesh of the dead. The time of Jacob's trouble, the time of Trial is coming to an end. After 7 long years especially for those who believed on Christ during that time. All the enemies of Christ will fall in battle. Christ will conquer them all! We see Prophecy fulfilled Ezekiel 39:17 "And, thou son of man, thus saith the Lord God; Speak unto every feathered fowl, and to every beast of the field, **Assemble yourselves**, and come; gather **yourselves** on every side to my sacrifice that I do sacrifice for you, even a great sacrifice upon the mountains of Israel, that ye may eat flesh, and drink blood." Now I know we saw this battle as pre-Armageddon earlier. But here too we have the calling of the fowl, every beast, coming on the Mountains of Israel to eat flesh and drink blood. Can you see judgment is coming? God will come soon in judgment! Each passing day is one day closer to Christ returning first for the church. Then at His second coming, first to avenge and judge then to rule upon this earth for 1000 years. Are you busy sounding the alarm? Are you telling those in the community you live in about the Lord, how about your family members and friends, how about your enemies are you sounding the alarm and telling them about Christ? You should be! We see now verse [19] "And I saw the beast, and the kings of the earth, and their armies, gathered together to make war against him that sat on the horse, and against his army." The enemy is gathered for battle. The beast of war are gathered, the kings of the earth, the leaders of all nations are here. Their armies are with them. They are here to make war against Him that sat upon the horse and His armies. Here we see the difference between the war in Ezekiel 38 & 39 and this one. We see verses 11 and 12 of Ezekiel 38, [11] "And thou shalt say, I will go up to the land of unwalled villages; I will go to them that are at rest, that dwell safely, all of them dwelling without walls, and having neither bars nor gates, [12] To take a spoil, and to take a prey; to turn thine hand upon the desolate places that are now inhabited, and upon the people that are gathered out of the nations, which have gotten cattle and goods, that dwell in the midst of the land." Notice in Revelation 19 they are gathered to fight against the one on the Horse and his armies. While in Ezekiel 38 we see they are gathered to take a spoil. They come to prey upon the land in Ezekiel and to make the land of Israel and others desolate. Here they are found in rebellion to Christ and are gathered to try and defeat Him and us. Revelation 16 verse 16 told us the place where these armies were assembled, the place in the Hebrew tongue is Armageddon! Where as in Ezekiel 39 we have these Armies defeated in verse [11] "And it shall come to pass in that day, that I will give unto Gog a place there of graves in Israel, the valley of the passengers on the east of the sea: and it shall stop the noses of the passengers: and there shall they bury Gog and all his multitude: and they shall call it The valley of Hamongog. And the name of the city in verse [16] And also the name of the city shall be Hamonah. Thus shall they cleanse the land." Do you see two entirely different locations? So here we have the battle of Armageddon. The battle and war are won! We see verse [20] "And the beast was taken, and with him the false prophet that wrought miracles before him, with which he deceived them that had received the mark of the beast, and them that worshipped his image. These both were cast alive into a lake of fire burning with brimstone." The beast the dictator of the Revived Roman Empire is captured. The false prophet and the anti-christ as well that is the false messiah are taken at the end of this battle though they had wrought miracles. They had deceived them into taking the mark of the beast and caused them to worship his image. They are both, we are told, cast into the Lake of Fire burning with Brimstone. The two greatest deceivers of mankind are destroyed! We see more about the Lake of Fire in Chapter 20 verse 14. But we see they are cast alive into this Lake. Physical death will probably be instantaneous. But they will suffer for all eternity. Many have asked if the Lake of Fire is a literal place. It is said here that these two are thrown into it alive! That sounds fairly literal to me! We see Jude 1:7 &8, [7] "Even as Sodom and Gomorrah, and the cities about them in like manner, giving themselves over to fornication, and going after strange flesh, are set forth for an example, suffering the vengeance of eternal fire. [8] Likewise also these filthy dreamers defile the flesh, despise dominion, and speak evil of dignities." That would be these two who are cast alive into the Lake of Fire, the beast and false prophet are like those in verse 8, aren't they! Sounds like a very literal place from this. This shows us it doesn't annihilate. Nor is it purgatory, it doesn't annihilate them nor does it purify them. They are cast there and we will see them in a few chapters. There will be 1000 years that passes and we are told they remain there in the Lake of fire. We now come to those who followed them those who never received Christ in the tribulation. We see verse [21] "And the remnant were slain with the sword of him that sat upon the horse, which sword proceeded out of his mouth: and all the fowls were filled with their flesh." Christ speaks and by the sword out of His mouth they are slain. We see here the fulfillment of prophecy seen in Matthew. We see, Matthew 24: [40]"Then shall two be in the field; the one shall be taken, and the other left. [41] Two women shall be grinding at the mill; the one shall be taken, and the other left. [42] Watch therefore: for ye know not what hour your Lord doth come." Those taken at this point in Matthew are the unbelievers they are taken and we see here in Revelation 19 they are slain by the Sword that proceeds out of Christ mouth. Their bodies now physically dead! The feast begins upon those being slain. The fowls were filled with their flesh. There is something else to notice here in a comparison to Ezekiel 38 and 39 war. The bodies of the dead in Ezekiel are buried over a long period. Here they are left for the buzzards we might say. They will no longer harm the sheep, the righteous. The feast of the fowls of the unholy fills them with their flesh. The return of Christ at the Second Advent will be a time of Judgment first in order to purify the earth. He comes with His bride and He defeats the wicked on the earth. The Lord accomplishes His mission, the defeat the unholy trinity. The Battle of Armageddon is complete here in Chapter 19. The beast and false prophet dealt with but what of satan, what is his fate?

4

Satan Bound, Christ Kingdom Begins

We finished the last chapter with the beast and false prophet being taken. They were cast into the Lake Of Fire burning with Brimstone and we saw they were cast in alive. For they had deceived mankind they had caused them to worship the image of the beast. The remnant of unbelievers was slain by the sword of Him that rode upon the White Horse that would be Jesus, He spoke and they fell over dead thus fulfilling Matthew 24:40-41. We now see satan's fate. What happens to him during the millennial reign of Christ during the Kingdom we see this in Chapter 20 and in O.T. prophecy! We come now to Chapter 20 verse [1] "And I saw an angel come down from heaven, having the key of the bottomless pit and a great chain in his hand." An angel comes and he is on a special mission. He has with him the keys to the bottomless pit. Remember that pit, the one which the locust demons were loosed from! He has a chain in his hand. This is going to be used to bind someone or something. We see satan now for the first time after the battle of Armageddon in Chapter 20 verse [2] "And he laid hold on the dragon, that old serpent, which is the Devil, and Satan, and bound him a thousand years," This angel laid hold on satan. We see all of his names being used here, the dragon, that old serpent. He is further identified as the devil. Then we see the use of the chain. Satan is bound and locked in the bottomless pit, for how long, 1000 years. We have the binding of man's enemy and God's enemy, satan. Cast into the prison known as the bottomless pit a.k.a. Tartarus. He will be there for 1000 years that is during the entire reign of Christ, in His Earthly Kingdom, can you see this isn't a figurative image but a real true event yet to occur! Satan's power and influence upon mankind and creation is completely removed, we don't have that in our current age. We see Ezekiel 28:14, the great covering cherub will be removed from the mountain of God. Who can chain satan you might asked? There are three, the first is of Course the conquering King of Kings and Lord of Lords, but verse 1 says it is an angel comes down from heaven. Christ had already come down and conquered, so I don't believe it is Christ, as some would say it is. Next is Gabriel the arch angel the Angel who announces the things God has accomplished or is going to accomplish. Again Gabriel usually announces or proclaims the things God has done or is about to do. That leaves Michael, God's war angel. It is Michael who has battled satan for the body of Moses as seen in Jude, Michael the arch angel who warred with satan and cast him out of heaven. Do you think we can believe this to be Michael? God's war general who fights the angelic battles with satan, I think we can, Newell and others agree. He bind's up satan with chains. Satan to be held for 1000 years in the bottomless pit his presence and influence will not be seen on earth again for 1000 years. Bound not able to deceive mankind, bound not even having the company of even his demon angels, separated from all contact. We see now where he is cast in verse 3, [3] "And cast him into the bottomless pit, and shut him up, and set a seal upon him, that he should deceive the nations no more, till the thousand years should be fulfilled: and after that he must be loosed a little season." Thrown into the bottomless pit, Tartarus, he does not join the other two members of the unholy trinity at this point. He is not cast into the Lake of Fire. God still has a purpose for him to serve. Not only is he cast down with force and vengeance but he is sealed in the abyss. Restrained with chains door closed locked and sealed. He has no way to escape. No means of disturbing the kingdom. No chance to deceive the nations. Sealed in by the authority of Christ and God, no one can unseal it until Christ allows it thus banished into darkness. The term is the 1000 years of the kingdom. The time of the direct government on earth with Christ seated on the Throne of David. Christ ruling and reigning with His saints that is the Tribulation Saints still physically alive as well as the church the Bride with Him the Bridegroom. Then satan we are told will be loosed for a little season at the end of the Millennial. We see why he wasn't cast into the lake of fire at this point! The Kingdom will have peace and prosperity for 1000 years. Christ will be in charge on the earth for 1000 years. Then at the end of the Millennial Kingdom satan has one last chance, one last opportunity! He will not come to persecute the Saints. He will come in spiritual conflict. We see now what will be occurring on earth as Christ reigns, of course we will need to study this section with Old Testament prophecy to connect all the dots. We see verse [4]"And I saw thrones, and they sat upon them, and judgment was given unto them: and I saw the souls of them that were beheaded for the witness of Jesus, and for the word of God, and which had not worshipped the beast, neither his image, neither had received his mark upon their foreheads, or in their hands; and they lived and reigned with Christ a thousand years." Thrones are seen here, who will sit upon these thrones? First we need to see 1st Corinthians 6: verse 2 & 3, [2]"Do ye not know that the saints shall judge the world? and if the world shall be judged by you, are ye unworthy to judge the smallest matters? [3] Know ye not that we shall judge angels? how much more things that pertain to this life?" As well as 2nd Timothy 2: [12] If we suffer, we shall also reign with him: if we deny him, he also will deny us:" It will be the Saints! Who are the Saints well there are 4 types of Saints which I see, there are the Old Testament Saints, there are the Saints of the church Age, the age in which we are living. There will be the Tribulation Saints, and the Millennial Saints, those born during the millennial reign and who receive Christ as their Lord and savior. Yes there will be children born physically during the Millennial they will need to make a decision for Christ. Yes we will reign with HIM, in the Kingdom! Here we need to interject something that I was taught about this time, look at Isaiah 65: [20]"There shall be no more thence an infant of days, nor an old man that hath not filled his days: for the child shall die an hundred years old; but the sinner being an hundred years old shall be accursed." There will not be an infant of days. There will be no old men that are waiting to die, for most will reign with him 1000 years. The child shall die at 100 years old that is the unbeliever, the person who has not received Christ as his or her personal savior will die at 100. As many of us believe that those who are infants and are covered until they reach the age of accountability. That is they come to the place where they know right from wrong and can decide to receive Christ, they are covered if they die before reaching that point in their lives. Here in the Millennial if they reach 100 years and have refused to receive Christ they will be put to death. The sinner being 100 will be accursed, that is those who received Christ and chose to fall back to sin will be accursed after 100 they will fall under God's discipline. They will live an unhappy miserable life.

As for the souls of the Tribulation Saints, those who were beheaded for their witness of Jesus and for the Word of God and those who died for not worshipping the Beast, neither worshipping his image they will be with Christ. Neither did they receive his mark upon their foreheads. Nor did they receive it in their hands. They live and reign with Christ 1000 years. Many in the past had a hard time understanding the beheading they said people don't do that anymore. What are seeing now with ISIS? They take a hostage and if they don't receive a ransom or if the prisoner doesn't renounce their faith they are beheaded. We can understand this perfectly now because it is becoming very prevalent in our world today. What we see here is anyone who dies for the sake of these things will rule and reign with Christ for the entire Kingdom Age. Many are going to die for the sake of Christ in Tribulation that we have seen in prior chapters of Revelation and in prior books written by this author. The thrones are real they will physically exist upon the earth. The souls of those who were executed for Christ sake are real souls not figurative; they will exist and rule on earth. The thousand years is a literal 1000 years of time on earth. Remember what Peter said in 2nd Peter 3:8 "But, beloved, be not ignorant of this one thing, that one day is with the Lord **as a thousand years**, **and a thousand years a**s one day." This is actually one day in the Lord's timetable. We need to go to the old Testament to see more of the time and what is occurring during the Millennial Kingdom, Isiah 11:6-9, [6]"The wolf also shall dwell with the lamb, and the leopard shall lie down with the kid; and the calf and the young lion and the fatling together; and a little child shall lead them. [7] And the cow and the bear shall feed; their young ones shall lie down together: and the lion shall eat straw like the ox. [8] And the sucking child shall play on the hole of the asp, and the weaned child shall put his hand on the cockatrice' den. [9] They shall not hurt nor destroy in all my holy mountain: for the earth shall be full of the knowledge of the

Lord, as the waters cover the sea." What Revelation doesn't show us in the things during the Kingdom Isiah does. The redeemer the branch from the root of Jesse will bring the Redemption of Creation. What Adam lost that is the dominion over the earth! Man has had to battle the forces of nature and until Christ returns and sets up His Millennial Kingdom this will continue. Fighting the weeds, thistles, insects, caterpillars, storms, droughts and floods and after the flood animals begin to prey upon one another. Death, groaning and destruction are everywhere. We see then that when His Kingdom is come all of the earth shall return to the original time of creation. The wolf will dwell with the lamb. The leopard shall lie down with the kid. The young lion and the fatling together, a little child shall lead them. It goes further; the cow and bear shall feed. Their young ones shall lie down together. The lion shall eat straw like the ox. The child shall play on the hole of an asp, that is the snake, and the weaned child shall put his hand on the poisonous snakes den. None will be harmed. This will be a time as the anti-diluvian period that is pre-flood. For in the original days before the flood there was longevity of life. Adam lived to be 930 years. Seth lived to be 912. Enosh lived to be 905. Cainan lived to be 910. Mahalaleel lived to be 805. Jared lived to be 962. Enoch lived to be 365 and he was translated, God took him. Methuselah lived to be 969 the oldest recorded until the Millennial. Lamech lived to be 777. It makes me wonder and maybe you too, will God replace the water vapor canopy over the earth, the canopy which many believe existed in that anti-diluvian world. Thus there would be a greenhouse effect upon the earth and life. Highly oxygenated air would make plant life thrive. Man with a higher oxygen level will be healthier and live longer as they did in pre-flood time. Less of the radiation would get through from the Sun's rays. The vegetation high in oxygen would also become high in nutritional value. God just may place that Water vapor around the earth because some folks in the millennial Kingdom will live to be well over 1000 years old.

Satan is bound during this Kingdom age. Yet we see from Isaiah 65 verse 20 many will reject Christ and the punishment when they reach 100 years will be death. The Saints of all ages will reign with Him on the earth literally. Those literally beheaded or killed for the sake of Christ and the Gospel those believers who refused to worship the beast or his image or refuse his mark who die will reign with him. All animal life will return to original creation state and live in peace, no meat eating animals and man too may not eat meat during this time.

We come now to Chapter 20 verse [5] "But the rest of the dead lived not again until the thousand years were finished. This is the first resurrection." The dead Saints of the Tribulation and for that matter Saints of all ages are raised from the dead, this completes the first resurrection. The resurrection of the dead began earlier in history. It began with Christ and over 500 souls were seen when Christ came out of the tomb. Then the resurrection of the dead at the trumpet call of the church age believers. Here now is the resurrection of the Old Testament and Tribulation Saints. Thus this is the first resurrection! So these are resurrected. They are delivered from the second death; they will not be eternally separated from God, which is the second death. The first Resurrection is completed. Here too we see the rest of the dead. They remain in the grave, why, because they are those who rejected Christ! Those of Old and New Testament, those of the Tribulation who rejected Christ! They must wait for their judgment. As we saw there will be those who reject in the Tribulation and they must join the rest of the dead. These souls spend 1000 more years in Hell, the torments abode. They must wait for final judgment! Not just theirs but the judgment of satan and the unbelievers of the Millennial Kingdom. Yes there will be those who reject Christ with satan bound! Even with Christ ruling and reigning on earth in a perfect world.

Next we come to verse [6] "Blessed and holy is he that hath part in the first resurrection: on such the second death hath no power, but they shall be priests of God and of Christ, and shall reign with him a thousand years." The Saints who all had a place in the First resurrection are said to be blessed and holy. Do you see here the second death hath no power over them? They will spend eternity with Christ. They will not be eternally separated from Christ, the Father nor the Holy Spirit because they trusted in Christ and were saved by Grace through Faith in Him. They will be priest. We are called by many, believer priest in our age. All the Saints will be priest in the Kingdom Age, Priest of God, and Priest of Christ. The Jewish believer will reign with Christ; He is not through with them either. The Gentile believers will reign with Christ that was in His plan all along. All on the earth that is all in His literal Kingdom, a Kingdom on earth as Prophesied by, Isaiah, Ezekiel, Jeremiah and all the Old Testament prophets. The term of the priesthood and reign is 1000 years. There are some that teach Christ has already returned, that it occurred in 70 A.D. and that the Kingdom is now occurring. They believe it to be a metaphorical Kingdom. A symbolic Kingdom, however this says they will reign with Him and no one is currently reigning with Him, and His Kingdom is to last 1000 years. That has not occurred because at the end of the 1000 years, we see now satan is loosed.

5
Final Battle and Judgment

We pick up in Verse [7] "And when the thousand years are expired, Satan shall be loosed out of his prison," The 1000 years ended and satan is now loosed for a short time. He has one last mission to complete, one final try to take control and dominion of the earth. One final battle to wage! Therefore, he is loosed from his prison. Here we see the purpose in verse [8] "And shall go out to deceive the nations which are in the four quarters of the earth, Gog, and Magog, to gather them together to battle: the number of whom is as the sand of the sea." He goes out to deceive the nations. Yes, those nations and people who have been with Christ. Who were born into the Kingdom age! Remember what we said about the child shall die at 100 years old that is the unbeliever, the person who has not received Christ as his or her personal savior and who will die at 100 years old, in Isaiah 65:20. As we have those who are infants and are covered until they reach the age of accountability, these reach that age of accountability here at the end of the Millennial Kingdom. They come from the four corners of the Earth. Notice too that one area in particular is mentioned, Gog and Magog, that is the Russian area of the nations. The biggest portion of those gathered at Megiddo in Chapter 19, were from that very same region. Those from the battle in Ezekiel 38 and 39 were from Gog and Magog. These will be the rebels yet again. The number that will gather is as the sands of the sea an enormous army coming to try to overthrow Christ, coming to try and set up the kingdom of satan over the earth. What does this reveal? That even in a time of perfect environment, the Perfect God, Jesus, ruling upon the earth we see the heart of man is deceitful and as Genesis 6:5 shows, man in the days of Noah, "And God saw that the wickedness of man was great in the earth, and that every imagination of the thoughts of his heart was only **evil continually**." Now the principle carries through here at the end of Christ Earthly reign in His Kingdom. There will be a great multitude in the end of the Kingdom who will revolt against Christ. We see how far they will go to overthrow Christ in verse [9] "And they went up on the breadth of the earth, and compassed the camp of the saints about, and the beloved city: and fire came down from God out of heaven, and devoured them." They go to the breadth of the Earth. They compass the camp of the Saints about, the beloved city! That would be Jerusalem. Guess what, God sends fire down from Heaven. It devours them! God always fights the battle for His Saints. The last rebellion and resistance against God is snuffed out! It was a foolish attempt, the finality and the end for satan. Now we see the end of satans attempts to rule over all of God's creation, in verse 10 His final sentence, [10] "And the devil that deceived them was cast into the lake of fire and brimstone, where the beast and the false prophet are, and shall be tormented day and night for ever and ever." The devil that deceived them is now taken and cast into the Lake of Fire. There to be tormented day and night. This is a life sentence, his final sentence. No parole! Notice here that the Beast and False Prophet are still there! They have not been annihilated as some want to teach. Nor have they been purified as the Purgatorial doctrine teaches. Notice it says they will be there for ever and ever. It says day and night for ever and ever. They have a life sentence, but their body and soul last for ever and ever. The Lake of Fire burns with Brimstone. That would mean a Lake of Molten Sulfur. No one is spared the intense torment; no one is given a cooler place in this Lake of Fire. That would dispel the thought of degrees of punishment in hell it would seem! The Lake of Fire is a literal burning furnace. All who end up there will be tormented day and night forever and ever.

Now we see the final doom of all the unbelievers, everyone from Cain to the final rebellion who rejected God and His plan of salvation. We see verse [11] "And I saw a great white throne, and him that sat on it, from whose face the earth and the heaven fled away; and there was found no place for them." The Great White throne of Judgment is now before us in Revelation. All the unbelievers will be judged here. Not one Saint that is a saved person will be judged at this judgment. Keep that in mind. Christ sits upon this throne in judgment. The day that all those who rejected Him will now face Him, Matthew 25 verse [41] "Then shall he say also unto them on the left hand, Depart from me, ye cursed, into everlasting fire, prepared for the devil and his angels:" Remember these had been taken in the beginning of the Millennial. They had been put to death as we saw and now they face their judgment. He will tell them depart from me I never knew you! Great will be their torment!

We see in verse 12 and 13 where these are gathered from, [12] "And I saw the dead, small and great, stand before God; and the books were opened: and another book was opened, which is the book of life: and the dead were judged out of those things which were written in the books, according to their works. [13] And the sea gave up the dead which were in it; and death and hell delivered up the dead which were in them: and they were judged every man according to their works." Notice no one will escape judgment if they rejected Christ. From the lowest of slaves to wealthiest people in the world, small and great will face the Great White Throne judgment! They will stand before God to answer for their rejection of Christ. Here again we see the book opened. The record of all their works, even those who did good works thinking it was for the cause of Christ. These will be there. We go to Matthew 7:22-24, [22] "Many will say to me in that day, Lord, Lord, have we not prophesied in thy name? and in thy name have cast out devils? and in thy name done many wonderful works? [23] And then will I profess unto them, I never knew you: depart from me, ye that work iniquity. [24] Therefore whosoever heareth these sayings of mine, and doeth them, I will liken him unto a wise man, which built his house upon a rock:" Everything these folks did is recorded in those books. We prophesied in your name, they testify, we cast out demons in your name! Their testimony goes we did wonderful works in your name! Yet His word will cut to the heart. Depart from me I never knew you! They depended on their works and never on Faith; they depended on what they were trying to do for Him, instead of upon His Amazing Grace, and placing their Faith in Him. They depended on what they thought the Bible said about Salvation instead of believing His word. They believed false teachers and deceivers. They never trusted in His blood and His Propitiatory sacrifice to save them fully once and forever, just as His word said. The sea gave up the dead! Think about those who have said God is going to have to find me, they had their body cremated and scattered over the ocean. Guess what He finds them one and all! Death and hell gave up the dead! All who were in the grave and all the souls in Hell stand before Him! They were judged according to their works. Here some will say see this shows degrees of punishment. Their works were judge and none were found worthy of salvation, do you see this isn't why they are told to depart from Him. We are not told that any were sent to the Lake of fire because of these books of works.

We see the final verses here in Chapter 20, [14]"And death and hell were cast into the lake of fire. This is the second death. [15]And whosoever was not found written in the book of life was cast into the lake of fire." All things associated with sin and doom are now taken care of death and hell were cast into the Lake of Fire. This means every soul and body of the unbeliever were brought together. Hell was taken and cast into the Lake of Fire, the temporary abode of the unbeliever is consumed in their permanent abode. We are told this is the second Death that means eternal separation from God, Jesus Christ and the Holy Spirit. Eternally lost not annihilated! Eternally lost not purified in a Purgatorial place to be later released to heaven from Torments abode of Hell into the eternal Lake of Fire forever a Lake which burns with Fire and Brimstone. Then we see why they were cast into this Lake of Fire! Notice it isn't because of their bad deeds nor is it because of any good deed. Whosoever, that is any and every one whose name was not written in the Book of Life, that is the Lamb's book of Life where all the names of those who trusted in Christ were written, will be cast into the Lake of Fire. They are cast in the Lake of Fire because their names failed to appear in the book. John 3:17 & 18, would apply here, [17]"For God sent not his Son into the world to condemn the world; but that the world through him might be saved. [18]He that believeth on him is not condemned: but he that believeth not is condemned already, because he hath not believed in the name of the only begotten Son of God." Do see it; those who believed not are condemned already! They are cast into the Lake of fire for unbelief and there can be no degree of punishment for unbelief. One sin is punished in the Lake of Fire one and one only. The sin of unbelief and for that there are no degrees, unbelief is unbelief. Because of their torments we see, Matthew 8:12, [2] "But the children of the kingdom shall be cast out into outer darkness: there shall be weeping and gnashing of teeth." We see Matthew 13:41 and 42, [41] "The Son of man shall send forth his angels, and they shall gather out of his kingdom all things that offend, and them which do iniquity; [42] And shall cast them into a furnace of fire: there shall be wailing and gnashing of teeth." Mark 9:44 "Where their worm dieth not, and the fire is not quenched." Here we see this fulfilled. Christ paid the price for sin, His blood paid for each and every sin. He became the Propitiatory sacrifice for all sin. Romans 3:25 "Whom God hath set forth to be propitiation through faith in his blood, to declare his righteousness for the remission of sins that are past, through the forbearance of God;" 1st John 2:2 "And he is the **propitiation** for our sins: and not for ours only, but also for the sins of the whole world." 1st John 4:10 "Herein is love, not that we loved God, but that he loved us, and sent his Son to be the **propitiation** for our sins." If there are degrees of punishment for those who are lost then God is guilty of violating the Law of double jeopardy. The sin is paid for; there can be no more punishment for sin, since Christ became the propitiation for the sins of the whole world. Do you see that? Everyone that ends up in the Lake of Fire is there because of rebellion; rejecting God's plan of salvation is rebellion. Satan wanted to ascend over God's throne that is rebellion. The book of Life was opened the one that contains the names of all the saved. None that were saved were missed but none who came before the Great White Throne's names were written in it and they were cast into the Lake of fire for ever and ever that is for all eternity. Do you see just how important it is to study Revelation? It should drive you to witness to friends and family, even to your enemies, if you don't they just might not have their name recorded in the book of Life and fall under sentence of the Second Death, eternally separated from God.

6 The New Heaven and Earth

We saw in the last chapter, the Great White Throne judgment. First they open the books containing the works of the unbelievers and none of their works were found acceptable for entry into Heaven. Then the book that counts was consulted and those whose names were not written in it were cast into the Lake of Fire and death and hell gave up their dead. All were cast into the Lake of fire and suffered the second death.

This Chapter we see the events unfolding in Chapter 21 of Revelation. Beginning in verse 1 "And I saw a new heaven and a new earth: for the first heaven and the first earth were passed away; and there was no more sea." We need to consult with Peter in order to see what happens after the Great White Throne. Look at what Peter had to say about this new heaven and new earth. 2nd Peter 3: [10] "But the day of the Lord will come as a thief in the night; in the which the heavens shall pass away with a great noise, and the elements shall melt with fervent heat, the earth also and the works that are therein shall be burned up. [11] Seeing then that all these things shall be dissolved, what manner of persons ought ye to be in all holy conversation and godliness," Peter says this earth which we live on will melt with fervent heat. All the human works will be burned up. He states "Seeing then that all these things shall be dissolved." Since all will be dissolved that is all that man has worked for, Peter exhorts believers with this question. "What manner of persons ought ye to be in all holy conversation and godliness?" This is the emphasis you and I should be working to accomplish; God's purpose not our purpose. We should be a witness for Him to others. That is the importance of a study of Revelation. In times past many would us Revelation to try and scare people into receiving Christ. This book should be a motivator to the believer, a motivation to witness to a lost and dying world. How are you living? Do you live with a Holy conversation? Do live a Godly life? Are you witnessing to others?

Here in Revelation 21 John now sees the New Heaven and New Earth. He goes a step further. There was no more sea! Everything this earth contained, everything man sees as precious is destroyed. This is again fulfillment of Old Testament scripture, Isaiah 65: [16] "That he who blesseth himself in the earth shall bless himself in the God of truth; and he that sweareth in the earth shall swear by the God of truth; because the former troubles are forgotten, and because they are hid from mine eyes. [17] For, behold, I create new heavens and a new earth: and the former shall not be remembered, nor come into mind. [18] But be ye glad and rejoice for ever in that which I create: for, behold, I create Jerusalem a rejoicing, and her people a joy." Coupled with Isaiah 66: [21] "And I will also take of them for priests and for Levites, saith the LORD. [22] For as the new heavens and the new earth, which I will make, shall remain before me, saith the LORD, so shall your seed and your name remain. [23] And it shall come to pass, that from one new moon to another, and from one Sabbath to another, shall all flesh come to worship before me, saith the LORD." God told Isaiah over 2500 years ago there would be a New Heaven and a new Earth. The old will not be remembered again. Just as we see at the end of Revelation here in Chapter 21. Then we get a glimpse of our New Home in verse 2, [2] "And I John saw the holy city, new Jerusalem, coming down from God out of heaven, prepared as a bride adorned for her husband." The Holy City it is called, "The New Jerusalem." The eternal city is coming to rest upon the New Earth. It has been in Heaven. Christ has been preparing it for us, do you remember His promise? In John 14: [2] "In my Father's house are many mansions: if it were not so, I would have told you. I go to prepare a place for you. [3] And if I go and prepare a place for you, I will come again, and receive you unto myself; that where I am, there ye may be also. [4] And whither I go ye know, and the way ye know." He was going to prepare a place for all Believers." He said He would come for us and in Chapter 4 He did exactly that He came for His Bride, the Church! We know the way, by Grace through Faith. Where He is, once He comes to bring His church home now we are told this city coming down will be our eternal Home.

As it comes down a voice is heard by John that says, [3]"And I heard a great voice out of heaven saying, Behold, the tabernacle of God is with men, and he will dwell with them, and they shall be his people, and God himself shall be with them, and be their God." Behold the Tabernacle of God is with men, His dwelling place is in this New Jerusalem. He is coming to dwell with mankind! Those who are saved shall all become His people. God will be with them. He will be their God. Do you see that those who say the earth will get progressively better couldn't be further from the truth? It takes God renovating it, destroying all the things man put on it to corrupt it. Even with perfect peace and a perfect environment, satan still found enough to muster an army to rebel. An Army out of Gog and Magog an army that is numbered as the sands of the sea comes together. But now for all eternity God will reside on the New Earth in the New Heaven. He will spend all eternity with us or should I say we will spend all of eternity with Him. The unbeliever is separated from Him, living in the Lake of Fire forever, there is no purification and they are never released. There is no annihilation. They are tormented day and night forever. Do you see why it is so important to be a witness? Even to those who hate you!

We will see friends and family members but we will only know we had a close relationship with many who were cast into the Lake of fire so we see, [4]"And God shall wipe away all tears from their eyes; and there shall be no more death, neither sorrow, nor crying, neither shall there be any more pain: for the former things are passed away." We will shed tears for those who are lost forever. God will wipe those tears away. All the effects of what has occurred, the former things have passed away. We will shed no more tears, this at the end of the 1000 years. You see we weep tears for the lost, and also we have happy tears for our new eternal home.

We see verse [5]"And he that sat upon the throne said, Behold, I make all things new. And he said unto me, Write: for these words are true and faithful." Just as He made us new by salvation He now has completed the redemption of the Earth and created her afresh. Old things passed away, 2nd Corinthians 5: [16]"Wherefore henceforth know we no man after the flesh: yea, though we have known Christ after the flesh, yet now henceforth know we him no more. [17] Therefore if any man be in Christ, he is a new creature: old things are passed away; behold, all things are become new. [18] And all things are of God, who hath reconciled us to himself by Jesus Christ, and hath given to us the ministry of reconciliation;" All things are of God even here now in Chapter 21 in the new Heaven and Earth! In the New Jerusalem, John is told to write for these words are faithful and they are true. Because God is truth and God doesn't lie! He promised a messiah, He came. He promised a Kingdom where the Messiah would reign, per Revelation that has come true. He promised a New Heaven and a New Earth and that too has now come. John is to write because God words are faithful and true.

Here are the words John was told to write, [6] "And he said unto me, It is done. I am Alpha and Omega, the beginning and the end. I will give unto him that is athirst of the fountain of the water of life freely." The one sitting upon the Throne says "It is Done!" "History's Finale God's Plan Finished." The end of Heaven and Earth as man knew it is finished. Psalms 33: [8] "Let all the earth fear the Lord: let all the inhabitants of the world stand in awe of him. [9] For he spake, and it was done; he commanded, and it stood fast. [10] The Lord bringeth the counsel of the heathen to nought: he maketh the devices of the people of none effect." All of God's Grace in the plan of Salvation, of Redemption is now completed. The One who sat upon the Throne spoke and it was done. All the Saints over every age are with Him. Changed from a corruptible body to an incorruptible one, or are they? The earth and Heaven changed from corruptible to incorruption. The whole of creation has now been made incorruptible and "It is done!" The Alpha and Omega, the beginning and the End accomplished His purpose in it all. The defeat of satan and the unholy trinity has been completed. The marriage of the Lamb to the Bride His church is done. The 1000 year Kingdom with Jesus Reigning on the Throne of David as the root of Jesse completed. The defeat of satan and his final place of torment has been accomplished! The renovation of the Heavens and Earth fulfilled. The New Heaven and New Earth are in place. New Jerusalem descending upon the New Earth, Christ says it is done! It is done right now as you read as if it were already done because God said it. It will be His glory to complete the work, His finished work, for all of creation.

The promise kept to those who Overcome, chapter 21 verse [7] "He that overcometh shall inherit all things; and I will be his God, and he shall be my son." Revelation 3:12-13, 12 "Him that overcometh will I make a pillar in the temple of my God, and he shall go no more out: and I will write upon him the name of my God, and the name of the city of my God, which is new Jerusalem, which cometh down out of heaven from my God: and I will write upon him my new name. [13] He that hath an ear, let him hear what the Spirit saith unto the churches." Revelation 3:21-22, 21 "To him that overcometh will I grant to sit with me in my throne, even as I also overcame, and am set down with my Father in his throne. [22] He that hath an ear, let him hear what the Spirit saith unto the churches" The promise to the churches fulfilled, those who overcometh shall inherit all things. How do we overcome, by Faith! It is not and cannot come by works, Titus 3:5-7 fulfilled here also, [5] "Not by works of righteousness which we have done, but according to his mercy he saved us, by the washing of regeneration, and renewing of the Holy Ghost; [6] Which he shed on us abundantly through Jesus Christ our Saviour; [7] That being justified by his grace, we should be made heirs according to the hope of eternal life." Here we see our inheritance of all things our becoming fully the Children of God. He will be our God forever and ever. God will be with us as we will soon see. Those who rejected Christ were cast into the Lake of Fire in outer darkness, forever separated from God which is the second death never to see the Light! He will be our God because we will have overcome by Faith in Christ. We will be His Children and live and reign with Him forever and ever as will the believers of all ages. New Jerusalem is descending upon the newly renovated earth. The now new Heaven and New Earth have come into being. Old things are passed away behold all things are become new. God has melted the Heavens and Earth with fervent heat; all the toys man has made are consumed in the fire. All is new and we are with our God and are His Children. God's plan is accomplished and "It is done!" But we have just a little bit more to finish in our Revelation study so hang on as the final portions are soon to come. Chapter 21 verse [8] "But the fearful, and unbelieving, and the abominable, and murderers, and whoremongers, and sorcerers, and idolaters, and all liars, shall have their part in the lake which burneth with fire and brimstone: which is the second death." The unbeliever will be in torments forever, a long list of their offenses is given while others are left out. Their offense as we saw in chapter 20 was their names not written in the Book of Life. Since they failed to receive the Lord Jesus Christ, they have their part in the Lake of fire. They die the second death eternally separated from God. There is no reprieve for them. Do you see why Revelation is so important to study? So that we ensure we witness to everyone that we try to lead them to the convicting power of the Holy Spirit. Then it is their volition to choose for or against Christ. A positive decision will make them one of the overcomers. A negative one will doom them to the Lake of fire, but you must be that witness.

Now we have yet another Angel a messenger come to John as we see in verse [9] "And there came unto me one of the seven angels which had the seven vials full of the seven last plagues, and talked with me, saying, Come hither, I will shew thee the bride, the Lamb's wife." One of the seven angels comes to John, one that had one of the seven vials full of the last plagues. He tells John come hither. The wife, the bride of Christ, the Lamb's wife will be revealed. We know the Lamb is Christ; He is the Son of God and heir to all things. The Bride His wife is not just one person who was saved. She is not one specific denomination or church. Not a Gentile or a Jew. She is All Believers. But is it all of one period of time? She is the Church of God in her Glorious, complete and victorious condition! John had seen the Holy City New Jerusalem. Now he is told to come closer, look into the city. John is carried away as we see in verse [10] "And he carried me away in the spirit to a great and high mountain, and shewed me that great city, the holy Jerusalem, descending out of heaven from God," This time John states he is in spirit for this vision. Carried to a high mountain, shown the Great city, Holy New Jerusalem. It is still making its descent to earth, the newly renovated earth coming out of Heaven from God. The city will reveal the Bride.

7

New Jerusalem Described

Now the description begins of this city, verse [11] "Having the glory of God: and her light was like unto a stone most precious, even like a jasper stone, clear as crystal;" First it contains the Glory of God, the Shekinah glory shines through! That which filled the Temple in Jerusalem in the Old Testament, 2nd Chronicles 5: [13] "It came even to pass, as the trumpeters and singers were as one, to make one sound to be heard in praising and thanking the LORD; and when they lifted up their voice with the trumpets and cymbals and instruments of musick, and praised the LORD, saying, For he is good; for his mercy endureth for ever: that then the house was filled with a cloud, even the house of the LORD; [14] So that the priests could not stand to minister by reason of the cloud: for the Glory of the LORD had filled the house of God." We see too Isaiah 60: [19] "The sun shall be no more thy light by day; neither for brightness shall the moon give light unto thee: but the LORD shall be unto thee an everlasting light, and thy God thy glory." That same glory which the priest of Israel could not stand to minister by the cloud is now in Holy Jerusalem, New Jerusalem our eternal home. Here we see her light described. It is like a most precious stone. Even like the Jasper we are told, Jasper a symbol of God's Diving Glory. This shows too that the city is invincible. We will be in peace for all eternity, with God reigning upon His throne. The wall is clear as crystal.

John can see in, one has to wonder can those in the Lake of fire see in! Will they be able to see for all eternity what was missed by their having rejected Christ? Showing them their eternal separation from God and this glorious city, that could have been their eternal home. This should motivate every believer to service, every believer to witness in order to win souls. We see verse [12] And had a wall great and high, and had twelve gates, and at the gates twelve angels, and names written thereon, which are the names of the twelve tribes of the children of Israel: [13] On the east three gates; on the north three gates; on the south three gates; and on the west three gates." A great and high wall is part of this city. Not to keep us in for we would not want to leave! Those in the Lake of Fire could not penetrate even if they were able. It shows the eternal security in eternity for all who Believe on Christ, Invincible, secure for all eternity.

There are names written on the gates which number 12, the number of Governmental perfection or completion. The city is Complete; the names on the gates represent the twelve tribes of Israel. We have here the fulfillment of yet more prophecy for Israel, Ezekiel 48: [31] "And the gates of the city shall be after the names of the tribes of Israel: three gates northward; one gate of Reuben, one gate of Judah, one gate of Levi.[32] And at the east side four thousand and five hundred: and three gates; and one gate of Joseph, one gate of Benjamin, one gate of Dan. [33] And at the south side four thousand and five hundred measures: and three gates; one gate of Simeon, one gate of Issachar, one gate of Zebulun. [34] At the west side four thousand and five hundred, with their three gates; one gate of Gad, one gate of Asher, one gate of Naphtali. [35] It was round about eighteen thousand measures: and the name of the city from that day shall be, The LORD is there." Here is the list of the tribes whose names shall be on that city. Reuben, Judah, Levi, Joseph, Benjamin, Dan, Simeon, Issachar, Zebulon, Gad, Asher, Naphtali, notice these are the exact names of the sons of Jacob! Not the tribes that the 144,000 represented.

Next we see the foundation, verse [14] "And the wall of the city had twelve foundations, and in them the names of the twelve apostles of the Lamb." The names of the twelve Apostles of the Lamb their work on Earth established the Church, the Bride of Christ! Now their names forever engraved on the pillars of this great city. They suffered and served Christ in establishing the Church. All but John martyred for the cause of

Christ and for His bride. Ephesians 2: [19] "Now therefore ye are no more strangers and foreigners, but fellowcitizens with the saints, and of the household of God; [20] And are built upon the foundation of the apostles and prophets, Jesus Christ himself being the chief corner stone; [21] In whom all the building fitly framed together groweth unto an holy temple in the Lord: [22] In whom ye also are builded together for an habitation of God through the Spirit." Do you see everything associated with the church has its foundation in the Apostles and the Prophets? The Apostles names will be on the pillars of our Eternal Home, deservedly so! Notice the number is Twelve; Governmental perfection is seen here also for the church. The number is significant, for if Matthias was the twelfth then Paul must be excluded! If Paul is the Twelfth then Mathias must be excluded. I believe it to be Paul, the Holy Spirit inspired scripture says so, Galatians 1:1 "Paul, an apostle, (not of men, neither by man, but by Jesus Christ, and God the Father, who raised him from the dead;);" Ephesians 1:1 "Paul, an apostle of Jesus Christ by the will of God, to the saints which are at Ephesus, and to the faithful in Christ Jesus:" Colossians 1:1 "Paul, an apostle of Jesus Christ by the will of God…;" 1st Timothy 1:1 "Paul, an apostle of Jesus Christ by the commandment of God our Saviour, and Lord Jesus Christ, which is our hope;" 2nd Timothy 1:1 "Paul, an apostle of Jesus Christ by the will of God, according to the promise of life which is in Christ Jesus;" and finally Titus 1:1 "Paul, a servant of God, and an apostle of Jesus Christ, according to the faith of God's elect, and the acknowledging of the truth which is after godliness;" If the inspired scripture says it is Paul as the Apostle then it is Paul! Since we have the foundation pillars of the Holy city with the names of the Apostles being twelve, then can we conclude the original eleven names are of no doubt and Paul not Matthias as the twelfth, to me there is no doubt.

We now see the measurements of the city in verses 15-17, [15] "And he that talked with me had a golden reed to measure the city, and the gates thereof, and the wall thereof.[16] And the city lieth foursquare, and the length is as large as the breadth: and he measured the city with the reed, twelve thousand furlongs. The length and the breadth and the height of it are equal. [17] And he measured the wall thereof, an hundred and forty and four cubits, according to the measure of a man, that is, of the angel." The messenger takes a Golden Rod to measure the city the gates and the wall.

As we see Ezekiel 40 we see the city measured beginning in verse 5. Here we see the angel measuring it. The city is four square. The length as long as the breadth, he measures the city with a reed. Twelve thousand furlongs the breadth and height are equal and the wall an hundred and forty and four cubits, according to measure of man. John says that is what the Angel measured. The size is enormous; we know the construction on the exterior is of Jasper, clear as Crystal. The New home, our eternal home is seen in its beauty and splendor. What a great eternity we as believers have to look forward too. Doesn't that make you want to tell as many as you possibly can about Christ?

Let's look at what a cubit of measure is as seen in the bible. This measure is used in many things we see built in the Bible, Noah's ark, the Tabernacle, the ark of the covenant, as well as the temple. Goliath was described in cubits concerning his height. Every description given of the city in Old Testament prophecy is given in cubits. So what is a cubit in our measuring system? A cubit was based on the distance from the elbow to the fingertips. Several different nations of biblical times used different measurements for a cubit. The average is a little over 18". Commonly though it is considered to be 18". So the square contains four walls 1500 miles long! It is said to be 12,000 furlongs. Therefore it will stretch 1500 miles east to west, 1500 miles north to south and 1500 Miles in height. It will be similar to a cube, as it comes to rest upon the earth. So let me put it in to terms you might can see to put this into perspective. It is 1519.5 miles from MacClenny, Florida which is on the western outskirts of Jacksonville to Deming, NM. It is 1448 miles from Deming N.M. to Prince Albert SK. CA. It is 1497.1 from Prince Albert SK. CA to La tuque QC. CA. and from La Tuque QC CA to MacClenny FL we see it is 1284 miles so you would need to go several hundred miles into the Canadian wilderness to gain the 1500 miles. That is the size of New Jerusalem.

We begin now with Chapter 21 verse [18]"And the building of the wall of it was of jasper: and the city was pure gold, like unto clear glass [19] And the foundations of the wall of the city were garnished with all manner of precious stones. The first foundation was jasper; the second, sapphire; the third, a chalcedony; the fourth, an emerald; [20] The fifth, sardonyx; the sixth, sardius; the seventh, chrysolyte; the eighth, beryl; the ninth, a topaz; the tenth, a chrysoprasus; the eleventh, a jacinth; the twelfth, an amethyst."

First the building of the wall that is the construction of the wall is of Jasper. The city inside that wall is of fine gold. Gold represents the deity of the Godhead. The gold was clear as crystal. Sounds like a beautiful place to spend all of eternity. The unbelievers were sentenced to the Lake of Fire forever. We are now getting the full description of our eternal home, New Jerusalem here in Revelation 21. Do you want friends and family in this with you? If they aren't here then they will be in the Lake Of Fire, do you really want to see anyone in that place?

Now we see the foundation of the walls in Revelation 21 verse [19] "And the foundations of the wall of the city were garnished with all manner of precious stones. The first foundation was jasper; the second, sapphire; the third, a chalcedony; the fourth, an emerald; [20] The fifth, sardonyx; the sixth, sardius; the seventh, chrysolyte; the eighth, beryl; the ninth, a topaz; the tenth, a chrysoprasus; the eleventh, a jacinth; the twelfth, an amethyst." The foundation is garnished with all manner of precious stones. The first foundation was Jasper, the symbol of Divine Glory. These jewels are the second Sapphire, the third chalcedony, the fourth emerald, the fifth the sardonyx, the sixth the Sardius, the seventh the Chrysolyte, the eighth the Beryl, the ninth the Topaz, the tenth the Crysoprasus, the eleventh a Jacinth and the twelfth and Amethyst. We were told the foundation had the name of the 12 apostles on them. These twelve stones are thought to represent two things, a variety and Excellency of the gospel or of the graces shown of the Holy Spirt. That being said these combined would represent the Excellency of Jesus Christ. Next we see the gates and as we hear them referred to the pearly gates. [21] "And the twelve gates were twelve pearls: every several gate was of one pearl: and the street of the city was pure gold, as it were transparent glass." Twelve gates as we were told for the twelve tribes of Israel. Each had one Pearl. These representing the Pearl of Great Price, the Lord Jesus Christ, thus we see the purity of Christ in these Pearls. Christ is the only way in which one enters into the New Jerusalem. Thus the price paid by the Pearl of Great price. The street of the city is of Pure Gold. It is as transparent as glass, golden glass. The transparent Glass Street shows us we walk on pure gold in heaven such beauty for the eternal home of all who believe.

There is no need for a temple and we are told in verse [22] "And I saw no temple therein: for the Lord God Almighty and the Lamb are the temple of it." No need to have a temple since the Godhead will dwell there. The True God, creator of all mankind will be the God who loves us and lives with us this being the place where God lives forever more. We are in a continual state of worshipping God.

Now we see just how much of the elements burned up as we were told in 2nd Peter with fervent heat. Revelation 21 Verse [23] "And the city had no need of the sun, neither of the moon, to shine in it: for the glory of God did lighten it, and the Lamb is the light thereof." There will be no more Sun or moon. We are told they are no longer needed. No longer are they required because there is a new greater source of light! The Light of the world is now the light of the New Jerusalem. John 8: [12] "Then spake Jesus again unto them, saying, I am the light of the world: he that followeth me shall not walk in darkness, but shall have the light of life." The light of life is with us forever in this city. The Father and Holy Spirit reside here with us all! Therefore no artificial light source is required. Nothing outside of the Glory of God is required.

Here we see verse [24] "And the nations of them which are saved shall walk in the light of it: and the kings of the earth do bring their glory and honour into it." All the people of the nations will walk in the light of New Jerusalem. The light of the Glory of God is seen and all the saved from all nations will come and walk in the light of this great city. The Kings of the earth will worship Him as the supreme ruler. He will truly be the King of Kings and The Lord of Lord's! The almighty ever present Lord of ALL! All rule, power and authority are done away. No more worldly riches or honor, nor will glory be brought to any nation. Neither are they needed here, for God is the authority, the supreme authority in this New Jerusalem.

We see verses, [25] "And the gates of it shall not be shut at all by day: for there shall be no night there. [26] And they shall bring the glory and honour of the nations into it." There is no danger of attack from outside the city. Satan and all the enemies of God are in the Lake of Fire forever, no means of escape. They will not be annihilated nor purified, no means of escaping the judgment of God! Yet more motivation for us today to serve God in being a witness for Him! Therefore the gates are not shut. There is no threat of war, only peace is guaranteed, continual, eternal peace in the lives of all who inhabit this city, New Jerusalem. The glory and honor of nations shall be in this city. Such glorious tidings will flow from her and there will not enter into it any sin, no abomination, not one lie is to be found in it.

Verses 26-27, [26] "And they shall bring the glory and honour of the nations into it. [27] And there shall in no wise enter into it any thing that defileth, neither whatsoever worketh abomination, or maketh a lie: but they which are written in the Lamb's book of life." Guess what we see here! We will no longer have the Old Sin Nature in our lives. No more sinful thoughts, no foul mouth our tongues will be cleaned. Only Glory and honor to God will be communicated in those walls. Isaiah 52:1 "Awake, awake; put on thy strength, O Zion; put on thy beautiful garments, O Jerusalem, the holy city: for henceforth there shall no more come into thee the uncircumcised and the unclean." Do you see yet another Old Testament prophecy fulfilled? No one who is self-righteous that is who tried to gain heaven by works or judging others as worse than they are, nothing like that will be permitted nor will it even come close to entering this city. The only thing allowed in it will be Glory and Honor to God. But sin will not enter in. That is great news! No tears or sorrow will enter in. All will be Praise and Honor given to the Lord! For all His greatness will He be praised!

We see New Jerusalem now coming to earth, our eternal home. We shall forever be with our Lord and Savior. Forever Praising Him and giving Him honor. This will be our eternal home and it will be a beautiful city, pearl gates, golden streets and our own Mansion. No harm, no sorrow, no pain and we will no longer be tempted to sin. This will be grand and glorious and the best thing of all is it is Eternal. This is or should be our motivation to spread the Good News to a lost and dying world.

8

Eternal Refreshing

God is the light, the Son is the Light of the world and He is the light of this city. Kings that is rulers will give glory and honor to Christ. Nothing will enter into the city that will defile it. Nothing that works an abomination, nothing that makes a lie only those things written in the Lamb's book of life will enter.

We begin this last chapter beginning with verse 1 of Revelation 22 as we enter the final chapter of our series of revelation. [1] "And he shewed me a pure river of water of life, clear as crystal, proceeding out of the throne of God and of the Lamb" We see that a pure river flows from the Throne of God and of The Lamb that is Jesus Christ. Crystal clear water the most beautiful water we will ever know, water that will never be contaminated. The head of this river comes from the throne and thus we see God's grace flowing throughout the city. The purity of God is seen in this river and his Grace makes us pure. Not only that but we find comfort in this water as it calms our thirst and gives us spiritual fulfillment. We find God's Glory pouring forth from it as it comes from His glorious throne. The quality of the water is pure, beneficial, these waters refresh. They are life preserving to those who drink it, which again shows God's grace.

We see verse [2] "In the midst of the street of it, and on either side of the river, was there the tree of life, which bare twelve manner of fruits, and yielded her fruit every month: and the leaves of the tree were for the healing of the nations." We see now what is in the midst of the street. We see Genesis 2:9-10, [9]"And out of the ground made the LORD God to grow every tree that is pleasant to the sight, and good for food; the tree of life also in the midst of the garden, and the tree of knowledge of good and evil. [10]And a river went out of Eden to water the garden; and from thence it was parted, and became into four heads."

Notice Eden the Paradise that man was created to live in had a river that went through it. In the midst of it was the Tree of Life. As man fell from paradise those who receive Christ will have paradise as their Eternal home. The tree produces 12 types of fruit. Ever ripe fruit for the residents of that Great city and those upon the earth, the tree of life produces fruit unlike the tree in Matthew 21: [18]"Now in the morning as he returned into the city, he hungered. [19]And when he saw a fig tree in the way, he came to it, and found nothing thereon, but leaves only, and said unto it, Let no fruit grow on thee henceforward for ever. And presently the fig tree withered away. [20]And when the disciples saw it, they marvelled, saying, How soon is the fig tree withered away! [21]Jesus answered and said unto them, Verily I say unto you, If ye have faith, and doubt not, ye shall not only do this which is done to the fig tree, but also if ye shall say unto this mountain, Be thou removed, and be thou cast into the sea; it shall be done." Christ cursed the fig tree and it withered.

The tree of life will never wither nor be cursed because it continually produces fruit. It yields fruit once a month; we get a monthly variety of food from this tree. The leaves heal the nations we are told. An abundant supply for all isn't that how God's Grace works, there is an abundant supply of Grace for all, but not all take part in that grace. Not all seek after salvation, many are called but few answer the call.

Why healing is needed in this perfect environment is not known, we are not told what happens to those of the millennial kingdom when it ends. We are not told what occurs with their bodies, we simply don't know. Maybe they are changed like we see in 1st Corinthians 15:52, but maybe they are in a perfect physical state and still need food, water and healing. Remember Jesus in His resurrection body broke bread and ate with the disciples, Luke 24 and the story of His followers on the road to Emmaus. We see in verses 30 & 31, [30]"And it came to pass, as he sat at meat with them, he took bread, and blessed it, and brake, and gave to them.[31] And their eyes were opened, and they knew him; and he vanished out of their sight." He sat at meat with them He ate with them in His resurrection body. So can it be surprising that we will eat fruit in the New Jerusalem? We will see this tree mentioned again later in this chapter.

In our resurrection body we will not have any infirmities. So what is the healing of the nations about? First we must understand it is not for the curing of diseases they simply will not exist. Nor will our health fail. We all will be changed, 1st Corinthians 15:50-52, [50]"Now this I say, brethren, that flesh and blood cannot inherit the kingdom of God; neither doth corruption inherit incorruption. [51] Behold, I shew you a mystery; We shall not all sleep, but we shall all be changed, [52] In a moment, in the twinkling of an eye, at the last trump: for the trumpet shall sound, and the dead shall be raised incorruptible, and we shall be changed."

We see 1st John 3:1-3. [1]"Behold, what manner of love the Father hath bestowed upon us, that we should be called the sons of God: therefore the world knoweth us not, because it knew him not. [2] Beloved, now are we the sons of God, and it doth not yet appear what we shall be: but we know that, when he shall appear, we shall be like him; for we shall see him as he is. [3] And every man that hath this hope in him purifieth himself, even as he is pure." Both these verses were written to the church. This new city is where the Bride dwells that is the church or should we say the church age believer. What we are not told is what happens once the earth has been renovated by fire. What of those alive at the end of the millennial reign. We are not told what type of body they have or if they too have a resurrection body like the Church age believers have. Those of the church will be like Christ scripture is clear on that. We also know that no sin will, nor will anything that defiles enter this city. We see here that we eat from the tree of life. The leaves are for the healing of the nations, this is a puzzling statement. These leaves must be for those who have a different type of body! It could be that the saved of the Millennial Kingdom have a physical body that needs renewing by these leaves. That God removes from them the Old sin Nature but like Adam and Eve in the original paradise, they must eat of the Tree and have its leaves for healing of that physical body. We simply are not told exactly what occurs, between the ending of the Kingdom age and the beginning of eternity.

Remember Adam and Eve began in innocence. Ezekiel 47:[12] "And by the river upon the bank thereof, on this side and on that side, shall grow all trees for meat, whose leaf shall not fade, neither shall the fruit thereof be consumed: it shall bring forth new fruit according to his months, because their waters they issued out of the sanctuary: and the fruit thereof shall be for meat, and the leaf thereof for medicine."

Remember we are told there is no end to Christ Kingdom reign over Israel. Remember too what we saw in Revelation 21:2, "And I John saw the holy city, new Jerusalem, coming down from God out of heaven, prepared as a bride adorned for her husband." The Bride that is the churches new home is "New Jerusalem." That could infer that the rest of the Saints, O.T., Tribulation and Millennial saints live outside the Great City and that they come to the tree of life for food and medicine. That appears to be what we have here, but no one is sure what occurs we simply are not told! We are left with speculation as to what the meaning is.

Now we see verses 3-4, [3] "And there shall be no more curse: but the throne of God and of the Lamb shall be in it; and his servants shall serve him: [4]And they shall see his face; and his name shall be in their foreheads." The earth is no longer under the curse that is what the Tribulation was for. The curse which came upon the earth when Adam sinned is totally removed. The redemption price was paid in the judgment which came upon the earth in the Tribulation. Sin that is the Old sin Nature no longer reigns in mankind.

Adam if you remember was created, Genesis 1:26-28, [26]"And God said, Let us make man in our image, after our likeness: and let them have dominion over the fish of the sea, and over the fowl of the air, and over the cattle, and over all the earth, and over every creeping thing that creepeth upon the earth. [27] So God created man in his own image, in the image of God created he him; male and female created he them. [28] And God blessed them, and God said unto them, Be fruitful, and multiply, and replenish the earth, and subdue it: and have dominion over the fish of the sea, and over the fowl of the air, and over every living thing that moveth upon the earth." God created man in His image. From all indications man did not have a sin nature at creation. We see Genesis 3:12-14, [12] "And the man said, The woman whom thou gavest to be with me, she gave me of the tree, and I did eat. [13] And the LORD God said unto the woman, What is this that thou hast done? And the woman said, The serpent beguiled me, and I did eat. [14] And the LORD God said unto the serpent, Because thou hast done this, thou art cursed above all cattle, and above every beast of the field; upon thy belly shalt thou go, and dust shalt thou eat all the days of thy life:"

Eve was not tempted from within as we are, the Old sin Nature came into us from our father Adam.

Here it seems man is back in the original state that is in the image of God as created at the beginning, no curse of the Old Sin Nature. Genesis 5 reiterates how man was originally created, [1]"This is the book of the generations of Adam. In the day that God created man, in the likeness of God made he him; [2] Male and female created he them; and blessed them, and called their name Adam, in the day when they were created." Man was originally created in the likeness of God, as body, soul and spirit a three part being. But man did not have a nature to sin in him at that point.

He did have volition the ability to pick and choose right from wrong, satan came and tempted her. We know she gave in and Eve gave Adam the fruit and he chose that is made a conscious choice, to eat of it. The curse of sin was not upon him at creation. The curse came at the fall and all of us born from the fall through the Millennial had the curse of the Old sin Nature upon us, in eternity there is no more curse.

Next we see the fact that "...but the throne of God and of the Lamb shall be in it; and his servants shall serve him: [4] And they shall see his face; and his name shall be in their foreheads." God's throne is in the city and in that city all the nations will come and worship Him. Christ sits upon His eternal throne here in the New Jerusalem. His servants will serve Him. We see His face continually. His name in their foreheads shows they are sealed! 2nd Corinthians 1:21-22, [21] "Now he which stablisheth us with you in Christ, and hath anointed us, is God; [22] Who hath also sealed us, and given the earnest of the Spirit in our hearts" Ephesians 1: [13] "In whom ye also trusted, after that ye heard the word of truth, the gospel of your salvation: in whom also after that ye believed, ye were sealed with that holy Spirit of promise, [14] Which is the earnest of our inheritance until the redemption of the purchased possession, unto the praise of his glory." Thus we see He sealed us for all eternity. Once we have been sealed with the Holy Spirit who came into us and indwelt us we remain sealed forever, do you see that here? Chapter 22 verse 5 says [5] "And there shall be no night there; and they need no candle, neither light of the sun; for the Lord God giveth them light: and they shall reign for ever and ever." No need for light. No candle needed. When God renovated the Heaven and Earth the sun was no more! The Lord gives us His light, the Light of the world is Jesus in this New Jerusalem. God reigns, Christ reigns, The Holy Spirit Reigns and their reign is forever and ever, Praise God! The inside of New Jerusalem is seen as it is now completely on the earth our eternal home. We shall forever be with our Lord and Savior. Forever Praising Him and giving Him honor. There will be a tree of Life and a river just like Eden had. Man shall dwell upon the earth for all eternity just as God intended for Him to do. Forever being renewed with 12 types of fruit and healing from the leaves of the Tree of Life. Forever seeing God and praising and worshipping Him every single day. This should stir up in you the desire to witness for Christ. In order that your family and friends as well as your enemy will be in New Jerusalem with you and they too will be worshipping God. Why study Revelation as a motivation to you that is why!

The curse is removed and God's throne as well as Christ throne is in the New Jerusalem. We shall see His face and His name will be written in our foreheads. There will be neither night nor day; For the Lord God gives us His light. We shall reign forever and ever. As we saw in Chapter 20 again we are told, [6]"And he said unto me, these sayings are faithful and true: and the Lord God of the holy prophets sent his angel to shew unto his servants the things which must shortly be done." Since God is a true and faithful God so too are these sayings.

What He told the Old Testament prophets is true and faithful. What God reveals to prophets will be fulfilled because God is True and faithful. All these things would come true and it would occur speedily when it occurs. We see verse [7]"Behold, I come quickly: blessed is he that keepeth the sayings of the prophecy of this book." When Christ comes it will be speedily. There will be no time for preparation. For many it will be everlastingly too late. We are blessed when we keep the sayings of this book! When we see this book as prophetic, we see it as a literal fulfillment not figurative or mystical.

Now we see verses 8, "And I John saw these things, and heard them. And when I had heard and seen, I fell down to worship before the feet of the angel which shewed me these things." John saw and heard these things. When he had heard and seen, we see him falling down to worship.

Next we see the Angel speak, verse [9] "Then saith he unto me, See thou do it not: for I am thy fellowservant, and of thy brethren the prophets, and of them which keep the sayings of this book: worship God." This Angel is not Christ as some would like to believe. Christ sits upon His eternal throne in the New Jerusalem. This angel is a fellow servant a servant of his fellow brothers in Christ. Just as the prophets, just as you and I who keep the sayings of the book. Just as all who worship God! John is rebuked again, showing us we should never worship angels.

The time for Revelation is at hand we see in verse [10] "And he saith unto me, Seal not the sayings of the prophecy of this book: for the time is at hand." John again is told not to seal the sayings of this book of revelation. God's word is never to be sealed. It is never to be held in. We are to proclaim God's glory! God's Faithfulness and God as Truth we are to do so "for the time is at hand." God's truth is always at hand. The time for witnessing to others is always at hand.

We continue with verse [11] "He that is unjust, let him be unjust still: and he which is filthy, let him be filthy still: and he that is righteous, let him be righteous still: and he that is holy, let him be holy still." When the time for New Jerusalem arrives with a new Heaven and New Earth, "he that is unjust, let him be unjust still" that is his fate for rejecting Christ, for the unjust will spend eternity in the Lake of Fire. They have not been justified by the Blood of the Lamb. We are to witness to the unjust. Once the unjust had passed on and at this point have been condemned to the Lake of fire he cannot be purified and brought to New Jerusalem. The unjust is eternally lost, forever and ever in torments.

He that is Righteous let him still be righteous. We are made righteous by our faith in Christ. Romans 1:16-18, is reiterated here in verse 11, [16] "For I am not ashamed of the gospel of Christ: for it is the power of God unto salvation to every one that believeth; to the Jew first, and also to the Greek. [17] For therein is the righteousness of God revealed from faith to faith: as it is written, The just shall live by faith. [18] For the wrath of God is revealed from heaven against all ungodliness and unrighteousness of men, who hold the truth in unrighteousness; " The just live by Faith and Gods righteousness is revealed in those who are believers from faith to faith.

God's wrath comes against ungodliness and the unrighteous that is the unjust. 2nd Peter 3:12-14, [12]"Looking for and hasting unto the coming of the day of God, wherein the heavens being on fire shall be dissolved, and the elements shall melt with fervent heat? [13] Nevertheless we, according to his promise, look for new heavens and a new earth, wherein dwelleth righteousness. [14] Wherefore, beloved, seeing that ye look for such things, be diligent that ye may be found of him in peace, without spot, and blameless." Once the old heaven and earth are dissolved there comes the time of righteousness in the New Jerusalem Righteousness dwells. Because of our Faith we had Righteousness imputed to our account. We shall remain righteous! Do you see that here?

If after seeing the truth of this prophecy one chooses to remain unjust, that is refuses to repent and turn to Christ let them remain unjust! It is clear the book of Revelation was given to reveal to all what eternity will hold.

For those who reject Christ and choose to remain unjust, choose to continue to reject Christ and remain unjustified, by their personal volition that is their personal choice. Romans 3: [28] "Therefore we conclude that a man is justified by faith without the deeds of the law." Romans 5: [1]"Therefore being justified by faith, we have peace with God through our Lord Jesus Christ: [2] By whom also we have access by faith into this grace wherein we stand, and rejoice in hope of the glory of God. Galatians 3: [24] Wherefore the law was our schoolmaster to bring us unto Christ, that we might be justified by faith." When those justified by Faith read this book that is the book of revelation then they are to remain just. That is remain in the walk of faith a holy walk, keep on serving God, this book is to motivate the just to continue in their Holy service with even more purpose.

We see Christ will move quickly when He comes for in verse [12] "And, behold, I come quickly; and my reward is with me, to give every man according as his work shall be." Christ comes to reward the Holy that is the just. Each and every believer will receive eternal rewards. The Old Testament believer will receive his reward. You and I of the church will obtain crowns or wood, hay and straw. The Tribulation saints will be granted to sit upon thrones in the Kingdom. The saints of the Millennial will receive their rewards; they will eat from the Tree of life and drink from the waters flowing from the throne.

Christ moves swiftly in judging the unjust! He has their sentence of dying the second death carried out and they are eternally separated from Him in the Lake of Fire forever and ever to remain unjustified. For Christ is, [13]"I am Alpha and Omega, the beginning and the end, the first and the last. [14] Blessed are they that do his commandments, that they may have right to the tree of life, and may enter in through the gates into the city." Christ is the beginning and the end.

Eternally, He created mankind and time for man. He will end time for mankind just as quickly. When we keep His commandments we are able to eat of the tree of life. We enter the gates of the city. What commandments, those which state "believe on the Lord Jesus Christ and though shalt be saved", "whosoever shall call upon the Lord shall be saved", and "whosoever believeth on Him shall have eternal life". All the commandments that tell us to have Faith that is believe in Christ "may have the right to the tree of life and to enter in through the gates into the city." Do you see salvation is by *Grace* through *Faith*?

Again we see what those who rejected Christ are, verse[15] "For without are dogs, and sorcerers, and whoremongers, and murderers, and idolaters, and whosoever loveth and maketh a lie." Those who rejected Christ that is, chose to live lives that resembled these things. They were like dogs that went after the things of the world, they were great sinners whose sin had been paid for by the blood of Christ but they refused to follow the commandments of God, refused to believe on Him. They are without, separated from Him, they are in the literal Lake of Fire forever tormented.

Jesus sent His messenger to testify to the churches, verses 16-17, [16] "I Jesus have sent mine angel to testify unto you these things in the churches. I am the root and the offspring of David, and the bright and morning star. [17] And the Spirit and the bride say, Come. And let him that heareth say, Come. And let him that is athirst come. And whosoever will, let him take the water of life freely." Every period of church History, every phase we saw the church go through as seen in my book "The Snatching Away of the Bride", has had God's messengers proclaiming the gospel. People heard the word, they heard the gospel. Every time the book of Revelation is taught the witness goes out. Christ the root and offspring of David. Jesus is the true Savior as promised. He is the "bright and morning star"

The Holy Spirit says come to salvation, the Bride that is the Church or every true believer says come. You see we are to be a witness, it is our job! Let those who are without hear and Come to salvation. Let those who are athirst for the true Spiritual water come. Whosoever will, that is by their own conscious choice may come. Take of the water freely, that water is Christ and the river flows from the Throne in New Jerusalem.

We finish the study with verses 18-21, [18]"For I testify unto every man that heareth the words of the prophecy of this book, If any man shall add unto these things, God shall add unto him the plagues that are written in this book: [19]And if any man shall take away from the words of the book of this prophecy, God shall take away his part out of the book of life, and out of the holy city, and from the things which are written in this book. [20]He which testifieth these things saith, Surely I come quickly. Amen. Even so, come, Lord Jesus. [21]The grace of our Lord Jesus Christ be with you all. Amen." We are not to add to the sayings of this book nor take away. This doesn't mean we cannot expound on the things written. This book is being endorsed by God. Many believe that adding to this book also entails adding to the canon of scripture. This was and is the Last book of the Bible, there were to be no more written. There was to be no more added. No one is to tamper with God's word. To do so comes with a very solemn warning. Christ will come quickly when He comes. Can we all say "Even so, come Lord Jesus"?

We see now what the future holds for the saved and the lost the warnings for the unjust that is those not justified by faith deal with their eternity. To us we are to testify to them that is we are to be a witness and the book of Revelation should bring us to be a stronger bolder witness. Because we see in the end God wins and we are His. We have a great and Beautiful home with Him for all eternity. Come to Christ is you haven't, "Even so, Come Lord Jesus."

CONCLUSION

It is that important that you know how you stand and how to receive so great a salvation! How do you stand today? Have you believed on Jesus as your Lord and Savior? If not you need to do so right now, don't miss being Snatched away in the rapture! Don't be one of those who will end up in the Tribulation facing the judgment of God! John 3:16" For God So Loved the Word that He gave His only begotten son, that whosoever believeth on Him will not perish but have eternal life." Do you see God by Grace gave His Son, Jesus Christ and you must believe on Him! Romans 10:13 "For whosoever shall call upon the name of the Lord shall be saved." Believe then call, is God's order. Look at what Jesus said in John 3:17-21; [17]"For God sent not his Son into the world to condemn the world; but that the world through him might be saved. [18]"He that believeth on him is not condemned: but he that believeth not is condemned already, because he hath not believed in the name of the only begotten Son of God. [19] And this is the condemnation, that light is come into the world, and men loved darkness rather than light, because their deeds were evil. [20] For every one that doeth evil hateth the light, neither cometh to the light, lest his deeds should be reproved. [21] But he that doeth truth cometh to the light, that his deeds may be made manifest, that they are wrought in God." Do you see believe and call upon Him, admit you are condemned already because you haven't believed on Jesus Christ? Believe you are sinner in need of salvation and believe that Jesus died for your sins. Call on the Lord and admit all to Him even that you believe Jesus died for your sins. You see it isn't a matter of your sin that has condemned you it is a matter of your unbelief. Believe and call upon Christ for Salvation and you too can be snatched away at the Rapture, you too can live eternally in the New Jerusalem. You too can drink from the water flowing from the throne of God. You too can eat of the fruit of the tree of life. There are two choices receive Jesus as Lord and Savior or reject him and live forever and ever in the Lake of fire, it is your choice!

Printed in the United States
By Bookmasters